W9-BCF-600

Children's Theatre

Play production

HARPER & BROTHERS, PUBLISHERS, NEW YORK

Children's Theatre

for the child audience ∾ ∾

JED H. DAVIS
University of Kansas

and

MARY JANE LARSON WATKINS
San Fernando Valley (California)
State College

With the collaboration of

ROGER M. BUSFIELD, JR.
Author of The Playwright's Art

CHILDREN'S THEATRE: PLAY PRODUCTION
FOR THE CHILD AUDIENCE

Copyright © 1960 by Jed H. Davis and Mary Jane Larson Watkins

Printed in the United States of America

All rights in this book are reserved.
No part of the book may be used or reproduced in any manner whatsoever
without written permission except in the case of brief quotations
embodied in critical articles and reviews. For information address
Harper & Brothers, 49 East 33rd Street, New York 16, N.Y.

K-K

Library of Congress catalog card number: 60-15622

792.022
D26c

To Winifred Ward

whose tireless spirit

and inspired teaching

guides us all

Foreword

·

WITH THE TREMENDOUS GROWTH of children's theatre activity in the past decade, it is indeed surprising that more books have not been written about playwriting for, and the directing, designing, producing, and managing of theatres for, children. *Children's Theatre* is a valuable and much needed addition to the field, especially since the authors approach children's theatre as an art.

Serious workers and students of modern children's theatre—directors, dramatists, designer-technicians, actors, and business managers—will each find here a rich storehouse of information to assist him in his role as a member of the children's theatre "producing team." Three groups should find it especially inspiring and practicable:

1. Individuals with educational theatre training and/or experience who need guidance in applying their abilities to theatre for child audiences.
2. Instructors conducting classes in theatre for children.

40697

3. Individuals without previous training or experience in adult theatre who are now becoming interested, eager, often inspired to work in children's theatre.

The authors are trained practitioners in the many aspects of children's theatre. Even more important, this book reflects also a rich background of child psychology and child audience study. While valid, practical suggestions are given for solving the many-faceted problems encountered in preparing various types of productions for child audiences, these are given not as ends in themselves, but as bases for "serious workers and students" to project their own imaginations and creativity. Such individuals will utilize the contents of this volume as a point of departure for their own creative endeavors. They can hardly help but be stimulated to carry out the philosophy of children's theatre that permeates this book: "Only the very best is good enough for children."

KENNETH L. GRAHAM

Preface

THIS VOLUME is addressed to the serious workers and students of the modern children's theatre. Into its pages are woven study of and experiences in several kinds of functioning children's theatre organizations—university and college, community, school system, and recreation programs. The authors have been privileged to take part in this vital phase of American theatre as actors, crew members, producers, playwrights, designers, directors, and supervisors of graduate research. While we ostensibly address ourselves to directors throughout the book, we hope all other workers will find a sympathetic approach to the fundamental *team* aspect of the activity.

We hope also that we have communicated our own profound respect for the potential that children's theatre represents wherever it is beautifully presented. Enthusiasm and dedication are obviously essential in children's theatre work, but we also advocate a high degree of scholarship. Without knowledge of basic theories and practices our work is bound to be hollow—truly "full of sound and fury, signifying nothing."

In the chapters which follow, we shall stress the central factor of the child himself and his relationship to each subject discussed. After a brief overview of the twentieth century and the development of the children's theatre movement in the United States, we shall examine the child and his role as a member of an audience. Next, for the benefit of playwright and director, we shall examine the script and the playwriting process as they apply to children's drama. Following this are two chapters devoted to the director's task as he prepares the play for performance, one dealing with his preparation and the other with his actual work with the actors. These are followed by two chapters concerned with designing and mounting the production. The final chapters are centered on the business and professional aspects of children's theatre.

Although it is quite impossible to give credit to all those who have influenced this work, we gratefully acknowledge the many ideas that have come to us from our students, co-workers, teachers, administrators, and eminent predecessors, even though we have not, in most cases, tried to trace the original source.

In great measure, however, we are happy to acknowledge the challenging influence of the Children's Theatre Conference of the American Educational Theatre Association. From its very inception in 1944, the Conference and its prominent leaders have given needed guidance and help, offering the necessary perspective on our own work as it became part of the nationwide scene. The sessions we have attended, the productions, and, yes, even the Board meetings, have given us an ever-growing sense of the importance of this total activity as the hope of the American theatre. To Winifred Ward, Campton Bell, Sara Spencer, Kenneth L. Graham, Eleanor Chase York, Dina Rees Evans, Dorothy Schwartz, Geraldine Siks, Albert Mitchell, the late Charlotte B. Chorpenning, and many others goes our unending gratitude. In a more specific sense we are grateful to Winifred Ward for her active encouragement in the writing of this volume, to Kenneth L. Graham for the Foreword, and to Mariam A. Duckwall for her work on the manuscript.

For permission to use photographs of their productions we are indebted to the following directors, designers, and publishers:

Katherine M. Sherman of the Long Beach, California, Children's Theatre, for Plate 2B.

Mary Gwen Owen of the Macalester College Theatre, St. Paul, Minnesota, for several audience photos and *The Sandalwood Box.*

St. Nicholas magazine for *Little Women.*

Kenneth L. Graham and Robert D. Moulton of the University of Minnesota Young People's Theatre, Minneapolis, for *King Midas and the Golden Touch, Seven Little Rebels, Alice in Wonderland, The Blue Bird,* and *Arthur and the Magic Sword.*

Lee Mitchell and Winifred Ward of Northwestern University and the Evanston Children's Theatre, Illinois, for *The Samurai Sword* and *The Princess and the Vagabond.*

J. H. H. Gaute, Editor, George G. Harrap & Co., Ltd., London, for Goncharova's design of *The Blue Bird.*

Richard Corson of New York City for his design of *Alice in Wonderland.*

Elemer Nagy and Howard F. Deming of the Julius Hartt College of the University of Hartford, Connecticut, for *Hansel and Gretel.*

Lee Mitchell, Dina Rees Evans, and Edith Underwood of the Cain Park Creative Workshop, Cleveland Heights, Ohio, for *Peter Pan.*

Dorothy Coit of the King-Coit School, New York, and Ruth R. Mayleas of the National Theatre Service, American National Theatre and Academy, New York, for *Aucassin and Nicolette.*

Hallie Flanagan Davis of Poughkeepsie, New York, for *The Emperor's New Clothes*.

Robert Darling of San Francisco State College for the photo of children meeting Clara after a performance of *Heidi*.

For their designs, diagrams, and working drawings, we gratefully acknowledge the cooperation and help of Herbert L. Camburn of the University of Kansas Theatre, Merlin E. Bement of Wesleyan College, Macon, Georgia, and Rosalind Mathews of Michigan State University.

The remaining illustrative material is the contribution of directors and designers who have worked with the Children's Theatre and the University Junior Players of Michigan State University, East Lansing.

To those who will find within these pages their first glimpse of the children's theatre or even their first exposure to the process of producing a play, a special word of welcome. We hope you will find your experience in the field immensely rewarding. We hasten to point out, however, that no single volume could contain all the information, thoughts, and techniques which have been painstakingly developed over the ages with regard to that enigmatic entity of the theatre. We urge you to extend your reading and study as far as you can. The references at the end of this volume may help you get started, but even they will be only a beginning.

Finally, we recognize that this book takes a stand for *strongly directed* theatre for children. We admit, furthermore, that the stand is controversial, but we hope the reader will find it justified and agree that it is the only way our stated purposes can be achieved.

J.H.D.
M.J.L.W.

July, 1960

Contents

	Foreword by Kenneth L. Graham	vii
	Preface	ix
1.	The Century of the Child	1
2.	Children's Theatre Is Good Theatre	15
3.	The Audience and the Play	22
4.	The Playwright at Work	51
5.	The Director Prepares	78
6.	The Director and Actors Work Together	110
7.	The Production Is Designed	153
8.	The Production Is Mounted	199
9.	Children's Theatre Is a Business	247
10.	Children's Theatre on Tour	279
11.	Children's Theatre Is a Profession	289

Appendixes

Sample Prompt Book Pages 300

Sample Light Plot 308

A Tabulation of 120 Children's Theatre Plays 320

Bibliography 402

Index 411

Children's Theatre

1 ⌒

The Century of
the Child

WHAT AN AGE we live in! What a breathless era, in which civilization moves at breakneck speed from one milestone to the next! In the fragment of time known as the twentieth century, man has experienced the chaos of wars, the headlong progress of boom prosperity, the despair of economic crisis, and the wonders of electric dishwashers, power lawn mowers, miracle drugs, and satellites orbiting in space. The rate at which these developments have occurred is unprecedented in the history of mankind.

But a blossoming technology has not been the only advance of our century. A serious, concerted study of man himself, both as an individual and as a member of society, has revealed a large body of knowledge of how people grow physically and mentally, how they behave in different situations, and how they communicate their ideas, desires, emotions, and dreams.

As the study of man has intensified and reached new heights, the child who would become the man has appeared more and more frequently under the microscope. One of the most startling changes in society's attitude toward itself is seen in the way we regard our children. Future generations may well think of this as "The Century of the Child." Ideas about children have surely changed more in the years since 1900 than in all the periods since antiquity. The few formal studies conducted before 1900 for the most part examined physical growth patterns. Although several case studies reported the language development of precocious sons and daughters, children were customarily regarded as miniature adults.

Early in the twentieth century, however, research coming from such child study centers as the Clinic of Child Development at Yale University began to indicate that, while he is not a separate breed, the child is unique in his physical and psychological structure. He is an individual developing mentally, emotionally, and spiritually as well as growing physically. Serious students of child growth and development began to turn to such diverse fields as biology, genetics, embryology, anatomy, pediatrics, sociology, social anthropology, psychiatry, mental hygiene, and psychology to gain an understanding of the needs and problems of children and youth.

The impact of research was widespread. As knowledge accumulated on how children grow and mature, how they develop in formation of concepts and reasoning powers, and how they behave in a field of constantly changing stimuli, laymen as well as clinicians began to give old words new meanings. Vocabularies began to swell with terms such as "frustration," "security," "adjustment," "maturation," "IQ," and "sibling rivalry." The facts brought forth by research and the ideas stimulated by the facts began to be useful in industry, in welfare work, and in advertising as well as in the classroom.

It is natural that all this new knowledge about children should have an effect on education. The modern school has largely abandoned the rote system of teaching isolated blocks of facts in favor of curricular and activity programs based on the true nature of childhood. Attacks on the system occur regularly and serve to keep educators on their toes. At times it seems fashionable to lay all our country's economic, social, and political ills at the feet of education. There are always those who would return to an earlier period, who would discount the value of research on the nature of the learning process, or who feel that this or that essential feature of education is being neglected in the schools. But the facts have generally upheld the progressive movement. Education built upon sound principles of child development will no doubt experience a scientifically based *evolution* in the years to come. The *revolution* has already occurred.

Taking their places alongside the schools have been the many government agencies on all levels, the community service organizations, the church and other religious groups, which have introduced or expanded programs specifically geared to meet the needs of children and youth. Few indeed are the youngsters who do not at some time come under the influence of the various "Y" programs, the Boy or Girl Scouts or Camp Fire Girls, municipal recreation summer activities, church camps, or service club baseball leagues, in addition to the rich and varied public school programs. The child of the twentieth century certainly leads a far more organized life than did his predecessors.

THE GROWTH OF CHILDREN'S THEATRE

Although the progress of children's theatre has been less widely publicized than the forward steps of other agencies concerned with young people, the growth of the movement has paralleled the acceptance of new concepts regarding children.

In the nineteenth century young people who lived in metropolitan areas might have seen an occasional adult play, but their theatrical fare was probably limited to scattered performances of plays based on stories now considered suitable for the child audience. There was, for instance, a production of *Rip Van Winkle* as early as 1828, and in 1865 Joseph Jefferson introduced his version of the same story in a series of performances which spanned almost half a century. Occasional references can be found to such productions as *Tom Sawyer,* first dramatized in 1875, the popular *Little Lord Fauntleroy,* and *The Prince and the Pauper*—both done before 1890. But these offerings probably were not planned exclusively for the delight and edification of children.

After 1900 plays suitable for child audiences began to appear more frequently in New York commercial theatres. In fact, by 1915 such favorites as *Peter Pan, The Blue Bird, Little Women, Snow White and the Seven Dwarfs, Racketty Packetty House, Alice in Wonderland,* and *Treasure Island* had been enthusiastically received by thousands of children. Even the critics hailed the incoming era with praise and thanksgiving. Talk about specially constructed playhouses for children became fashionable, and one, the Children's Playhouse atop the Century Theatre, actually materialized. Despite generous private endowments, however, commercial producers gradually abandoned their dreams of elaborate and specialized children's theatre buildings as they recognized that fixed locations and engagements confined to week ends and holidays severely limited their potential audience.

One door was left open to those who would produce on a commercial basis for children—"the road." An enterprising and talented young man named Stuart Walker conceived a production plan whereby the settings, lights, costumes, as well as the entire theatre itself could be packed into a few crates and shipped anywhere in the country. His "Portmanteau Theatre," which could be set up in any large room or hall, operated only from 1915 to 1919, but in that time he brought living theatre and extremely progressive staging methods to thousands of children and adults from New York to Chicago. By 1920, however, leadership in both quantity and quality of plays for child audiences had passed from commercial to noncommercial producers.

The established children's theatre programs which thrive today can most accurately trace their ancestry to an enterprise which began in 1903 among the Russian-Jewish immigrants on New York's lower East Side. The Children's Educational Theatre, guided from 1903 to 1908 by Alice Minnie Herts Heniger, produced two plays a year on the little stage of a building which belonged to the parent organization—the Educational Alliance.

Miss Herts established her pioneer program for specific educational purposes which are as valid today as they were in 1903. She recognized a crying need for beauty in the lives of the neighborhood children. They were wasting their time on the streets and in the pool halls. They were pouring by droves into the readily accessible, new, and fascinating nickelodeon—the forerunner of the modern movie palace. Seriously questioning the artistic stimulation most of those children received, Miss Herts was impelled to maintain a democratic program in which children alternately performed in the plays and worked backstage. Dramatic classes were conducted for them under the supervision of Miss Herts and Emma Sheridan Fry. No "stars" were allowed, and productions were mounted with care despite the ever increasing deficit and burden on the Alliance. Ill health and a city-wide ban on Sunday performances forced Miss Herts to close the project in 1908; but she continued to urge the establishment of subsidized children's theatres wherever she went, and her many writings have come to be regarded not only as a chronicle of the Children's Educational Theatre of New York but as formulating a basic philosophy for the budding movement.

Variations of the pattern which Alice Minnie Herts established soon began to appear in expanding municipal recreation programs in several parts of the United States. Dramatic activities with and for children came to be recognized for the values they brought to average as well as to underprivileged youngsters, to young residents of Cleveland and San Francisco as well as to settlement house children of New York and Chicago. As the community theatre movement began to sweep the country, several of the leading organizations began to include a play for children in their regular seasons. Constance D'Arcy Mackay, director and playwright, recorded in her many books and articles the growing link between the community theatre and the children's theatre movement. By 1919 the first college program of children's theatre activities—on both curricular and extracurricular levels—had been established at Emerson College, Boston, under Imogene Hogel.

Indeed, during the first twenty years of our century, energetic and dedicated individuals had succeeded in laying the cornerstone for a strong cultural influence in this field. The next ten years saw the completion of the foundation and even some of the superstructure which are still evident today.

The decade of the 1920's was extremely important in the development of children's theatre in the United States. In 1921 the Association of Junior Leagues of America inaugurated what was to become its present extensive program. In that year, the Chicago League, under Annette Washburn and Alice Gerstenberg, produced the latter's *Alice in Wonderland,* using an all-League cast and a professional production staff. In succeeding years, the Chicago League continued its unique operation in the Playhouse of the Fine Arts Building. Soon other Leagues instituted their own systems for presenting plays to local and outlying audiences. By 1928, more than fifty Leagues were engaged in children's theatre activities. In the years that followed, national Junior League leaders encouraged the extension of operations to include publishing and distributing plays, sponsoring professional and nonprofessional performances in local communities, and trouping plays to schools and auditoriums within a limited radius. Today representatives of the Junior League are likely to be found on boards of directors of many community-sponsored children's theatres. On both national and local levels the contribution of this civic service organization to the growth and prosperity of the children's theatre movement cannot be overestimated.

Another cooperative project between the commercial and the noncommercial theatre was instituted in 1922 at the Children's Theatre of the Heckscher Foundation, New York. In a magnificently constructed and mural-decorated auditorium in the Heckscher Building, a combination of professional actors and settlement house children opened what seemed to be a most promising venture with a production in which the fairy tale murals came to life on the stage. Clare Tree Major soon assumed the management of a company of young professionals who performed alternately at the Heckscher and the Princess Theatres. After two years Mrs. Major left the Heckscher. Since then, except for scattered productions by drama schools and other outside organizations, this beautiful theatre has remained without a regular program.

The Clare Tree Major players, however, continued to expand their activities in other locations. In 1928 a system of touring was begun which, for a quarter of a century, brought the exciting magic of theatre to children from coast to coast. Both large and small towns were included in the itinerary of the several companies of each play which Mrs. Major sent out on the road.

In addition to her active production program, her original scripts kept expanding the repertoire of plays available to the rapidly increasing number of producers throughout the country.

With the exception of the Clare Tree Major trouping units, however, the field was more and more dominated by municipal recreation and community theatre programs. Children's theatre productions were given in Rose Valley, Pennsylvania; Poughkeepsie, New York; Highland Park, Michigan; Oakland and Los Angeles, California; and elsewhere across the land. Then in 1925, two pioneering programs, initiated in neighboring communities, ignited the fire in many educational institutions in the years that followed: the Children's Theatre of Evanston, Illinois, and the Goodman School of the Theatre, Chicago.

From several points of view, serious concern for the children's theatre movement in this country can be said to have begun with the work of Winifred Ward at Northwestern University. Through her foresight and inspired leadership, a system of cooperation between the University and the Evanston Public Schools was established that continues to the present day. Miss Ward's high production standards, her knowledge of children, and her well-founded teaching methods placed her program in the vanguard of the advancing forces. Scarcely a children's theatre director practicing today has not come under the influence of Miss Ward herself or been swayed by one or more of her many publications which began appearing in 1926. Miss Ward has been the movement's prophet and its guide—inspiring, advising, organizing, and writing as actively after her retirement as in the first days of the Evanston-Northwestern Children's Theatre.

Though the year 1925 also saw the first productions for children at the Goodman School of the Theatre in Chicago, the outstanding contribution of this program did not really begin until later. In 1931 Charlotte Barrows Chorpenning assumed the directorship of the children's theatre and began the intensive period of playwriting, production, and experimentation for which both she and the Goodman will always be remembered. Both alone and through collaboration, this prolific playwright more than doubled the repertoire of good scripts for children's theatre in her lifetime.

Several other schools began productions for children within the same decade. The University of Tulsa Children's Theatre, under Josephine Layman Story, began to produce with child actors in 1926. Several high schools, among them Santa Monica and Bakersfield, California, presented plays for children as part of their season's offerings. An unusual kind of children's theatre program was begun in 1924 by Edith King and Dorothy Coit at their school in New York City. Under their guidance the children immersed themselves in the culture and art of a period and country for several months, studying and then dramatizing one of that country's famous legends. Such unusual stories as *Aucassin and Nicolette, Nala and Damayanti, Kai Khosru,* and *The Image of Artemes* were presented with a "relief stage" technique. Critics hailed the King-Coit enterprise as America's first "Art Theatre for Children," although emphasis was put upon the child as a performer and upon the cultural broadening of the participants rather than upon the child audience.

By 1930, the major patterns of children's theatre activity in the United States were crystallized, though organizations varied widely as to purposes and methods. Some stressed the recreational or social-cultural broadening of the performers through participation in plays. Others stressed both the artistic growth of the participants and the enjoyment of the child audiences who attended the performances. Still others stressed the educational value students of the drama received from working with child actors, observing child audiences, and performing in plays for children. Some were set up to utilize adult actors exclusively;

others used only children in the casts; a few audience-oriented groups saw the obvious advantages of casting children in youthful roles and adults in mature parts. Actually, in this early period there was little apparent interchange of ideas and only a few publications in the field; no two children's theatres were very much alike.

With the development of radio and motion pictures as the popular mass media of entertainment in the 1930's, research was rather extensively conducted to determine their effects on children. The increased power of persuasion through drama, the longer retention of facts graphically presented, the somewhat ephemeral nature of the isolated, though intense, emotional experience on children who saw movies or listened to the radio, and the existence of rather clear age-interest patterns were conclusions systematically recorded through experimental studies.

The literature which children read was also scrutinized. Bloody and cruel aspects of fairy tales were being questioned by both educators and psychologists. Old tales were rewritten in the light of a new philosophy. Children's interests in stories and illustrations were studied, and the results were turned to practical use in schools, homes, and publishing houses. Some of the research conclusions of the 1930's have been negated or modified by more recent work, and the pendulum, prone to swing to extremes, has begun to return again. Nevertheless, much of what was discovered during the depression years has supported the work of the children's theatre.

During these lean years two important commercial ventures, both related to the demands of humanity, appeared on the national scene to further the growth of children's theatre. 1933 saw the beginnings of Junior Programs, Incorporated, under the leadership of Dorothy L. McFadden. This nonprofit operation, begun to satisfy the entertainment demands of children in Maplewood, New Jersey, eventually developed into an organization which acted as intermediary between professional entertainers and sponsors throughout the country. Before long Junior Programs was a producer in its own right, sending out the best professional groups available. The Edwin Strawbridge Lyric Theatre productions first toured under its auspices. Junior Programs soon sprang up in other cities, though the commercial aspect was modified. Seattle and Denver set up organizations which sponsored or imported entertainment for their children. Playwriting for child audiences was encouraged through contests, and close contact was characteristically maintained with the many agencies in the community that work with and for children. Some of these groups still continue to explore further possibilities for community service.

The other significant commercial operation of the 1930's was the Federal Theatre of the Works Progress Administration. Established by an Act of Congress in 1935 and closed by the same body in 1939, the Federal Theatre Project carried out its purpose of bringing theatre at modest admission prices to thousands of Americans who had never before seen a live performance. As a part of its program, productions for children were staged outdoors in city parks, inside ordinary halls and school auditoriums, as well as in regular theatres closed by the depression. Yasha Frank's *Pinocchio,* Chorpenning's *The Emperor's New Clothes, Little Black Sambo,* and a number of scripts which remained unpublished were presented to youngsters in many parts of the country in a conscious effort to keep youth from inheriting only the despair and uncertainty of the times. That the Federal Theatre provide a livelihood for professional actors was its first concern. That it brought exciting stories beautifully, if economically, staged to at least some of our children was an assurance of public funds well spent.

Set up to operate on a commercial basis within a limited radius of Pittsburgh was a company of young professionals organized by Grace Price in 1934. Still active today, the group performs for thousands of youngsters annually in school auditoriums under the sponsorship of local groups. The Grace Price Productions have served as a model for many other regional professional touring groups on the west coast, in the Chicago and New York areas, and in other parts of the country.

As in the previous decade, the great bulk of children's theatre activity during the 1930's continued to be carried out by an ever increasing number of community theatres, recreation programs, Junior Leagues, and college and university theatres. One of the most elaborate of these community children's theatres was the one at Palo Alto, California, established in 1933 by Hazel Glaister Robertson. An average of one play a month was presented during the first season, and so valuable did the experience prove for the children involved that the community eventually erected one of the nation's very few specially constructed playhouses for children. As the years went on, the program expanded to include film work in addition to stage plays.

Other community theatres with such established names as the Omaha Community Theatre; the Town Theatre of Columbia, South Carolina; and the Cleveland Playhouse were added to the list of those producing plays for children. An important program with and for children developed at Cleveland Heights, Ohio, in the late 1930's. Dina Rees Evans, founder and for many years director of the summer program at Cain Park, set up a schedule of classes and productions which were supervised by a large staff and attended by children of the area. Full advantage was taken of the natural beauty of the outdoor setting for classes in art, puppetry, dance, creative dramatics, and radio-television. Extensive training was given to aspiring and practicing children's theatre workers who joined the staff. The Cain

Park program established by Dr. Evans continues to function vigorously today.

The depression years saw literally scores of producing groups introducing children's theatre productions. The Ohio Wesleyan Players and the University of Minnesota Theatre were among the established organizations which added children's plays to their seasons, forwarding the movement and reflecting the utmost faith in the future.

Even World War II did not slow the tide of the advancing forces of hardy and dedicated children's theatre enthusiasts. In 1944, undiscouraged by travel restrictions, a group representing many programs across the land responded to the call of Miss Ward to meet at Northwestern University for the purpose of forming a national organization. The Children's Theatre Conference was the outgrowth of that meeting, and the new body allied itself with the American Educational Theatre Association. Hazel Glaister Robertson of Palo Alto was elected the first chairman. In the years that followed, the Children's Theatre Conference became the strongest national influence for the encouragement of dramatics with and for children and for the elevation of production standards. Its membership today numbers more than 1,200. Its annual meetings draw representatives of schools, colleges, universities, community service groups, churches, special institutions, private studios, recreational organizations, and the commercial theatre.

Immediately following the war two promising commercial ventures appeared and soon built up enviable reputations. The Children's World Theatre, operating from headquarters in the Barbizon Plaza Hotel in New York, continued its extensive touring operation until the death of its founder, Monte Meacham, in 1955. The other, the National Youth Theatre, continued its touring program for a somewhat shorter time. Still others—the Merry Wanderers, under Gian Pace and Dick Dun-

ham, and the Equity Library Children's Theatre booked by
Briggs Management—have been organized in recent years to
fill the vacancies left by Clare Tree Major, Monte Meacham,
and others on the commercial scene.

No accurate count of the number of children's theatre programs existing today is possible. Estimates vary between 500
and 1,500 groups engaged in the production of children's plays
in the United States. A Children's Theatre Conference survey
indicated that in 1957 some 200 colleges and universities in the
country were engaged in some form of children's drama activity, about 50 of them offering formal courses in the field. These
figures indicated almost a 30 percent increase over the results
of a similar survey conducted four years earlier.

Organizational patterns and methods of functioning will be
discussed in detail in Chapter 9 of this volume. Even though
only a few past and existing children's theatres have been mentioned in our summary of the progress of the movement, we
should note that a wide range of organizations has taken up
the work and that a wide range of specific objectives is represented by these groups. Not all of them would subscribe to the
purposes and aims stated at the close of this chapter, but the
eclectic nature of these groups has brought about a healthy
growth of the movement as a whole, a development based upon
continuous examination and re-evaluation.

The children's theatre of the twentieth century is not an isolated phenomenon. Its growth has reflected a general concern
for the children of our times. It has thrived as an implementa-
tion of research, as an example of curricular and cocurricular
activity in schools on all levels, and as a community effort to
meet the demand for programs serving our youth. The final development has not yet been reached. As Nellie McCaslin, children's theatre historian, declared, "Children's theatre in the
United States has been one of the youngest and most vigorous
movements in our cultural history."

2 ∽

Children's Theatre Is Good Theatre

THE ORDINARY PROCESS of living our daily lives frequently brings with it experiences we call *dramatic*. These are moments of crisis, of decision, of giving battle, or of resolving conflict. They are memorable moments, ones we recall later with a chuckle or a shudder or a tinge of guilt. We do not have to work hard to recall these incidents. They are at the root of our learning and are an inseparable part of us. We remember them because they really happened to us; we were involved in them and lived through them ourselves.

In the theatre we are permitted to experience these same moments of crisis or conflict in a slightly different way. Obviously the incidents are not actually happening to us—they are happening to others, and we are looking on. We are, nonetheless, *experiencing* these moments because we are involved with them through our senses. As we sit in the darkened auditorium we seem to become, at least to a degree, the people to whom the incident is happening. We experience *vicariously*—that is, we participate sympathetically in—the dramatic situation. We discover that occurrences in the theatre can also become a part of our background and can contribute to our learning almost to the extent of dramatic occurrences in life.

We may all have *dramatic* experiences every day, but the *theatre* experience can occur only to an assembled audience at the performance of a play. The actors in the play may be reliving an actual dramatic incident, but the theatrical event is experienced only by the spectators.

More and more frequently nowadays the spectators who gather in auditoriums across the country to share a theatrical event are children. Our major purpose as producers of plays for children must be to provide them with a true *theatre* experience. Since we want these children to derive the age-old satisfactions from vicarious dramatic involvement, we must exert every effort to assure them a play within the range of their understanding and a production directed toward their characteristic reaction patterns. Unless we can guarantee these things, the children's time would be better spent on the sand lot or around the house where actual *dramatic* experiences are more likely to occur.

But if the theatrical event is true, there are certain results which we have come to expect. Through vicarious involvement in a dramatic event and through the process of identification with the characters who are living the event, children will gain insight into their own actions; and as they understand themselves better they will begin to understand others. Such empathic involvement with a dramatic event, vividly and effectively portrayed upon the stage, may furnish a basis for future thought and action in the same way as an actual dramatic experience. The dramatic event may not be a substitute for an actual experience, but it may augment it or clarify it by focusing the child's attention on its essence, stripping it of the myriad complications which surrounded it in life.

What theatre experience can impart to the child audience is

almost limitless. The accumulated knowledge and wisdom of the ages can be painlessly, even joyously, conveyed if emotional involvement is aroused. Obviously it is our responsibility as producers to see that what our children derive empathically is worthy of being learned. Patterns of response which are acceptable in our culture can be suggested to children as they take part in the theatre experience. These patterns, as well as facts, are learned; and they can be learned in a natural manner through the process of identification. What is learned with the heart is absorbed into the personality through the back door, almost unperceived, scarcely even recognized. There it dwells to be drawn upon in the child's independent living.

Sympathetic participation in events and emotions portrayed on the stage is just as pleasurable to children as it is to adults. Sitting in an auditorium, they can experience grief without pain, wickedness without guilt, selfishness, cruelty, and greed without remorse. Here is an acceptable way to try out behavior patterns forbidden by our culture but still lurking as part of our animal nature. The joy which comes as the child associates himself with the play's action, its succession of events, and its final climax is unmistakably indicated at the moment of release. Shouts and bodily activity are the sure signs of the pleasurable release of tension in the final resolution of the dramatic conflict. We have come to value this final joyous release as the very essence of the theatre experience. It will not occur if children are asked to identify themselves with a tragic hero. We cannot expect them to derive pleasure from an apparent defeat of the character with whom they have associated their highest aspirations.

We have long known of the power of the theatre to influence human behavior and relationships—it has been alternately embraced and rejected by both government and church, depending upon whether its influence was sought or feared. The theatre will effectively sway society only if our youth, motivated by an adient drive to perpetuate early pleasurable experiences, continue to attend and support it. The future of the American theatre and certainly its standards may well be in the hands of today's children. We producers and playwrights of the children's theatre can therefore follow only one principle: CHILDREN'S THEATRE IS BASICALLY GOOD THEATRE. This principle cannot be compromised.

WHAT CHILDREN'S THEATRE IS AND IS NOT

A children's theatre exists whenever a production of a written script is directed specifically for the child audience. The players may be children or adults, but preferably they are a combination of both—adults in adult roles, children in child roles. If children are used in the cast, they should be children who are ready to take part in an activity in which "the play's the thing" and the director is not necessarily concerned with the play's therapeutic value to his actors but rather with its dramatic value to his audience.

Any activity which does not provide the child audience with a true *theatre experience* is not children's theatre. Creative dramatics, the process of extemporaneous situation and story playing under the guidance of a leader, is frankly not audience centered. Where creative dramatics is concerned solely with the participant and his growing ability to analyze and portray characters from imagination or literature, in children's theatre the *product* is of primary importance. The greatest value to children in creative dramatics is the *process* itself. The story being played may never reach a polished "performance" quality, but if it does the only presentation it is likely to receive is a *demonstration* for the parents or classmates of the group.

It sometimes happens that a story which is played creatively

reaches such a state of development that the leader may decide
it shows the potential of performance quality. When this happens, a script will be written, parts will be assigned, lines will
be learned, and the action and business will be blocked out by
a person with directing ability. Every effort will be made to
polish the performance, to supply the necessary technical aids
such as scenery, costumes, properties, lights, and make-up which
contribute to a total theatre experience for the child audience.
When this happens, the activity is no longer creative dramatics
but children's theatre.

Creative dramatics and children's theatre should be treated as
separate—though mutually complementary—phases of a total
children's drama program. Children under ten should not be
encouraged to perform on stage before a paying audience. We
should be most reluctant to take a chance that an unfortunate
incident or a sense of failure on stage may destroy a child's
desire ever to try again. The place for young children is in creative dramatics where they will learn the process of characterization and the mastery of the means of expression through a
natural channeling of their imaginative powers. Children so
trained will be most valuable to children's theatre groups when
they have reached the age of active participation in formal
theatre.

CHILDREN'S THEATRE WITH CHILDREN

Aside from the fact that the community which supports a
children's theatre is entitled to see a performance in which dramatic values are respected and technical competence maintained,
the director of any group using child performers would do well
to examine his motives carefully. If in reality he is merely
exploiting the children for his personal gain or need for ag-
grandizement, he would do the community a favor by seeking

another kind of occupation. If, on the other hand, he is convinced of the values which child participants can gain from formal theatre, he will bend every effort to see that the goals listed in the next section are actually accomplished.

A child actor can further his sense of self-sufficiency by subjecting himself to the severe discipline required for a consistent character portrayal. A specific objective, obtainable through concerted effort, is set well in advance. The satisfaction that comes as the child actor begins to see himself as a living link between the playwright's script and the audience is a feeling not soon forgotten.

While only a few of the thousands of children who perform in children's theatre every year will ever find their way to the professional stage, all of them will find their way into the society which nurtured their development. The understanding of people which comes from the concentrated study of characters, their backgrounds, their motivations, their frustrations and aspirations will form a solid basis which child participants will find helpful in establishing their own interpersonal relationships in the years ahead.

The exchange of ideas which always occurs in a well-run rehearsal is actual—not contrived—practice in the democratic process. As a child learns to submit to others or to win his point without gloating he acquires an ability which will be the cornerstone of his future success. There are no stars in the children's theatre, and children who have been led to believe they can perform a play successfully without the full cooperation of everyone involved will soon learn otherwise. The child exhibitionist will disappear into an ensemble concentrated on one main effort: to bring the play to life in a perfectly balanced form for the child audience.

BASIC ASSUMPTIONS

As we proceed through the present volume, our discussion will be founded on the primary premise that children's theatre is good theatre. Five assumptions are inherent in this approach:

1. Children's theatre must be undertaken from the point of view that an artistic and communicative relationship inseparably binds the playwright, the director, the designer, the actors, and the audience.
2. A firm and studied direction by an imaginative artist of the theatre is needed to assure a true theatre experience for the child audience.
3. The theatre experience for the child audience is best assured by convincing and genuine characters working as an ensemble in a situation which arouses empathic involvement.
4. Formal theatre for the child audience must be characterized by especially high technical production standards.
5. Under proper direction, child performers can gain much from formal theatre production, though creative dramatics—a separate phase of drama work with children—is a more natural means of expression.

3 ∽

The Audience and
the Play

THE YELLOW SCHOOL BUSSES pull up to the curb in front of the auditorium. With the air of a holiday excursion the children climb out and shuffle toward the door through the early November slush and snow. Boys and girls chatter excitedly, playfully pushing each other now and then as the double lines move into the lobby. Each room teacher hands the correct number of tickets to the attendant at the door, and ushers busily escort the groups to assigned sections of the auditorium. In a matter of ten minutes the seats are systematically filled—lower grades toward the front where they are sure to see easily, larger and older children toward the back. The teachers are near their own groups to keep them under control and to answer questions. A few preschool children are sitting with their parents in a separate section of the auditorium. The air is filled with anticipation, the suspense of an atomic bomb ready to explode, and the smell of wet wool.

While the conditions are probably not ideal, this description is quite typical of the arrival of the most important single factor in children's theatre—the child audience. Out front the house committee sees it as a vast ocean of little people, some of them barely visible over the backs of the auditorium seats. A strange mixture of feelings takes hold of these adults. How gratifying to see the concrete results of their publicity and their careful organization come pouring through the door! Yet how will the production hold down the tide of mounting excitement and weld this colossus into a concerted response? Though acutely conscious of their purpose, these adults cannot help feeling a little apprehensive.

Backstage the cast listens nervously to the rising din that filters through the curtain. Will the children like the play? Will they even listen to it? What will they do if they lose interest? What can the players do to make sure of the audience's attention? So few against so many! Will it be a pitched battle? Or is there really nothing to fear after all? Hesitantly the actors reassure each other. Surely the playwright knew what he was doing. He wouldn't leave them out on that stage unprotected! He must have known well the audience to whom he was addressing his work, and everything about the play must have been calculated to hold in abeyance the potential bedlam of which these children are assuredly capable! Here there can be no half-success as with an adult audience. There will be no polite tolerance of unconvincing acting or sloppy production. Instinctively the actors sense that even their best efforts will be none too good.

In a moment a resounding cheer greets the first flicker of dimming house lights. Did ever an adult theatre give such a sendoff to its favorite stars? As the curtains part, that wonderful suspense-filled hush descends. The actors are amazed, the house crew relieved. Actors sense the complete trust which is placed in their care. The child audience is no longer a sea or colossus, but an assemblage of brothers and sisters willingly entering the world of the imagination.

We do not suppose that anyone fully *understands* the child audience. As in the adult theatre, each one is a little different. Some follow predictable lines of response. The children laugh, cheer, sigh, and listen attentively as one would expect such reactions to occur. Others sit silently with little or no evident involvement in the play. Still others may use the performance as a background for their own amusements. Nevertheless some things have been observed and a few facts have been experimentally ascertained to help us gear our plays and our productions to the audiences for which they are intended.

THE SUM OF EXPERIENCE

Psychologists and educators have done much to lead us away from the old belief that children are little more than "miniature adults." Now we have come to regard the period from infancy to maturity as one of continuous personality development. The youngsters who fill the seats at the children's theatre already have experienced a certain amount of living, and each one of them brings his experiences with him in his conscious or subconscious mind where dwells his every experience ready to interpret, reject, or qualify what takes place before him on the stage. If the story he sees being played out before him can be related to his actual or imaginative life, the child will be caught up in its spell. He will live the life of the characters. He will be led willingly, as the children followed the Pied Piper, beyond the mountains into new and fascinating experiences.

That these journeys into the world of imagination justify the faith with which they are undertaken places an undeniable burden on playwrights and producers. Both need to be unrelenting in their search for knowledge about this audience to whom they are addressing their efforts. They must experience, insofar as possible, the child's world—his beliefs, his feelings, his desires—so that both the plays themselves and the manner of presentation capture the interest of the children and provide food for thought long after the curtain is down.

DEVELOPMENTAL GROUP INTERESTS

The response of children to artistic or imaginative material follows a regular—if not hard and fast—pattern. Tastes, if properly led, progress steadily upward. Experiences with literature, art, music, and drama proceed from the simple to the complex, as to both form and content. They proceed from the literal to the abstract or symbolic as the ability of children to translate and interpret becomes more pronounced. The growth of concepts in the child's mind—images and abstractions which become reinforced through repeated exposure—generally parallels the physical growth and maturation which proceed at a regular rate from early childhood to adolescence.

Because this development occurs regularly in normal children we find it possible to specify certain interests which are likely to appear at various ages, even though we recognize in any given group of children some deviations from the norm. Furthermore, a child does not "step neatly" from one stage to the next. Rather, he gradually expands his interests to include new material while still keeping his foothold on the old and familiar. Just because he has "outgrown" former interests does not mean he may not return to them with great satisfaction. Watch a group of adults at almost any children's play to see the effects of a new exposure to old material!

UNDER FIVE. Children under five years of age are getting their feet firmly planted on the ground. Theirs is a realistic world, modified by mothers and fathers, brothers, sisters, milkmen, postmen, household pets, toys, and weather. All of these exert their influence on them in one way or another as they try to find their place in the vast scheme of life. Some contribute to their frustration; others reinforce their quest for self-realization. Some bring interesting things—surprises and fresh stimulation, new vistas, and fun. Others quietly contribute a warm sense of security. The child is rather self-centered, but he is making an effort to share his things with others at the urgent request of mother. The difference between "mine and thine" is being pointed out regularly. The futility of losing one's temper is being stressed, as are other simple rules of behavior and morality. Youngsters who attend nursery schools are more advanced in these social skills.

Rhythm and repetition are delightful to youngsters of five and under. Funny names, animal characters who have human traits, nonsense rhymes, and jingles capture their interest. The consequences of willfulness, breaches of confidence, misconduct —all on an obvious and simple level—generate suspense. People who fall down, who get paint or mud splashed on them, or who get chased are the funniest things in the world. But people who are lost, left alone, or ostracized are likely to arouse a fear which is overpowering. Music and dancing gain a most favorable response at this as well as at most ages. When rewards for virtuous actions are distributed, these must be quite tangible in nature. All of these things are part and parcel of children's normal experiences, and the fact that they are depicted in their plays does not strike them as being in the least mundane.

Few plays will appeal in their totality to this age group. Few have been written for them. One- and two-year-olds seldom are brought to the theatre for other than baby-sitting reasons, and even three-year-olds are usually sent only by ill-advised parents who are taken with the idea of a play "for children." However, a surprising number of four-year-olds find their way into children's theatre audiences across the country. Unless the plays are written for them and take into account their brief span of interest, this group is likely to become restless quite soon, displaying all the signs of boredom. Producing groups will find that youngsters under five are much better served by a separate series of plays especially written and planned for them than by being encouraged to attend plays for older children.

THE AGE OF FANTASY.   Since many plays of the adult theatre as well as of the children's theatre are fantasies, it may be a mistake to label any single age the "fantastic period." However, children as young as five years of age frequently show signs that simple unrealistic characters are beginning to attract their attention. Even their own dramatic play at five and six is likely to involve realistic family situations which are mixed with elementary fantasy gleaned from books, stories, or television programs.

How soon children embark into the realm of the fairy tale is largely a matter of how soon they feel secure in the world of reality. Characteristically, these stories are peopled with wicked witches, ogres, and evil fairies who wreak horrible vengeance on their victims; so children not well grounded in actuality are likely to feel quite ill at ease with these unsavory figures. Even so, by six or seven, most children have reached the point where they not only feel safe with unreal and frightening characters (from a distance!) but actually revel in the "delicious fear" these characters arouse. By this age, also, children are ready to concentrate longer on the inherent complexities of plot structure and to infer the moral values which are a part of the classic fairy tale. The romantic nature of the subject matter—kings and queens of long ago, poor stepdaughters and farmer lads who win fame and crowns—opens ever-new and fascinating vistas. Through such characters the youngsters experience extremes of fortune which may color future concern for people caught in the web of circumstance.

After five, children are learning systematically to regard the rights of others in their schoolrooms, to apply their best efforts to whatever task they undertake. The vast world of knowledge is beginning to unfold. It is not strange that this would be the age of interest in the fairy tale simply because the child begins to see limitless horizons beyond his little world. Between six and eight, this interest appears to be at its height in most children, but a certain fascination, especially with the wicked characters, continues when they pass on to other interests. (Indeed, extensions of these figures can be found every week on the screen in the form of the "teen-age thriller.") Lines of battle are clearly drawn in the fairy tale; good overcomes evil despite the odds of supernatural powers. The child recognizes the justice of the ultimate punishment and approves the reward of a rise in social status. Since the classic fairy tales are produced more frequently than other plays, many children are likely to get their first theatre experience at a performance of one of them.

THE AGE OF HEROISM.   As early as seven or eight years some boys develop a strong desire for adventure. While certain fairy tales satisfy the craving to some extent, interest is primarily reserved for realistic or historical figures who have achieved heroic proportions through a mixture of fact and legend.

The ages of nine to eleven are considered to represent the height of interest in heroism. This may be due to the fact that exposure to history in school has stimulated an urge to relive the past conflicts and to regain the glory exemplified by these men or women. Modern heroes are as well liked, if somewhat less known, as historical characters.

Young folks of this age are especially well suited to theatre attendance. They are able to concentrate for longer periods of time; they can follow more involved plots; and they are able to interpret to some extent the conventions of the stage. They no longer expect rewards always to be tangible and will accept successful fulfillment of an assigned duty as sufficient recognition in itself. They take special delight in figuring out the "how" of stage effects.

The interests of boys and girls begin to divide rather sharply in this age group. The more rapid maturing of girls places their interests at a considerably advanced level. While the subject matter remains realistic for both sexes, girls seem to be more interested in plays of family and home life, of solving home problems, and of stories containing central girl characters. Boys will show little interest in such stories and will tend to scoff at them, outwardly at least. They will be much more interested in stories of western heroes, pioneers, soldiers, and boys much like themselves who are capable of doing clever deeds to save the day.

These sharply divided interests are probably due to the successful implantation of the sex role in our society: boys to careers combined with adventure and girls to careers as homemakers. While the development of this concept is a steady one throughout early life, by ten or eleven young people are showing the results in their outward behavior.

Historical themes have an appeal to the nine-to-eleven age group for another reason. Until some point during these years, children have not had much concept of time. The "past" could be anything from yesterday to last month. Until young people have had enough experience with time to form an image of its relationship to life and growth, a historical period is nothing more than some nebulous age in which people dressed in a peculiar way. There is no idea of the relationship of one period to another, no idea of progression from age to age. By the time he reaches eight or nine, however, the child is fairly well oriented to the idea of "years ago," and after he begins to study some history he is able to place in time certain important events. As soon as this concept becomes established a new horizon is opened up to the inquiring mind, and a whole new set of fascinating characters awaits acquaintance. This, too, is an excellent age for young folks to discover the children's theatre.

THE AGE OF IDEALISM.   By the age of twelve for boys and somewhat earlier with girls, young people show a marked preference for stories which exemplify an idealistic dedication on the part of the central characters. The adventures of these characters are usually rather romantic in time and place, adding to their grandeur. Characters who fight tremendous odds in search of truth or to further a cause have the complete sympathy of the preadolescent.

On the verge of adulthood themselves, preadolescents are ready to accept subject matter and structure which forms a natural bridge into adult theatre fare. Plot lines can be rather complex; abstractions may be introduced to some extent; and the audience can be expected to follow the story without difficulty. Appreciation of subtleties within lines, irony of situation, and humor of dialogue can be expected to accompany the increased command of language which these young people have acquired.

The fact that few children's theatres pay much attention to this age group is particularly deplorable since it is the link between children's and adult theatre. The junior high school age is almost forgotten in the repertory. These young people are reluctant to think of themselves as "children" any longer and hence do not respond favorably to a "children's" play. A "Youtheatre" or "Young People's Theatre" is far more to their liking. Perhaps this is the reason why a general fall-off in attendance at this age is noted by most children's theatre producers. It may also be part of the reason why theatre-going is not as general among adults as might be wished.

CONSIDER THE INDIVIDUAL

The general pattern of advancing interests and interpretative skills which children display from the early years to adolescence is an important key to the production of plays addressed to them; but one must also realize that there will be some deviations from the pattern, depending largely upon the cultural environment in which the children are growing up.

The speed with which children develop interests has something to do with how soon and how frequently they are exposed to new material. There are differences between a child who has older brothers and sisters and one who is alone in the family. Precocious children seek to expand their experiences sooner than others. Children to whom stories are read or told consistently or who have television in the home are often exposed to material prematurely, and their rate of development may actually be hastened.

Many conditions which affect the rate of literary development can obviously be related to the socioeconomic level of the community from which the children come. Those from wealthy residential districts can be expected to respond quite differently to the same material than their peers from a foreign-speaking industrial center. Children from progressive school systems in which a premium is placed on individual exploration will probably be more advanced in their tastes than those from less modern schools. Variations may be noted from section to section of the country as different occupational groups are encountered.

So rapidly do these conditions change in modern society that it is dangerous to generalize about which group will be advanced and which retarded in its artistic tastes. Mass ownership of television sets even among low-income groups may have a profound effect on any existing pattern.

THE MIXED AUDIENCE

Ideally, our child audience is composed of one age group whose interests are likely, in spite of some variation, to be homogeneous. For a fairy tale we should be able to confine our audience to six-, seven-, and eight-year-olds. For an Arthurian romance, we should invite only children in the sixth grade or above. Both plays and productions should be geared to the specific age group which has shown interest in the particular subject matter. If we are fortunate, the school system will present the play on school time, and only the specified grades will be allowed to attend.

More often than not, however, we look in on a week-end performance of an exciting western story and see scattered throughout the house a large representation of kindergartners and first and second graders for whom neither the play nor the manner of presentation was intended. There seems to be no way of preventing this short of literally denying admission to children under the specified age. Many producers are reluctant to take this step for several reasons, the main one being the complete disappointment the child feels when he has been anticipating his trip to the theatre. Even so, the presence of the wrong age group is likely to be a source of consternation to both actors and producers, as well as to other members of the audience. The following observations will, however, help us to take strength until the ideal condition of strict limitation can be realized.

Fortunately, many of the plays in current repertoires have been written as total works of art rather than as strict fairy tales, adventure stories, or romances. Playwrights have mixed appropriate elements of other kinds of stories into their playscripts. They have tried to include several "levels of meaning" which will be recognized by children at whatever degree of understanding they have achieved. The rather universal concepts of suspense and humor are generally interwoven with the subject matter in a way that makes the play reasonably interesting for those below or above the "recommended" age. Each child will draw from the experience whatever has meaning to him at his stage of development.

In the mixed audience we will find children who range from the most naïve to a rather mature point of view. In such groups the more mature children are likely to "trigger" responses throughout the auditorium by laughing at the humor of a line or by suspensefully hushing the younger children as they try to catch subtleties of situation or character. A characteristic of the "psychological crowd" is the collective response which may be led by a relatively small group. The older members of the audience will tend to "draw" the less mature up to their age level in response patterns. Frequently when no older children are in the audience an expected response will not occur at all.

Children certainly have an effect upon each other in the audience situation, but that effect is somewhat different from the psychological crowd in the adult theatre.[1] Whereas adults will generally show some reluctance to respond in an individual manner without group support, a single child can frequently be seen jumping up and down in his seat, laughing gleefully, without getting so much as a sideward glance from the others. Adults tend to relax their individual restraints in order to react as a group, but children are not necessarily conscious of a total group response at all. Youngsters do, however, take "cues" from fellow audience members. If a small group starts buzzing

[1] For an account of the theatre audience as a "psychological crowd," see Barnard Hewitt, *The Art and Craft of Play Production*, Lippincott, 1940, pp. 31-35.

in boredom at a certain spot, this reaction may spread like a wave throughout the auditorium. In the same manner, the excitement response may build to deafening heights, not necessarily because the suspense of the play is building but because more and more of the children are caught up in the stimulation of the response itself. Fortunately, then, the children who are younger than the intended age group will to some extent be "led" in their response patterns by the older children, who note subtleties which even the desired age group may miss.

For a Common Response: Rhythm

While interests change from age group to age group, while they develop at different rates of speed in individuals, rhythm is one factor which can be relied upon to establish a common ground among children of all ages. Rhythm is so basic to life itself, founded upon the heart beat, the regular intake and outgo of air through the lungs, the pattern of waking and sleeping, the regularity of all movement, that it has become recognized as the very foundation of all artistic response.

Children's normal rhythm patterns are different from those of adults. These differences are not entirely a matter of tempo, although certainly this is part of rhythm. A normal child's pattern is built upon sudden and complete changes. He partakes of active living at an exhausting degree of intensity for a brief time; then he releases almost completely. The lull is followed by another period of activity during which the body tires and demands release from tension. As the day wears on the successive periods of release and tension become more frequent, cannot be sustained as long, and begin to show signs of fatigue and irritation. The younger the children, the shorter are the alternating periods.

Playwrights, directors, actors, and technicians are all made painfully aware of any disrespect they may show for these normal rhythmic patterns of children. Scenes in a successful children's play will alternate between tension and release, excitement and quiet, pageantry and reflection, action and conversation. We soon discover that errors in calculating the length of these alternations may result in inattention and rejection on the part of children. Children have less control over their rhythmic patterns than have adults and will not make necessary allowances. The playwright, especially, must arrange his dramatic material in a sequence which takes this basic physiological factor into account.

Thus, it is necessary to know the general development of interests and response patterns through the childhood years, recognizing that socioeconomic factors, intelligence levels, and cultural environments will effect changes in these patterns. But it is also helpful to realize that the concept of the "psychological crowd" and the somewhat eclectic nature of plays in the modern children's theatre repertoire can provide some basis for a common response—at least partially satisfactory—for those groups which must produce for a mixed audience.

THE THEATRE AND THE NEEDS OF CHILDREN

Children sitting in the darkened house sigh with rapture at the unworldly splendor before them. They are sensing something beyond, something deeper than momentary delight in the trappings of the stage. From their seats in the auditorium they are reaching out for a fuller life. The theatre, for the brief span of the play and, we hope, for long afterward, is touching the innermost being with its magic.

EXPERIENCE THROUGH IMAGINATION

The bonds of time and space are just as real to children as they are to adults. Yet there is within us all the capacity to experience in a vicarious way the adventures, the situations, the exploits which expand our knowledge and satisfy our desires. A child may have a deep sense of inadequacy built through incident after incident of apparent failure; but in the theatre he becomes through his imagination the youthful hero who is not only adequate but unquestionably victorious. The achievements of the hero become his achievements. A lonely child who wants companionship experiences through the leading characters a very real sense of belonging and being needed. For a time, at least, he is not ostracized but taking part in the action with others.

While adults experience the same kind of satisfaction at the theatre, children seem to sit breathlessly waiting for the "magic moment" to arrive when they will depart—heart, soul, and body—into the realm of make-believe. As the house lights start down, the children give audible evidence of their impatience to begin. As the curtain opens, the world of reality slips away into the dark house, and only the unearthly light on the stage is truth. When the "moment" arrives—and it should come quite soon in a children's play!—the children are caught up in the action so literally that one can easily observe muscle tensions, facial expressions, and even actions identical to those occurring on the stage.

Actually, many "moments" will come throughout the play. But the first moment is of the utmost importance. Children want action to begin immediately. They are impatient with delayed curtain times, long introductory speeches, and extended exposition, so anxious are they to experience the first great "moment" of transport, to suspend their disbelief in the contrivances of theatrical art.

Children should find in a theatrical performance the same escape from the humdrum of daily living that adults crave. The quest after beauty has not yet been dulled in their minds. They may live in squalor among the smokestacks of the factory district, but they will not fail to appreciate the efforts of a thoughtful producer who has been successful in providing true beauty for them. For a while, at least, these youngsters will live in a new and glorious world where color, grace, and harmony are in abundance.

But it is not just the factory district children who find in the theatre a chance to expand their experience. All children construct for themselves mental pictures drawn from bits and scraps of life, stories they have read or heard, pictures they have seen —all of an existence beyond their high walls. At the theatre, these pictures come to life. The desire to see them in concrete form is one of the very real drives which can be counted upon to fill the auditorium for the performance of a familiar story. An unfamiliar story will require more effort on the part of the producer; but if he is painstaking in his publicity he will be able to build in the children's minds new pictures which will prepare them for the new play's reception. Incidentally, he will not have the problem of a discrepancy between the production and a preconceived image of it, and he may very well provide a theatre experience which is more satisfying than one which comes from a familiar play bounded by strong preconceptions.

A Thin Border Between Actual and Imaginary

Observation of a child audience during a performance will quickly confirm the truth that children do not make much distinction between various levels of reality and make the transition from reality to unreality with little difficulty.[2] This ability to enter into imaginary situations with little reservation or, indeed, little consciousness of the unreality of it all is characteristic of children from early childhood to adolescence. While the phenomenon was first noted in connection with literature,

[2] For an extended discussion of this point, see Kurt Lewin, *A Dynamic Theory of Personality,* McGraw-Hill, 1935, pp. 104-107.

the presence of the living actor supported by all the visual aids of the theatre tends to make the experience more literal.

The willing suspension of disbelief which children show in the theatre often leads them unwittingly into a desire to change or interrupt the action on stage. Adults may wish to interrupt, but they seldom call out to the characters in warning of impending disaster. Children can be expected to take advantage of their superior knowledge of the situation on stage by giving advice rather freely to the players. For the time being, at least, it does not occur to them that the play is imaginary and that they are only observers without the power to take part in it. Though the house lights will again return them just as easily to the world of reality, the extent of children's involvement in the imaginary situation suggests that they have been contacted at the very roots of their being and that a lasting impression has been made. This goes beyond mere sensation. It is a thing which will modify behavior in general living.

Children do not appear to make much distinction between a character and the actor who portrays that character. The performer of an unsympathetic role will have a hard time overcoming the aura which surrounds him on stage when he appears among the children afterwards. They will have very little to do with such unsavory personalities but will often regard them with fascination from a safe distance. This identity of character and actor in the child's mind has many implications for producers of children's plays.

IDENTIFICATION: THE BASIS OF THE THEATRE EXPERIENCE

The process of *identification*—the tendency to "become" at least partially and for a limited time the person whose problems are being perceived—is central to the theatre experience. Children identify themselves to the extent that the character possesses traits or desires which they recognize within themselves.

Their inner fantasies are displayed before them, and they watch a portion of themselves achieving their desires. It is through this process that imaginative experience can be so satisfying, that some of the basic needs of childhood are met, and that attendance at the theatre can become a meaningful thing.

Most children recognize that they are a mixture of good and bad traits, that they think thoughts and do deeds that are alternately desirable and undesirable. Images of perfection are constantly held up to them for comparison with what they themselves are, and the inevitable result is a feeling of guilt, the development of conscience.

Through the process of identification children see in the villainous characters the "badness" that is in them. As they identify with these antagonists (and they unquestionably do) they experience the power of being antisocial, if only for a moment, and then the purging that comes through punishment. Their guilt is salved, and they can go on secure in the thought that they have paid the price for the escapade.[3] The shrieks of delight in a child audience as the villain gets his just reward are perhaps not so much pleasure in the thought that good has overcome evil as a deep sense of relief that the children's own "bad" actions have been punished.

The child audience will derive more satisfaction from protagonists who overcome their weaknesses than from those who are perfect from the start. Children need the reassurance that they, too, can conquer the evil that is within them. They know the hatred and feelings of aggression which plague them in their daily lives. As diminutive members of an essentially adult society, they rebel violently against their comparative weakness. They contemplate hateful actions against those they love. It is through identification with meek and lowly characters who

[3] Herbert Kupper, "Fantasy and the Theatre Arts," *Educational Theatre Journal,* March, 1952, p. 35.

battle and defeat the powerful that children experience a safe outlet for feelings which bring on a strong sense of guilt if allowed to fester within them. Those who would "water down" the conflict in traditional tales by softening the strong, primitive, sometimes gory action in them must recognize that in so doing they are likely to rob the stories of their ability to satisfy the natural hostilities of children.

The degree to which children identify with characters in a play depends entirely on the extent to which the performance transports the children into the realm of make-believe. While theatre-going should remain an aesthetic experience for children, anything which interferes with the identification process will tend to weaken the value of the play. The skill of adult actors is considerably greater, as a rule, than that of child actors; and since adults are able to tell the story more effectively, children will identify more closely with them. If the audience recognizes its peers on the stage, an inability to believe in the characters completely may result. For this reason a play by a child cast will improve when taken to a school where the actors are not known.

The psychological process of identification with characters in the children's play is thus seen to be the key to enjoyment of the play. It also is the touchstone by which the child audience is led on a journey through new experiences, the channel through which vicarious success over seemingly insurmountable odds is achieved, the poultice which draws out the infection of guilt and leaves the soul purified.

EXPECTED PATTERNS OF RESPONSE

When children have been properly prepared for an emotional experience in the theatre, sponsors, producers, and actors are always delighted to find their efforts so unmistakably appreciated. Children react to the imaginative situation with definite and overt displays of humor, excitement, and fear, while boredom and even embarrassment will likewise reflect developmental interests.

The mode of presentation—the actors' method, technical accoutrements, and general "spirit" of the production—influences the nature of the reaction to the content itself. The difference between children's and adults' reactions is principally a matter of degree rather than kind; but actors who are accustomed to playing before adult audiences soon learn that the *loudest* response from children is not always the most desirable one, and that it is not necessarily the reaction of the majority of children. Though it may attract the most attention, it is not always a clue to the general response of the audience.

HUMOR

One of the most bewildering sights, but not uncommon, for a director seated among the children in the auditorium is an individual child rocking and squealing with laughter at something on the stage, completely unmindful that his glee is not shared by anyone else in the audience. Such a reaction illustrates the tendency of children to respond individually even though they are part of a large group. The laughter may have been brought on by a complete misinterpretation of a line, a word, or a situation—but it is nonetheless very real and very satisfying to the child. Obviously, teachers should not try to quell this kind of reaction in an effort to make the child conform.

Children under twelve (sometimes even older) find humor in simple incongruities, feelings of superiority, funny-sounding words and names, and farcical situations. They will laugh at the combination of stupidity and pomposity in a character, at the underling who is "putting one over" on his superiors. They will squeal with laughter at the moment of consummation of a trick or even during the preparation period as they anticipate the climax. They will respond with loud laughter as people fall, are tripped, slide the full width of the stage on their stomachs, are kicked, bitten, or tickled by hidden or "invisible" forces.

Adults frequently err in what they think children will find humorous. They may well ask themselves whether a thing appears funny because it makes an essentially adult comment on childhood. "Cuteness" in dialogue, characters' names, or in the staging may seem quite delightful to adults but seldom to children. Young people take themselves very seriously, and they regard with contempt any tendency on the part of adults to look down on them or to think of them as "cute." Playwrights or directors who cannot resist the temptation to perpetrate their own private little jokes at children's expense have no business in the profession. The sincere, naïve laughter of a child audience, given in complete faith, should be sought by playwrights, actors, and producers in the spirit in which it is given. Laughter should be recognized as a frequent reaction to both humor and excitement. As suspense mounts in a children's play, a combination of laughing and shrieking is likely to be the normal outlet for pent-up emotions.

EXCITEMENT

Children will display a general emotional state of excitement when their interest in the dramatic situation is sufficiently strong to stimulate a desire to enter into the action. Frequently one can observe the children duplicating every muscle tension on the stage as they vicariously experience the conflict along with the characters.

Excitement is unfailingly generated by scenes in which the principal character is chased and eventually caught by antagonistic forces. Such sequences occur in many plays for most age groups, and the response is always the same. On the other hand, intensely quiet scenes, in which someone is sneaking around the dimly lighted stage, will produce a suspenseful hush, much leaning forward and nail biting, and suppressed squeaks of apprehension. During scenes of crisis, in which it appears as if all is lost for the protagonist, children will jump up and down in their seats, call advice to the players, and occasionally start down the aisle to lend a hand in a more physical way. Sword fights and contests of all kinds will generate excitement in the form of wide-eyed, breathless watching. Children do not miss a detail, so anxious are they to experience the victory of the favorite character.

While overtly expressed excitement cannot automatically be considered "overstimulation," there is always a danger that the border line will be crossed. It is certainly undesirable to have children completely lose perspective, forgetting the theatrical situation and the external nature of the stimulus. A reasonable degree of involvement in exciting situations should be encouraged for the emotional release it can afford; but moments of intense conflict in the children's theatre should be achieved through a pooling of the artistic sensibilities of the people involved: the playwright, the director, the actors, and even the technicians.

FEAR

Some of the general excitement responses are perhaps more accurately classed as fear, since children may be showing apprehension for the safety of characters caught in certain intense situations. Fine distinctions between these emotions are difficult to draw, since many of the same patterns appear whether the children are excited or fearful.

Clear-cut fear responses are likely to occur as a result of sudden shock—a flash of light, a loud explosion, a quick transformation, a sudden entrance. Certain forms of stage magic also seem to trigger this response. However, if the situation quickly returns to normal the fear subsides and no harm is done. Nevertheless, very young children may fail to enjoy the rest of the performance because they anticipate a return of a similar shock.

As we have already noted, children, especially in the early years, do not differentiate their own experience from what they see. If the imaginative situation on the stage reminds a child of his own secret fears, or if it calls forth violent fantasy desires of which he is ashamed, he is likely to experience a severe reaction and display intense rejection behavior. Parents and producers frequently are bewildered when a younger child must be carried from the auditorium in a state of mild panic. Cajole and comfort as we will, the child refuses to go back and take his seat. Such a reaction to the imaginary situation can usually be traced to a chronic anxiety that comes surging forth.

Fortunately, severely frightened behavior at the theatre is exceptional. Most well-adjusted children are able to experience the fear and suspense inherent in drama without harm. A few, however, will not only show extreme reaction at the moment but will also continue the experience in their dreams. One obvious purpose of children's theatre is to provide an outlet for pent-up hostilities, to broaden experiences which presumably point the way to healthy psychological adjustments. However, the theatre can hardly be expected to provide therapy for neurotic children, and it is a mistake to condemn a play as being too frightening merely on the basis of an isolated reaction.

It is equally a mistake to ignore the possibility that a given dramatic situation may prove overly frightening for a large number of children. As early as 1908, for this very reason, the Moscow Art Theatre decided to omit the Forest and Graveyard scenes in its production of *The Blue Bird*. Subsequent producers of the play have recognized the validity of the objection and have either cut these scenes or tempered them in production. In other plays a few extreme characters, such as barbarians, Indians, ogres, and witches may tip the delicate balance between "delicious fear" and serious fright. The long, pointed fingernail is the very essence of terror for the young child.[4] Many children display an extreme rejection of shrieking women characters who scold loudly and threaten their adversaries. As we describe later, in Chapter 6, producers and actors can usually modify a performance in accord with the sensed response of the children. Such tactics seldom call for compromising the dramatic impact of the play. They are simply good sense.

BOREDOM

The child audience lacks the basically adult sense of social decorum which prevents it from showing boredom. The signs are unmistakable: shifting in seats, talking to neighbors, standing up and looking around, and even an occasional trip up the aisle for water. There is nothing quite so deflating to an actor as the undeniable and obvious fact that no one is paying attention to him. If once they experience the indifference of a child audience, actors will usually go to any limit to prevent its recurrence.

It should be noted, however, that there is a difference in degree between the undesirable reaction of boredom and the normal release which comes after scenes of high tension. The rhythm of a children's play requires these "releases" for the specific purpose of preventing overstimulation. If the play does not provide them where they are needed, the children themselves will insert them—much to the consternation of the actors.

Certain conditions on stage almost invariably call forth a boredom response. Such "wiggle spots" are likely to occur in

[4] Leo Angelo Spiegel, "The Child Concept of Beauty: A Study of Concept Formation," *Journal of Genetic Psychology*, 1950, p. 20.

scenes of exposition without action. Sequences depending entirely upon comprehension of dialogue and denying the language of children—which is basically action—may easily lose attention. Long speeches by a single character and sequences which develop character rather than plot will probably lose the audience. Characters who sit down to talk are not likely to be interesting to children. Long explanations of off-stage action will likewise bore them, since they would much prefer to see what is happening rather than hear about it. Adults will sit quietly and cough, perhaps even shuffle their feet, at boring points in the drama, but children will not be so reserved in their comment.

A character who makes an entrance during a "wiggle spot" will attract the audience's attention immediately. The children seem to feel that once a new person has arrived things will "get going" again. Even though the entering character may eventually add to the boredom response, his arrival at least is accorded undivided attention.

The fact that entrances, changes of pace, or the introduction of new plot elements may immediately eliminate boredom and crystalize attention would seem to indicate that at least some heed has been paid to happenings on the stage throughout the sequence. Actors disturbed by apparent indifference are often amazed to note how quickly attention is regained.

For evidence that peripheral attention is functioning at such times, we need only observe adults and children in the presence of a television program. They can be doing many other things during the course of the action while still keeping "half an eye" on the screen and "half an ear" on the loud speaker. This is apparently true in the theatre as well, for at least some of the exact quotations reported to producers in letters and conversations have been delivered during the "wiggle spot" segments. At times producers and actors would swear that no one heard a word of what was said in certain scenes, but they are amazed to discover that the scenes not only have received their share of attention but are sometimes cited as the "favorites" of the children and are remembered almost verbatim!

As with excitement and fear, this boredom response should not be prolonged unnecessarily. While few plays will hold undivided attention throughout the performance, especially among a mixed age group of children, actors and producers should try to recognize the distinction between boredom and the normal release. Actors have been known to "release" the audience so far that it is never really regained, with a result that is closer to bedlam than to any kind of artistic experience. Every effort should be made to prevent the vicious circle of "inattention→ noise→inability-to-hear→more noise→lost audience."

Embarrassment

Since children usually rate kissing among the "funniest things" adults do, their reaction to a scene of love-making in the theatre is often one of embarrassment or open rejection. Boys, particularly, may whistle, catcall, or boo if the situation on stage even remotely suggests a personal love between characters. Oddly enough, they seem to make a subtle distinction between the impersonal love of the princess for the prince and love inspired by other motives. Marriages of state and "convenience" appear to be a matter of course in traditional tales, and so children of all ages are rather accustomed to them. Sex relationships other than these are seldom approved. The affection of friends and coconspirators, however, is within their experience, and finds sympathetic reception in the children's theatre. The love of mother and father *for their children* likewise receives sympathetic attention.

Not until young people are well into adolescence will they be comfortable viewing scenes of passionate emotion. The very young are bored by them; intermediate grade children wonder what all the fuss is about; in the upper grades and junior high school, the girls begin to understand, but the boys will usually busily look the other way or mimic the self-conscious rejection of the older boys. It would therefore seem wise to eliminate such scenes from a children's play, since the reception is likely to be quite different from that desired.

Admittedly, most of these reaction patterns are typical of a hypothetical "middle" group of children. Variations will occur with children older, younger, more advanced, or less sophisticated than this middle group. The suitability of the material and the method of presentation will have much to do with the reactions of any given audience. Each producer is urged to study the responses of the children of his own region and cultural climate; he should take copious notes during the plays, interview, and use any other research device which occurs to him in order to build his own knowledge of children's reactions to the imaginative situations presented in plays. The benefits of such procedures to directors, actors, and technicians will be immeasurable.

PERPETUATION OF THE EXPERIENCE

The curtains close, and the performance is over. By the time the house lights come up, half the children already have on their coats, caps, and mittens. Teachers lead their groups up the aisles in an orderly manner, and the smiles on the children's faces proclaim better than words that the experience has been a happy one. If the actors are in the lobby to meet the children on their way out, the youngsters may go directly to their favorite player and bombard him with questions about the background and skills which the character displayed in the course of the performance. Or they may shyly regard the actors from a distance, unwilling to break the illusion of the story. Regardless of the factors and motives which combined to bring them to the theatre, the children who leave the performance carry away with them a new experience, a new attitude, a fresh point of view which will be food for future thought.

Responses Are Fed Back

If the producers are fortunate, they will receive an invaluable collection of letters in which children record their impressions of the play. These provide a concrete guide to the probable lasting effects of the performance. Frequently children's letters will compare the current production with past ones they remember. Titles may have escaped them, but the breadth of detail they recall will amaze the recipients. Usually the points of greatest audience involvement at the performance are mentioned as the favorite spots. But directors who study these letters can frequently discover references to concepts and incidents which needed a period of thought and gestation in order to find their place in the child's scheme of life. These are the lasting impressions for which workers in the children's theatre strive. They serve to emphasize that during every moment of the play children are watching, listening, and interpreting a message. The message had better be one we wish them to carry throughout life.

Sometimes a producer is fortunate enough to observe the children of the community giving rather concrete evidence of the play's impact. The carry-over from the theatre to children's own dramatic play is usually a clear indicator of the impression created. Neighborhoods may get together and present their own version of the story for astonished parents and friends. Informal play may include verbatim passages from the most immediate experience with the drama, or even a strange mixture of passages and incidents from several recent offerings. An

40697

alert producer will make it known throughout the community, to parents and teachers, that he is vitally interested in receiving reports of such incidents to add to his file. Through careful examination of these reports he can gain valuable insight into the child mind and consciousness. He will learn that his job is not completed with the closing curtain, that the results of his work are more far-reaching than he imagined—it is not too farfetched to suggest that the concepts learned today in vitally stimulating form at the children's theatre may appear tomorrow on the floor of the United Nations General Assembly.

4 ∾

The Playwright
at Work

THE PLAYSCRIPT is the heart of the production. Careful direction, excellent acting, and magnificent staging mean nothing unless the play itself is worthy of its audience.

The constant search for quality children's theatre playscripts provides a strong challenge to the imaginative playwright. As the number of producing organizations increases, the demand for plays becomes intensified. To vary their seasons' offerings, children's theatres seek realistic and historical dramas, fairy tale and fantasy plays, romantic or idealistic tales and scripts based upon familiar stories or upon some new and different theme which will provide a change of pace. It is up to the children's theatre playwright to supply these plays.

There is no formula for turning out a good children's theatre playscript any more than there is a rigid prescription for writing adult dramas. The principles of sound dramaturgy apply in either case. Essentially, the mechanical aspects of play construction remain the same, regardless of the audience to which a playwright addresses his work. Any differences are a matter of

degree or emphasis. This chapter is designed to guide the dramatist in his writing and the director in his selection of plays for
the child audience.

All children's plays have a central figure or figures, a protagonist force through which the audience sees the play. Every
children's play has a plot, a story arranged into a meaningful
pattern which depicts the struggle of the protagonist to achieve
or gain an objective. If either the objective or the protagonist
force is unworthy of our interest, if we cannot care about them,
then there is no play at all. The meaningful pattern of the play's
plot will determine its theme—an important element of a children's play. But *the most important quality of any children's
drama is the story,* and it must control the play. All other struc-
tural elements must be considered in reference to story.

STORY AND PLOT

The plot of a children's play is the arrangement and amplification of its story in terms of the playwright's purpose. The
relationship between plot and story is sometimes confused, and
there are even those who claim that the two are synonymous.
The story, however, is only part of the plot. It is what happens
to the characters, what they do. The manner in which the story
is told is the plot of the play. For example, there are several
dramatic "versions" of Cinderella. Each is basically the old
familiar story, and, in that respect, all are identical. However,
in each play the story is told or plotted differently.

Every children's play must have a story which includes a
logical progression of events depicting the struggle of a protagonist to achieve his goal. The plot should develop simply and
clearly, avoiding complications and subplots which do not move
the story forward. This is generally true of adult drama, but it
is especially true of children's plays. Any intrusion of extrane-

ous material, any temptation to halt the progress of the story while a character mouths platitudes or thematic concepts the writer wishes to impart to his audience, should be rigorously avoided by the playwright. Epigrams, gags, and jokes divorced from character or plot should be similarly avoided. After witnessing some existing children's plays, a writer may feel obliged to include a big fight, a chase scene, or a scene heavily dependent on broad physical movement. True, children like such action, but this alone is not sufficient reason for superimposing exciting scenes. If they are used, it should be only because they contribute to the normal development of the play.

Closely allied to arbitrarily intruded extraneous material is the danger of getting the story so involved or complicated that it becomes necessary to introduce an outside force to extricate the protagonist from his dilemma. This problem has probably faced every playwright in the history of written drama, and it constantly confronts the children's theatre playwright as he constructs his play. Obviously, if his protagonist can merely reach out and obtain his objectives there is no conflict and consequently no drama. Obstacles must therefore be thrown up to prevent the simple attainment of the goal. These may be in the form of antagonistic forces seeking the same goal, or the goal itself may become an antagonist as it struggles against attainment by the protagonist force. Whenever the playwright allows the complications he erects to become insurmountable by the protagonist force, his only alternative is to introduce an outside element or force to resolve the difficulty.

The ancient Greeks referred to the use of this outside element as the *deus ex machina*. The term "god out of a machine" had a literal application then, but it is still applicable to modern drama—only the means of introducing the "god" differ. All of us have seen dramas, especially on television or in the motion pictures, where the protagonist is hopelessly lost until the *deus ex machina* appears at the last possible moment to save the day. This technique tends to destroy our belief in the artistic reality of the drama.

What implications does this have for the playwright constructing a fairy tale drama? In fairy tales the protagonist's problem almost invariably is solved through the good offices of a supernatural force. However, an examination of the vast majority of fairy tales which have stood the test of time will reveal that an aura of magic surrounds the entire story: supernatural forces are at work almost from the beginning; they come to the aid of a protagonist who is clearly worthy of their aid; the expectation of such assistance is inherent in the development of the story. If in plotting a fairy tale play the dramatist carefully prepares for the arrival of the element of magic, he does not deceive the audience. However, if he introduces it without prior motivation and preparation, he violates a basic principle of artistic honesty.

Since the plot of a children's play should remain relatively simple and uncomplicated, the introduction of a strong subplot is questionable. Subplots may be useful in unfolding the action, but in a children's play they should retain a direct relationship to the major story line and actually contribute to the rise of the play to its climax.

A climax is necessary whether a play is for children or adults. As members of an audience we expect, no, we demand, a climax to resolve the major question posed by the drama and to provide a release from the tensions which have mounted steadily to that moment. The release which occurs as the conflict is resolved allows the audience to have a theatre experience, which, after all, is the purpose of theatre. Minor climaxes or high points are essential as various smaller crises emerge in the plot of the play, but these should contribute to the rise toward the play's major climax.

Some confusion exists regarding the terms *crisis* and *climax*.

The *crisis* is the intensification of a question to the point where the outcome is in doubt. The moment when that doubt is removed is the climax of the crisis. In children's theatre the playwright should see that his play ends soon after the climax. His audience will not wait around for a gradual denouement.

In spite of all these cautions, if the playwright who starts out to write a children's play is so aware of all the "do's" and "dont's" that apply to him, he is in great danger of losing the creative spark entirely. Children's theatre playwrights should shape their plots, write rough drafts of their plays, and then concern themselves with suiting the material to a particular group or age level. Sometimes the greatest strength of a play lies in its appeal to several age groups. Often a play resolves the question by naturally inclining itself toward one group or another. If, without damaging the plot or characterizations, the playwright can adjust his play and its attendant action and dialogue to meet the needs of a certain group, then, and only then, should he do so.

Normal plotting procedure requires that each scene of the play leave a question unanswered, the curtain falling at a moment when the outcome of one of the smaller crisis situations is clearly in doubt. However, when the final curtain falls there must be no question as to whether the protagonist has achieved his goal. In the children's play the final climactic moment often is written to allow for a spectacular closing with many characters on stage to reinforce the ultimate triumph of the protagonist and leave the audience fully satisfied that this triumph is an occasion for widespread rejoicing. In Chapter 6 we shall observe how such an ending also can assist the director in planning the curtain call.

An Original Drama or One from Literature?

Since many directors prefer to offer their audiences the stories and characters children know and love best, the playwright often feels pressure to turn to familiar works of literature for his dramatic material. This preference for familiar stories and characters is understandable. Parents are eager to have their children share the childhood experiences they held dear. Traditional stories are proved entertainment. They call out to children with voices from another age—perhaps one that never really existed except in the imaginary world of the young, but that was, is, and always will be a world of reality to the growing child. Stories from this realm are in a sense timeless. They possess a universality of mood and emotion and, therefore, pose little challenge to the playwright to anchor them in time and place. Familiarity with the stories they are to witness on the stage not only does not dampen the interest of children, it seems to have the opposite effect, since it enables them to follow the story easily, to concentrate more intensely upon the characters and their struggles.

However, despite the popularity of tried and true material, there is much to be said for using unfamiliar stories from children's literature. For some reason or another a number of stories, many excellently written, have not become popular with children. A dramatist approaching them anew can frequently instill the spark necessary to translate these stories into excellent dramatic fare and thus reintroduce worthy literary works to the child audience. The playwright turning to the children's theatre field for the first time may well be advised to try translating a little-known story from the printed page to the living stage.

As the playwright gains experience in writing for children he undoubtedly will eventually want to attempt an original play. Nothing can be more rewarding to a writer than originating all elements of a drama from his creative imagination. Children's theatres will always lean heavily upon the traditional repertoire but, recognizing the need for more and better plays, they will always welcome the well-conceived, well-written original play.

Some playwrights have enriched children's dramatic literature by writing original plays around characters already well known. For example, when Albert Mitchell discovered a genuine interest in the character of Miles Hendon in *The Prince and the Pauper,* he built a completely new play around this familiar character and called it *The Prince and the Knight.*

SELECTING STORIES FOR CHILDREN'S PLAYS

The children's theatre playwright employs the mechanics of dramatic construction and utilizes the elements of drama primarily to communicate the all-important story, but unless the story itself is adequate in the first place there is nothing he as a playwright can do to bring it to life. He must therefore evaluate his choice of story on the basis of the elements a story must contain if it is to serve his purpose: the plot, the theme, the characters.

Whether the story chosen as the basis for a children's play is original or borrowed, it must present a problem with a complication or obstacle which has to be overcome before the problem can be resolved. Overcoming the obstacle must involve conflict which builds to a strong climax. As we have noted earlier, this is the plot.

The playwright must also give careful thought to the theme or idea of any story he is considering. Most themes can be reduced to simple statements of universal truths such as "honesty is worth any sacrifice" or "rewards gained falsely can never be lasting." As we have previously remarked, obvious moralizing is never justified in children's plays; however, worthy ideas must be inherent in them. An important reason for examining the theme before giving serious consideration to any story is that unless the central idea is worthy the story should be abandoned.

Evaluation of the central character is especially important, since it is through identification with this character that the child responds to the story. To make a strong protagonist, he—or she—must have the qualities of attractiveness, credibility, and strength of will. The characterization of the protagonist, the antagonist, and other characters of a children's play is discussed later in this chapter.

Dialogue is unimportant in selecting a story for dramatization, since its function in the story is materially different from its function in the play. The story writer has no need to rely on dialogue to tell his story; instead he writes descriptive passages which serve his purpose far more adequately than conversation. He also has the advantage of being able to explore the thoughts of his characters and record their reactions to other people and situations, reactions which may never be translated into overt actions. The playwright can reveal such things only through externalized actions and actual dialogue.

Rather than taking dialogue directly from the story the playwright should write his own lines, using standard criteria for dramatic dialogue as his guide. Since stories seldom have much dialogue that truly characterizes individuals, he will have to be most inventive to convey through the spoken word the traits of each character as created in the literary story. If he captures the spirit of the original story and its characters and then writes his own lines he is almost certain to find that his dialogue is not only consistent, a necessary quality in any drama, but also more spontaneous and natural.

In some cases a universally familiar story will contain certain lines of dialogue so well known to children that they will be disappointed if these lines are not heard in the stage version. These lines, borrowed directly from the story, will sound natural if the playwright has made the characters and plot of the story *his* characters and *his* plot.

The foregoing criteria are generally applicable to selecting story material for any dramatic medium. An additional consideration must be given to stories for children's theatre plays: if a story is to provide a satisfactory basis for a plot it must be suitable for children, and it should be the kind of story children enjoy. For example, no story will hold the interest of a youthful audience if it is built upon maturity of character relationships which make it difficult for children to follow and understand. Furthermore, no story will make enjoyable theatre fare unless it can be translated into visually observable action. The aspiring children's theatre playwright must certainly acquaint himself with youthful tastes, as described in Chapter 3, for example. In addition, a knowledge of children's literature will serve him well. There are many fine critical studies in the field of children's literature, and these will provide him with authoritative opinions to assist him in selecting story material for his plays.

From Storybook to Stage

Having selected the story from which he will fashion his play, the writer's immediate problem is that of translating material from one medium to another. There are several basic differences between writing stories and writing plays that will affect his ability to translate any story to the dramatic medium of the stage. The difficulties presented by these differences must be surmounted if his work is to be successful.

In the first place, dramas are not actually written—they are "wrought." The spelling of "playwright" indicates a person who *makes* plays, dramas. Composition in the usual literary sense is almost foreign to the playwright. He must think in terms of action—of characters acting and reacting upon one another. His powers of visualization are not necessarily more acute than those of the novelist. However, the playwright must be able to turn his visualization into clear-cut dialogue and stage business that will effectively convey his story on a stage.

The produced play is a time-art, whereas the published story is a nontime art form. The playgoer has no control over the time element. Once the curtain rises the action proceeds until the story is told. The reader of a story, however, is in complete control of the time factor. He may read as little or as much as he wishes at any one time, or he may reread passages or entire sections before continuing. Since the theatre audience lacks this advantage, the playwright must utilize every word, every phrase, every piece of business to convey his story the first time it is told. He cannot stop his action to explain the motivations, history, or background of a character. Everything must be revealed to the viewer as the story unfolds and be so well incorporated within the unfolding that forward progress is never impeded.

The time-art element of a produced play offers the child audience a startling contrast to literature. On stage the play is actually happening, uninterrupted in its flow. This places great demands upon the playwright, since in the unfolding of the play everything must be unquestionably clear to the children. Only when this happens can they fully understand and appreciate the drama they are witnessing.

Exposition poses few problems to the writer of a story or a novel. If necessary he can use an entire chapter to develop the background of a situation or to explain his characters to the reader. The playwright, however, must be able to motivate his characters and keep their actions consistent with what has been disclosed to the audience about them, thus developing situations that clarify themselves in their very unfolding.

ADHERENCE TO THE ORIGINAL STORY

A major problem facing the playwright using material selected from literature is the question of adherence to the original's story, characters, and theme. With what degree of faithfulness must he treat the story being translated to the dramatic medium? He can vary this from absolute adherence to the original to a relatively liberal interpretation in which he borrows as much or as little of the material as he chooses in terms of his own specific purpose.

Some story material contains elements that make it suitable for almost literal transference to the dramatic medium, while other works of fiction are suitable for dramatic interpretation only in certain respects. In the latter case the playwright must interpret the borrowed material freely in order to create a dramatically acceptable stage piece. The playwright is making a children's drama, and it is to this end that he must make all decisions regarding adherence to original material.

The very term *dramatization* implies a faithfulness to the story, characters, and theme of the original work. If the material lends itself to such literal transference the playwright may, if it suits his purpose, accept the plot, characters, and theme and give them dramatic life. In such a case he should clearly label his work a "dramatization."

Not many stories lend themselves to simple dramatization. *Adaptation,* on the other hand, is quite a different matter. When performing the task of adaptation the playwright's purposes may supersede those of the original author. An adaptation is somewhat faithful, at least recognizably so, to the original material, but the playwright may take greater liberties with plot, character, and theme in terms of their dramatic feasibility than he would when doing a "dramatization."

In some cases, what the playwright does is neither dramatization nor adaptation. He may decide only to *base* his play upon the story, in which case he will take over only certain portions of the original story and its characters, as they suit his dramatic needs. More liberal changes in plot, character, and theme are possible when basing a play upon an original story. The term *suggested by* is applied when only an idea or ideas expressed in an original work are borrowed and amplified by the playwright, perhaps to such an extent that they lose their identity in the plot of the play.

If a children's play is an adaptation of a familiar work, be it of literary or of folk origin, the director will surely evaluate it on the basis of the original, and the playwright must recognize this fact. He is safe in making major departures from the original only when he is dealing with a little-known or completely unknown work.

In recent years there has been much discussion of the effect folk literature may have upon the growing personality, and many works, both literary and traditional, have been either condemned or rewritten on the basis of their "suitability" for children. Ugliness, lack of breeding or even petty criminal acts, and the "unrealistic" aspects of fairy tales are sometimes condemned as harmful. Frequently, removal of the unpleasant or supernatural elements from a work of children's literature will weaken the story and characters, and when the story is a familiar one, this elimination in turn will weaken the play. There is an essential realism in fairy tales in that they are true to human nature but not necessarily to human powers. Human traits are so specifically highlighted that there can be no mistaking them, even when the play reaches into the supernatural and the characters allegorically represent good or evil. The playwright should avoid falling into the trap set by those who would remove all "objectionable" elements from stories which in their original form have delighted and edified generations of young people.

Careful scrutiny of the theme remains a basic criterion for choice of stories to be made into plays. If the central idea is acceptable but the playwright seriously questions other elements which are an integral part of the story, he may be well advised to make another choice. It is better to discard the total work than to destroy its strength by making radical alterations.

THEME

Themes of plays are usually serious in nature or intent. In every case, let us repeat, they should be imparted implicitly *within* the action, not explicitly stated or pasted on like a label which calls out, "This is my theme; this is why I wrote the play!"

All worthwhile themes are calculated to move men toward good acts rather than evil. Living in a moralistic society, a playwright cannot avoid stating a point of view as he arranges the elements of his play. The arrangement of those elements will determine his message. His purpose may be so important to him that he will select a character to mouth his own feelings. If he submits to this urge to preach or moralize, his play will almost certainly fail. Children, like adults, detest being admonished, and they are not deceived when moralizing is woven into the dialogue of a play. They instinctively react with, "We are being lectured, and we don't like it."

Even a strong theme can be imparted implicitly, within the action of the drama. Showing a point of view—demonstrating it in terms of understandable action and dialogue—is far better than telling it. The very act of telling a message erects a barrier to its reception. Besides, a drama is a doing, a showing, not a statement of a lesson to be learned. If the playwright coats his message with sugar, it is easily digested, and its effect is more penetrating. The audience will take the message from the theatre, and it will become a part of a total experience, its effect being judged in terms of its lasting power.

The extreme of explicit statement of theme is the tacked-on message, telling the children to be good, to eat their vegetables, to believe in God, and to get plenty of sleep. This usually differs from the main theme of the play and is often an added thought. We have even seen a play, otherwise excellently constructed and staged, that ended with an added scene beyond the story line in which members of the audience were urged to brush their teeth twice a day and see their dentists twice a year.

Most experienced playwrights recognize that they do not start the creative process with a theme or message in mind. Rather, they find a story or a set of characters that fascinates them. They arrange their incidents and build their play, and when it is done they discover that their work expresses a point of view and really has a theme. While this discovery may come as a complete surprise to the writer, the theme's presence is inevitable.

CHARACTER

Character creation draws heavily upon the imaginative powers of the playwright. He is faced with the problem of creating believable characters an audience can care about. The children's theatre playwright is often faced with the additional task of bringing to life characters the children already know from their storytelling and reading experiences. To create dramatically acceptable characters without destroying the established images held by the children is a real problem.

MAJOR CHARACTERS

Although simplicity is the keynote of character development in children's drama, the playwright still has an obligation to portray his characters vividly. Major characters in a children's play tend to be semidimensional in nature, falling somewhere between the extreme of flat stereotypes lacking any dimension whatsoever and highly developed, complex personalities.

PLATE I

The nucleus of theatre for children. (Macalester College Children's Theatre, St. Paul, Minnesota)

PLATE 2

Above. *Individuals will react differently to the same scene. (Macalester College Children's Theatre, St. Paul, Minnesota)*

Right. *The child in the theatre. (Long Beach Children's Theatre)*

Below. *A mixture of ages usually attends. (Macalester College Children's Theatre, St. Paul, Minnesota)*

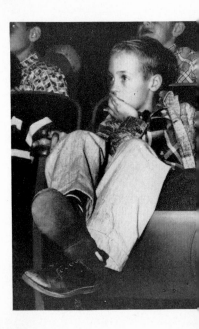

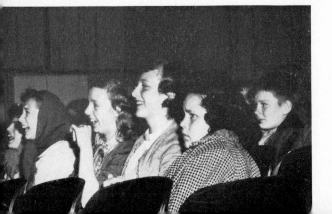

PLATE 3

Above.   *Note the possibilities for movement and pictures with this floor plan. J. Morton Walker's design for Chorpenning's* King Midas and the Golden Touch; *University of Minnesota Young People's Theatre production, directed by Kenneth L. Graham, 1951.*

Below.   *Note the placement of the throne and other key properties. Herbert L. Camburn's design for Watkins'* The Rose and the Ring, *Michigan State University Junior Players production, directed by Mary Jane Larson Watkins, 1955.*

PLATE 4

Characters grouped meaningfully and interestingly around the central action. Lee Mitchell's design for The Samurai Sword, Children's Theatre of Evanston production, directed by Winifred Ward, 1934.

PLATE 5

Above. *Naturalistic design for William Brady's production of Marion DeForest's* Little Women, *New York, 1912.*

Below. *Vern Adix' realistic design for Musil's* Seven Little Rebels, *University of Minnesota Young People's Theatre production, directed by Kenneth L. Graham, 1941.*

PLATE 6

Above. *Simplified realism in Lee Mitchell's design for* The Princess and the Vagabond, *Children's Theatre of Evanston production, directed by Winifred Ward, 1930.*

Below. *Stylization in Merlin E. Bement's design for King's* Peter, Peter, Pumpkin Eater, *Michigan State University Children's Theatre production, directed by Mary Jane Larson Watkins, 1956.*

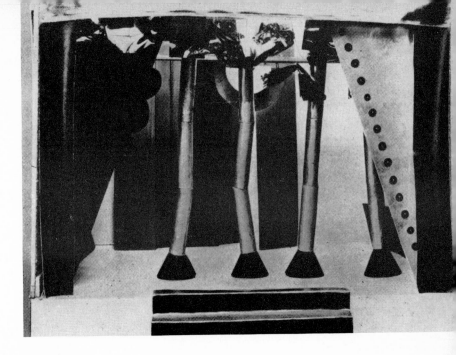

PLATE 7

Above. *Extreme expressionism in Gonchorova's design for* The Blue Bird, *Russia, ca. 1925.*

Below. *Capricious expressionism in a design by Daniel Covell for Chorpenning and Tully's* The Elves and the Shoemaker, *Michigan State University Junior Players production, directed by Mary Jane Larson Watkins, 1957.*

PLATE 8

Above. *Wendell Josal's theatrical design for Moulton and Ware's* Alice in Wonderland, *University of Minnesota Young People's Theatre production, directed by Robert Moulton, 1954.*

Below. *Theatricalism and stylization in Elemer Nagy's design for Humperdinck's* Hansel *and* Gretel, *the opera for children produced by the Hartt College of Music of the University of Hartford, directed by Elemer Nagy, 1942. Note the use of a portal.*

Within this semidimensional pattern major characters may exhibit genuine traits without being either too simple or too complicated for the child audience. Above all, playwrights must avoid subtlety in creating these characters; otherwise their meaning will be lost for all but the most perceptive children.

The real danger in keeping a major character semidimensional is a possible failure to provide the actor with a role he can bring to life by utilizing his talents to their fullest extent. However, the playwright can impart an impression of simplicity to a characterization without sacrificing his challenge to the actor for a penetrating analysis of the role.

Since the average children's play runs for considerably less than two hours, the children's theatre playwright does not have the time allowed the writer of adult dramas to reveal his characters. And since plays with small casts of characters are rare in children's drama, the playwright must also face having the time he can spend developing any one character greatly restricted.

This time limitation handicaps the children's theatre playwright. A character is revealed largely through his own words and actions. When the opportunity for this revelation is restricted, the playwright must make certain that the traits he wants revealed are established quickly and economically. Since the forward progression of the play cannot be halted for character development, all characterization must be achieved in the normal unfolding of the plot.

Each character's actions and lines reflect his reactions to the dramatic situation and the other characters involved in it. In order to see a person dimensionally we must witness his reactions to these different people and events. The sum total of these reactions constitutes a view of his personality. In creating major characters for children's drama the writer must fight a tendency to allow them to become one-dimensional by reacting to everybody and everything in the same way. Granted that the inherent limitations of the medium preclude creation of fully dimensional characters, the semidimensional character does have some breadth and depth. His dimensionality is best revealed by the varying ways in which he meets his changing environment.

THE PROTAGONIST

Every play needs a protagonist, a person or group of persons about whom the play revolves. Even experienced playwrights have made the mistake of writing a play which is one character's story, only to discover in performance that the audience identifies with another character altogether. While he is working the playwright should continually ask himself, "Whose play is this?" That character should be the protagonist, and the drama should be written to insure that it is his play as well as his story that is being told.

No playwright can ask his audience to accept a central figure who is neither credible nor attractive. The audience must believe in the hero and care what happens to him. He must be believable in terms of human life and human values. Although he need not be a "realistic" figure, the qualities he displays will be interpreted as desirable human characteristics by the children identifying with him. He therefore must be worthy of the faith placed in him by members of the audience.

Realizing that he cannot hope to establish complete dimensionality in his major characters, the children's theatre playwright may err in creating a protagonist who is too good, too perfect. Such heroes are as unacceptable as those lacking attractiveness. Children find it difficult to identify with the superman character who displays no weakness or apparently makes no mistakes. Such characters convey an impression that they are superior to anyone else. Children dislike this attitude in life and tend to reject it in their theatre experience. Examination of the protagonists in the best-loved stories from children's literature will reveal that most of these characters do exhibit failings which make them more credible in human terms. Even Sleeping Beauty has a fault—a fatal curiosity which carries her to the tower room. But she is more acceptable as a protagonist because she is not 100 percent perfect!

The children's theatre playwright should avoid rushing into the actual writing of his play with only a detailed plot outline to guide him. His characters, especially those involved in the basic conflict, should be fully conceived before writing begins. It is the clash of characters upon one another that produces drama. If the playwright does not have a vivid picture of his characters and their strengths and weaknesses it is almost impossible to generate genuine conflict. Carefully established characters can only act and react as they have been created. In a sense they take over the playwrighting task, writing their own dialogue and, in a broad sense, resolving their own difficulties.

The playwright should ask himself the following questions about his protagonist: Is he merely *acted upon*, or does he move with strong volitional motivation toward his objective and thus bring about the action of the drama? Does he, chiefly by his own abilities and efforts, bring about or cause to be brought about the resolution of the plot? If he must rely entirely upon an outside force to extricate him from what appears to be a hopeless situation, he is not a very strong or worthy protagonist for children's drama. The child audience expects the protagonist to win, but he must always remain worthy of his victory. This is the reason there are no tragic heroes in children's drama. All authorities are in agreement that good must always triumph in children's theatre and that triumph must be demonstrated in more concrete than abstract terms.

Many children's theatre plays are written with two equal

protagonists linked together by a common quest or peril. Zar and Zan in Chorpenning's *The Emperor's New Clothes* are examples of a pair of characters acting more or less as one. It is more common for one protagonist to be a boy and the other a girl, thus providing identification possibilities for both sexes. Beauty and Prince Elano in Chorpenning's *The Sleeping Beauty* do not really act as a unit, but they provide identification possibilities for both boys and girls.

In some children's plays the protagonist is a group, such as the family in *The Utah Trail* or *The Five Little Peppers*. Identification with the various members of the family as each in turn takes up the main action is a normal extension of the familiar process. In general, however, multiple-identification plays should be reserved for audiences over eight years of age, since they are likely to be somewhat confusing—therefore unsatisfying—to younger children.

THE ANTAGONIST

The antagonist, either as a force or as an individual, is usually a much greater problem to the children's theatre playwright than is the protagonist. Young children are easily frightened, and it is possible for an animal antagonist such as a wolf or crocodile, even an obviously make-believe one, to terrify this group unless it is tempered by humor or made to appear ridiculous or ludicrous or ineffective. Walt Disney and Walter Lantz, pioneers in the motion picture cartoon field, developed one method of handling the animal antagonist. The cat chasing the mouse is a humorous character who always is outwitted. The fox trying to trap the roadrunner is treated in the same way.

The fear provoked by antagonists in the theatre is different from the emotion aroused when the same characters are told or read about in a story. In the theatre the antagonist's presence is immediate and concrete, whereas in a story told or read from the printed page he remains an abstraction. For this reason the antagonistic force in plays for the preschool child should never represent pure evil. The playwright's care in handling the antagonist in this case probably will exceed his concern for the protagonist, so important is it not to trigger a deep fear-response in this age group.

If the playwright has aimed his play at the middle group described in Chapter 3 (ages six through eight), the antagonist may be clearly evil, especially in dramatized fairy tales, since this age group will accept what the younger group will not. Even for these children, however, various techniques are frequently used to temper the total impact of the forces of evil. For example, three characters comprise the antagonistic force in Chorpenning's *Cinderella*—the mother and the two sisters. The sisters are made comical, and this softens the force; the mother, however, remains a relentlessly insidious influence. The antagonist in White's *Snow White and the Seven Dwarfs* is consistently cruel, but she is made ridiculous at the end of the play when she sprouts a long nose which she can never slough off. Furthermore, this cruel antagonist is softened by a force allied to her, since the witch who assists her is a clearly comic character.

In writing plays for older children it is possible to view the antagonist more realistically. The principle works on a sliding scale: the younger the audience, the less threatening the antagonist; the older the audience, the more realistic the antagonist. In Chorpenning's *The Prince and the Pauper,* for example, the antagonist is John Canty, who has no redeeming feature except that he is the hero's father. His presence in the play is not likely to constitute a personal threat to the older audience to whom the play is addressed, since its members all have heard of such fathers and rejoice that their own parents are not like John Canty.

Minor Characters

In order to throw more emphasis on the development of major characters, the children's theatre playwright will usually find that minor characters of necessity run more or less to types. Because minor characters in children's plays tend toward the one-dimensional, they pose few problems for the dramatist.

Nevertheless, determining the relative importance of each minor character is a key decision for the playwright. If he does not exercise caution in this regard, undue audience interest may be aroused in a character planned to serve a minor and temporary plot function. If such interest is aroused the audience wishes to see more of the character; but if the playwright has dismissed him from the scene there is no way to bring him back into the action.

A general rule of thumb is first to determine the basic function of each minor character. If a minor character is merely to perform an essential bit of business or to assist briefly in furthering the plot, he should be kept one-dimensional and not allowed to have an individualized personality. For example, a guard may be employed to conduct a major character on a journey or to prison. The playwright need go no further than making him "the guard." If he endows such a character with interesting personality traits, the playwright not only endangers his emphasis when he dismisses him, but he also misleads the audience.

Children's theatre playwrights are well aware of the demand for scripts with large casts. Furnishing such scripts bothers many playwrights, because they dislike sacrificing character creation for the sake of providing large numbers of parts. The wise dramatist keeps his principal characters few in number regardless of the number of minor characters he chooses to employ. They at least will assume some stature and will become semidimensional.

MOTIVATION

The playwright must prepare the audience to accept whatever he has his characters do and to believe these characters capable of performing every action in which they are involved. In other words, every action of every character must be motivated and consistent with what the audience has discovered about him.

As characters encounter other characters and become involved in the situations of the plot, they will of necessity react. If at any time the playwright wants a character to react in an unusual manner, he must carefully establish the plausibility of the response by preparing for the unusual behavior. Establishing plausibility or potentiality in no way tells the audience what is going to happen. It does, however, prepare them to accept actions and reactions as consistent with the character as he has been revealed to them.

Acts which are accepted as a matter of course in everyday life will have no meaning in the theatre unless they are motivated. In real life, for example, people enter and leave rooms, seldom offering an explanation of where they have been or where they are going. On the stage, however, a character's entrances are not acceptable unless there is some explanation of where he has been, what he has been doing, and why he has come. The same is true of exits. The playwright must be extremely careful in bringing characters in and getting them out of the immediate action.

All action, including scenes of spectacle, should be motivated in terms of the plot. Here is where many children's theatre playwrights err, succumbing to an impulse to include such scenes as songs, dances, chases, and comic bits for their own sakes. To be sure, the child audience may delight in such sequences, but unless they can be logically motivated in terms of the plot, they have no place in the children's play.

DIALOGUE

The dialogue of the children's play poses more of a problem to the playwright than it does to the director. While the director will judge it on the basis of the function it serves in the total production, the playwright is acutely concerned with dialogue as the medium whereby his artistry succeeds or fails.

The function of dialogue in children's drama is to further plot, reveal character, and clarify situations. To achieve its purpose it must be simple, direct, and economical. However, simple, direct language does not mean language geared to the lowest grade levels. Clarity of expression rather than difficulty of individual words should be the criterion. Flowery speeches and long conversational sequences revealing the inner thoughts and psychological complexities of characters are certainly to be avoided. The character-revealing function of dialogue in children's plays will best be served when each character's lines quickly and clearly distinguish him from the other characters and keep him consistently individualized throughout the play.

In furthering plot, dialogue must contain nothing that will deter the play's action or cause it to digress. Frequently dialogue in the children's play is of secondary importance compared to action. Therefore, in scenes where visual stress is more important than auditory, dialogue should be used sparingly and only when necessary to explain meaning or purpose or to motivate a piece of action not completely clear in itself.

Dialogue is what gives a play life and magnetism. Lest the children's theatre playwright feel unduly limited by his potential audience, let him remember that thorough understanding and appreciation of the story and its characters will assist him in painting vivid portraits. His technique will include economical use of language to avoid wordiness, choosing words which will impart just the right flavor to each character speaking, and permitting himself to be so caught up in the forward movement of the plot that he cannot possibly allow its progress to be interrupted.

THE PLAYWRIGHT IMPARTS RHYTHM TO HIS PLAY

Many playwrights and directors prefer to ignore the question of a play's rhythm. To them it is a mysterious occurrence defying explanation. As we remarked earlier, rhythm is essential to life itself, and without rhythm the play, like the body, will die of malnutrition.

Every element of a play is related rhythmically. A character is created with a basic rhythm of his own. He comes into contact with other characters possessing their own basic rhythms, and the ensuing scene has a rhythm of its own. The speeches, the scenes, their growing relationship to one another, constitute the rhythm of the play. Interrupt it, or break it, and the play either dies or is so badly damaged that it limps through to its concluding curtain.

The adult play usually begins slowly in order to accommodate late-comers and to allow the audience to settle down and prepare for the theatre experience. In children's theatre such waiting is disastrous. Therefore, the playwright sets out to establish interest at once. He also is charged with a responsibility to keep the opening action clear, relatively simple, and not cluttered by the immediate introduction of a large number of characters. An opening scene involving pantomimed action is not only arresting, but it also establishes the overall rhythm of the play, suggests the prevailing mood of the story, and points ahead to subsequent action. In addition, it gives the audience an opportunity to orient itself to the environment in which that action will take place.

Examples of this type of opening are readily found. Tully and Chorpenning's *The Elves and the Shoemaker* opens on a dimly lighted shoemaker's shop; soft music is playing; suddenly the door opens, and three small figures enter in a shaft of moonlight. Martha Bennett King's *Peter, Peter, Pumpkin Eater* has a clearly rhythmic opening as Peter's mother and sisters are discovered making pies with the action carried out in a unison movement almost suggestive of the dance. Whiting and Rickert's *Huckleberry Finn* begins with a furtive escape followed by a silent chase which introduces the major action. The director must realize that the rhythm of any play actually begins before the opening curtain. His role in establishing this rhythm will be discussed in Chapter 6.

In the children's play, rhythm is most noticeable in the relationship of scenes. While each scene must contribute to the forward movement of the story and build toward the climactic moment when emotional intensity reaches its peak, a steady and unrelieved increase of tension could tax the emotions to the breaking point. Careful plotting should prevent this from happening. Tension is built as each minor crisis is reached. Then, when the obstacle is overcome and the crisis reaches its climax, a moment of release precedes the next rise in intensity. The play for children accomplishes these build-ups largely in terms of overt, often vigorous, action. Each such scene should be followed by a quiet scene.

The playwright should recognize that he places almost insurmountable obstacles in the path of the children's theatre director when he ends one act with a conversational scene and begins the following act with a similar conversational sequence, when he prolongs the more static scenes, or when he places two rhythmically similar scenes together.

The director should always subject the rhythmic structure of a playscript to careful scrutiny before he decides to produce the play. His handling of the playscript will have much to do with the overall rhythm of the performance, but if the playwright has not provided him with a rhythmically sound drama, no amount of effort on his part will rescue the play.

THE LENGTH OF A CHILDREN'S THEATRE PLAY

The running time of a play is a major problem in children's theatre and thus an important factor in playwriting. Producing groups often insist upon a two-hour play in order to satisfy parents that full value has been received for the price of the child's ticket or to keep children in the theatre for the same period customarily occupied by the Saturday movie. Either point of view is a mistake.

Despite the compelling nature of a live theatrical performance, the attention span of children is relatively short, and to sacrifice the theatre experience the event is intended to provide is not justifiable under any circumstances. A play running from forty-five minutes to an hour is quite long enough for the very young. Older children usually will remain attentive through a play which lasts approximately an hour and twenty minutes.

When a play is overly long, the simple factor of physical fatigue can play havoc with attention. When a play is reasonably short and lively and colorful in writing and staging, the period of concentration goes unnoticed, and subsequent retention of the theatre experience will be stronger and more lasting.

COVER SCENES

In a children's play every scene must serve the primary function of furthering the plot. However, many scenes have a strong mechanical function as well. These are known as cover scenes.

Typically they are sequences arranged to bridge intermissions, allow an actor sufficient time to change costume, or maintain interest to mask a technical movement in lighting or scenery.

Some children's theatre playwrights anticipate intermission problems and write scenes to be played in front of the curtain. Such a scene is usually brief and is an integral part of the play. It may involve a group of characters in action, or a single character presenting a narrative of details occurring during the time lapse in the dramatic action. Musil's *Robin Hood,* Mitchell's *The Utah Trail,* and Whiting and Rickert's *Huckleberry Finn* are examples of plays utilizing such techniques to advantage.

Many children's plays are capable of including such scenes, and if the playwright has not provided them, the director may elect to write them in, using either a single-character narrative or a group scene. Bridging scenes, however, must be extensions and amplifications of what has been and will be occurring in the play. They should be written in the same style as the script itself with no apparent break in either dramatic action or writing technique. Under no circumstances should they be added as afterthoughts the day before the play opens.

SELECTING THE TITLE

Selecting a title for a play may not at first appear to be a playwriting problem, but many writers actually handicap their works by making a wrong choice. Finding an intriguing title poses no problem when one dramatizes a familiar story, since the choice is automatic in that case. However, providing a title for an original play or one based upon an unfamiliar story is not as easy as one might think.

Although a title may accurately describe the story, it may not capture the fancy of a potential audience; and all too often a play draws crowds on the basis of its title alone. Worthy as an unfamiliar work may be, it will compete on the season's bill with plays bearing established and recognized titles. If the name of the play suggests that its story will appeal to the child audience, it is more likely to succeed.

Theatre involves the collaboration of many artists. In children's theatre each of those artists bases his work on the premise that he is producing *good* theatre. Working from this point of view the playwright devoting his talents to writing dramas for the child audience will discover that he faces essentially the same problems and applies the same basic techniques in this field as he does in the adult theatre. His task will be more enjoyable and the results of his efforts more successful if he becomes familiar with all the aspects of children's theatre.

In a very real sense the playwright is the key factor in the collaborating team of artists who work to produce fine plays for the child audience.

5 ∾

The Director
Prepares

THE ROLE of the director in children's theatre is to bring the play and audience together in performance. He works with the actors and technical staff to make the production artistic, finished, and capable of arousing delight in the minds and imaginations of the children who view it.

The basic principles of good theatre are the same, whether they apply to plays with adults, with children, or with mixed casts. The present discussion of the complex subject of directing is applicable to all types of producing organizations, though, recognizing that some problems are unique to a specific kind of group, we shall from time to time suggest techniques and procedures having special application to one or another. The present chapter covers only preparation for rehearsals; the following chapter is concerned with director-actor relationships through rehearsals and performances.

CHOOSING THE PLAY

The director's first important decision is the selection of a suitable script. One unfortunate experience with a poor script quickly demonstrates how important this decision is. No amount of directorial skill, no amount of clever design and staging, can make up for a basic inadequacy in the text itself. On the other hand, a strong script can gain and hold the attention of the child audience in spite of many production faults.

The primary requisite of a children's theatre script is that it exemplify the qualities we have discussed in the previous chapter. These specific demands of theme, plot, character, and dialogue must be uppermost in the director's mind as he reads, so that the script he selects will provide a worthwhile activity for the players as well as a rewarding theatre experience for the audience.

The director should be equally concerned that the script be suitable to the particular audience for which it is intended. He tries to ascertain whether the situations and characters are within the comprehension of the children who will be the audience, whether they are likely to be of sufficient interest to hold the attention of those children, and whether the dialogue clarifies the story on that level. He must decide whether the script will satisfy the needs of the children who will see it or whether it contains situations that would be better avoided in his community. A working knowledge of the development and needs of children as discussed in Chapter 3 will guide the director through this phase of the process.

Finally the director decides whether or not his own producing group can be successful with the script. The number and complexity of the roles are of considerable importance, especially when child actors are used exclusively. The technical demands of the play must be taken into account, and some consultation with designers and costumers may be needed before making a final decision. The fact that the production may be given in many different auditoriums and must therefore be transported may also have a bearing upon selection. Moreover, the director himself may feel more secure with one script than he does with another because of his own experience or lack of it.

Above all, a director should never elect to produce a play which he does not like, for he will live with it for a considerable period of time. If it does not at the first reading set his imagination afire with production possibilities, he should leave it alone. But if he is impelled to read it at a single sitting, is unable to put it down until the final curtain, and if he is set ablaze with enthusiasm and ideas, then this is the script for him. Regardless of the demands upon his time, ingenuity, and stamina, he will find a way to bring this script to life and share his thrilling experience with child audiences wherever the production goes.

GETTING STARTED

The imaginative children's theatre director will probably visualize action, characters, and environment as he reads a play that interests him. Just as his subjective response to the play will be instrumental in his decision to produce it, his initial visualization will influence his overall concept of the production.

Once the play is selected, the director must study it carefully to arrive at a clear-cut production concept which will then serve as his master guide through each of its phases. If no historical period is specified, as is the case with many fairy tales and fantasies, he will decide what period is best adapted to enhance the qualities of the script and what type of setting will provide the best environment for the action. He will become acquainted with the play's characters as individuals, determining their roles in the unfolding plot. Until he knows what the play says and how it says it, he is not prepared to cast and rehearse his actors or to work with designers or technicians toward the integrated artistic production that is his goal.

The director who wishes to leave nothing to chance will formulate a careful preparation check list. Such detailed advance planning of every phase of production will free him to exercise his creative role unhampered by confusion and last-minute panic over forgotten details.

TRYOUTS

ADVANCE PLANNING

For most children's theatre directors the process of casting the play is one of the more harrowing aspects of production. Will the right kinds of people turn out? What if unmanageable mobs show up? How will he be able to remember who came, how various individuals read, what qualities they exhibited? How can he be sure the cast he chooses will be the right one? Careful preplanning can alleviate many of these problems, and evidence of planning and organization can be instrumental in setting the tone for the entire rehearsal and performance period.

Casting should never be a hasty process. Choosing a cast is a calculated gamble at best, and it is impossible to do an adequate job of selecting actors in a single tryout session. Whether one is casting adults or children, a series of tryout sessions is needed. Three open sessions plus a call-back allow the director time to acquaint himself with prospective actors, to note evidence of growth and interest as candidates become familiar with the script, and to give a hearing to those whose schedules might have prevented attendance at an earlier tryout.

Fortunate indeed is the director who can hold his tryouts in the auditorium where the play will be produced. Lacking that, he needs a room large enough to provide an open area where readers can stand and move about, and where he can be far enough away to check vocal quality and projection. If the play is to include song and dance, separate rooms should be secured for these auditions; and if he has enlisted the assistance of a dance director and singing coach, they should hold simultaneous tryouts so that candidates for roles can go from one audition to the next.

The director is advised to recruit assistants to distribute and collect scripts, see that tryout cards are properly filled out, and answer routine questions. It is next to impossible for the director to handle all the mechanics of tryouts without such assistants. He should be able to devote undivided attention to the business at hand, which is giving a fair hearing to the candidates for roles.

When he is casting a play with adult actors he can save much time by duplicating for distribution a brief synopsis of the play, short character sketches, a tentative rehearsal schedule, dates and places the production will be presented, and information about the obligations the company will be expected to assume. If the play it to tour, such expectations should be made clear. A frank statement of what the actor's obligations will be if he is selected for the company will provide an immediate "out" for candidates whose motives for coming to tryouts may be somewhat vague in the first place. For child actors this necessary information should be presented verbally. Distributing such material to children in initial tryout sessions is likely to arouse false hopes.

Tryout cards are an invaluable aid to the director. The sample illustrated here suggests typical information that should be readily available to him. Some directors record their reactions directly on the cards, while others prefer to keep separate notes. However they are kept, written notations should be made as each candidate reads.

Starting at the beginning and reading straight through the play, merely changing characters from time to time, is not a satisfactory audition method, since random readings reveal little of the actors' potential. Scenes in which the characters

TRYOUT CARD

(Name of Theatre)

Name

Address

City   Phone

Grade   Age   School

Height

Special Talents

Other Obligations

(Do not fill in below this line)

Date   Play

Comments

Fig. 1. A sample tryout card.

appear in a variety of moods and relationships should be carefully selected in advance.

TRYOUT PROCEDURES

When the time for tryout arrives, the director warily surveys the waiting group of hopefuls who have assembled to display their talents. He knows only too well that the best director can make mistakes in casting, and that the most he can expect to discover during readings is the possibility of a possibility. Nothing is more discouraging to him at this point than to have to share this responsibility with a disinterested "casting committee," made up of children or adults untrained in the ways of the theatre. Democracy has little to do with casting, and selecting a cast by majority vote is ridiculous. On the other hand, a few trained and interested assistants can be of great help to a director in discussing reactions and possibilities after tryouts have been completed, provided the final decision belongs to him alone. He alone is responsible for bringing the play to life, and his instruments are the actors. He must be free to choose those who capture and project the qualities he seeks. If the producing organization has placed its confidence in him, assuming that he will be able to direct and coordinate the production, it also should allow him the privilege of selecting his own cast.

In screening actors for children's theatre productions, the director applies the same principles of sound theatre practice he would observe in casting a play for adults. Producing a play for children requires the same seriousness of purpose as does any other theatrical venture. In children's theatre our major concern, as we have remarked several times, whether we are casting adults or children, is to provide the child audience with the best possible entertainment. However, since children and adults pose their own problems in the audition situation, tryout techniques differ. We shall first consider the selection of the adult cast.

CHOOSING THE ADULT CAST. One problem in selecting an adult cast for a children's play is that those coming to try out often have no idea what a children's play is, how it will be produced, or why. They may be bewildered by what they face. In this event it is the director's responsibility to orient them to children's theatre in general and to the specific nature and requirements of the current production. He must communicate his own seriousness of purpose and his belief in children's theatre as a worthy art form.

In actual tryouts many factors may work against candidates. On any age level, oral reading difficulties give an unfavorable initial impression. Many adults read inaccurately or so mechanically that the sense and rhythm of a scene is lost. The director must train himself to see through the limitations of interpretative reading. Ability to give a fluent initial reading does not necessarily indicate acting ability. In fact, the glib reader may lack other qualities which ultimately make for excellence in performance. If quality of reading does not afford an accurate measurement, what, then, must the director look for as he selects his cast?

The essence of sincerity must pervade in performance, and many keys to actors' attitudes can be noted during tryouts. For example, a smirking, offhand approach to reading suggests an attitude of condescension that should immediately put the director on guard. He may have to help adult actors look beneath the surface simplicity of the script to find the meanings and challenges it presents. Happily, the actor who approaches tryouts for a children's play with misgivings frequently changes his attitude as he becomes familiar with the script and its characters.

One of the prime keys to success in children's theatre is convincing characterization. No actor, however skilled he may be, can present a character convincingly unless he himself believes that character to be genuine. Rejection or supercilious attitudes in performance will lead to audience rejection and ultimate failure of the production as an artistic success. The director therefore carefully notes signs of negativism at tryouts.

Closely allied to sincerity in the actor is the intangible quality we call empathy, which has nothing to do with beauty or handsomeness in the conventional physical sense. Child audiences often respond to a character the instant he enters the scene; even before he speaks they will decide whether they like or dislike him. Such immediate acceptance or rejection is especially important in the case of the protagonist and the antagonist. The director takes an unwarranted chance with the success of his production if he casts in a role requiring sympathy and audience identification an actor who projects a negative quality.

Coupled with sincerity, empathic quality ultimately adds up to convincingness. Probably the best definition of this quality was provided by a child actor in a production of *Beauty and the Beast*. The adult actress playing Beauty was not physically beautiful, but the warmth emanating from her was so great that the child was prompted to remark, "I like Beauty because she is so caring." For the clearly antagonistic character the director seeks a quality which will assist the child audience to revel in his downfall.

Vitality and physical flexibility and control are obvious factors which can be discovered through objective observation of actors in the tryout situation. The actor's physical bearing, facial animation, and vocal projection are all indicators of the presence or absence of energy and zest. He may be sincere and eager to participate in the production, but his personality may lack the inner strength to project a believable character. On the other hand, initial shyness or insecurity may give an impression of languidness; where this is a possible factor the actor should be given more than one opportunity to read so that the director can determine whether lack of vitality is habitual.

While the "slice-of-life" play still largely dominates adult theatre, the children's play usually requires much purely physical action. Therefore the children's theatre actor must generally be agile and endowed with considerable physical stamina. A flexible body and the ability to handle it with grace are particularly important in romantic fairy tale and fantasy plays where characters are presented in a more-or-less grand style. The director must have a general idea of the physical demands to be made on each actor in the cast so that he can determine whether candidates are equal to them.

A sensitive imagination is also essential to acting success. Frequently an actor will appear to take on added stature as he discovers meanings and subtleties in the script and gives himself to its rhythm and mood. In some cases this response is immediately apparent. In others several readings are required before evidence of imaginative response begins to emerge. If the director schedules a series of tryout sessions he has more opportunity to note qualities that will enable actors to play roles convincingly.

After candidates have done some line reading and have listened to the script, the director should attempt improvisation. Many children's plays have at least one scene which is entirely pantomime. The director can describe the situation and action and then talk it through as the actors play, watching for signs of imagination and total physical response and control. At other times he can ask a group to play a familiar scene with improvised dialogue and action to see what they are like when the script is not binding them, to note whether they capture the spirit of the scene, to see if they attempt to play together

—in other words, to catch a glimpse of what they might become during rehearsals. During tryouts the director should certainly note whether individual actors tend to work in a vacuum or attempt to relate to the other characters in the scene. Improvisation is a valuable means of determining the actor's willingness and ability to fit into the ensemble.

As tryouts progress the director can give suggestions about the purpose of a scene, the effect it should create or the meanings it should convey, noting how well candidates are able to assimilate these ideas. Evidence of flexibility and versatility can be observed by having each actor read more than one role. If he reads the protagonist and the antagonist with the same expression, he is likely to be a poor casting risk. If, after reading one role several times and hearing others read it, his interpretation remains unchanged, or if he seems unable to utilize the director's suggestions, it is likely that he lacks necessary qualities of imagination and responsiveness.

The voice cannot be overlooked during casting. Mere volume is not enough to meet the vocal demands of theatrical production. Pitch range, vocal quality, flexibility, clarity of diction, ability to project without evidence of strain, and absence of inflection pattern all should be noted. If he is to be convincing, the basic quality and pitch level of the actor's voice must be suited to the character he portrays. Further, he must be heard and understood. Generally speaking, the pressures of the rehearsal period are too great and time is too short for the director to undertake major voice and diction training with his cast. Certainly play production is an excellent way to develop good speech habits, but basic voice and speech qualities must be more than adequate to begin with.

At the close of each tryout session the director appraises the possibilities he has discovered. Some candidates will definitely be eliminated; others will be singled out as strong possibilities; some will be listed as questionable. In a series of open tryouts the director can expect that a number of hopeful actors will attend more than one session, sometimes creating a problem because they obviously cannot be used in the production. However, common courtesy dictates that they be given opportunities to read each time they come to try out. Furthermore, the keen interest which repeatedly brings them to auditions often can be channeled in other directions, and the director may draw some of his most valuable backstage workers from this group.

In casting adults an invitational call-back session is essential. Such a tryout enables the director to concentrate on candidates who are being seriously considered. If the director is working toward an ensemble approach to the production—and this certainly should be his goal—it is extremely unwise to cast actors in isolation. Evaluated separately, a number of individual actors may seem to be completely right for specific roles in the play. However, when they are brought together as a group, the potential cast that emerges may be quite unconvincing. Physical relationships are of major importance in achieving a quality of believability: a family group should be acceptable in terms of relative sizes; Prince Charming must not be smaller than Cinderella; there must be a strong contrast between Jack and the Giant. Size discrepancies are not easy to correct, and all too often even the most skillful attempts to increase the stature of an actor to any measurable degree are completely unconvincing.

Voice balances also must be considered in assembling the cast. Each actor should have a pleasant and distinctive vocal quality which not only suits his character but which blends harmoniously into a pleasing auditory pattern of balance and contrast. Casting actors with similar voices leads to monotony as well as to confusion in identifying characters. If unusual vocal demands are to be made on any actor, the director should make certain that he will be able to produce and sustain without undue strain the rough voice of the giant or the quaver of the witch, for example.

In addition to assuring the director that he is assembling a cast capable of presenting the play artistically and convincingly, the call-back session has further merit. Gathering a small group of candidates for readings and discussion provides an opportunity to determine the extent and sincerity of their interest. At the call-back meeting the director discusses in detail his plans for rehearsals and performances. He checks on outside obligations of potential actors and makes clear what will be expected of the actors should they accept roles. Then if anyone feels he cannot devote the required time, energy, and effort, he may drop out before his withdrawal creates a serious problem.

After the call-back session the director can be reasonably certain that, barring emergencies, he has assembled a cast that will remain together, working harmoniously toward a successful theatrical venture.

CHOOSING THE CHILD CAST.   If a production is to fulfill its purpose of providing a sound aesthetic experience for those who come to see it, the director seeks the same qualities and characteristics in child actors that he hopes to find in adults. This does not mean that he expects children to come to him fully trained, nor does he expect to make unreasonable demands on them. It does mean, however, that he chooses the best possible cast and then works with them in such a way that participation in play production becomes a sound artistic experience for them, even as watching the play provides aesthetic benefits to the audience. All producing organizations must have a definite policy regarding the age of children who may participate in formal drama. The Children's Theatre Conference suggests that children below eleven or twelve years of age should not be in formal plays; at lower age levels they benefit more from creative dramatics.[1] Some organizations place the lower age limit for participation in formal drama at the fifth grade level. Casting children younger than this is a questionable practice from two points of view: the developmental benefit to the performers, and the quality of the production as a work of art.

The organizational pattern for production should allow for children to work backstage as well as to act in plays. If we are to give more than lip service to the educational purposes of children's theatre, our producing organizations should offer children opportunities to discover, through actual participation in all its phases, that theatre involves more than acting. Starting with tryouts the director helps children realize that actors are only one part of the team responsible for bringing the play to life. Crew work should be glorified, and an opportunity to work backstage should be presented as a privilege rather than as a second-best substitute for acting. Such a plan assists in solving the problem of numbers which so often arises in a children's producing organization.

This problem of numbers must frequently be faced in the tryout situation. The degree to which it arises depends largely upon the organizational framework and fundamental purposes of the producing group. These vary widely. The philosophy of one producer may favor opening tryouts to all interested children in the community. Perhaps a loosely knit organization of several hundred members is involved. Sometimes a play is cast within a single school, youth organization, or recreation center. Sometimes a relatively limited group from a drama studio or organized community theatre operation is involved. Whatever the organizational structure is, it has a direct bearing, both on how many children come to tryouts and on the knowledge, skills, and understandings they bring with them.

[1] Ann Viola, "Drama with and for Children: An Interpretation of Terms," *Educational Theatre Journal,* May, 1956, p. 141.

If the director also works in regular classes or in creative dramatics with children eligible to try out he will know them well, and casting is relatively easy. However, most directors lack the advantage of either long acquaintance or of control of numbers. The average director may have to prepare to handle a hundred or more children at an announced tryout, in which case he must discover an efficient and time-saving method of judging fairly what each child can do. This involves enlisting a group of adult assistants for at least the initial stages of the tryout process. He should do everything possible to avert the disconcerting confusion of a sea of eager faces and waving hands—not to mention potential disciplinary problems inherent in keeping large numbers of children waiting through a conventional reading tryout.

Adult assistants should be carefully selected on the basis of background and understanding and thoroughly briefed by the director. He should make clear to them the qualities he seeks in child actors, sharing with them his philosophy of children's theatre production. Each assistant should have a specific assignment covering one phase of the tryout process.

When large numbers of children are expected at an audition a system of tryout stations is helpful. Such a system would function about as follows: As soon as the candidates arrive, one assistant helps them fill out tryout cards. Then the children move to other stations to participate in the various phases of an initial screening. One phase may involve presentation of a short memorized selection; at another station children may be given a brief selection for impromptu reading. They may be asked to pantomime some commonplace activity. After moving through the various stations each child has completed his initial audition and is dismissed.

Some plays lend themselves to a simultaneous three-phase tryout. If there is to be considerable song and dance, the adults who will coach these phases of the production may each take a third of the children for special auditions while the director holds conventional readings for another third. The groups would then rotate, each child having an opportunity to try out three times during the first screening session.

Unless the director's purposes are made clear, any form of mass tryouts may be bewildering to children and misinterpreted by their parents. Giving each child a written statement to take home with him can do much to eliminate misunderstandings and hard feelings. The message should explain that this first tryout constitutes an initial screening and that many children will, of necessity, be eliminated from further tryouts for the current production, reassuring parents that elimination this time should not discourage a child from coming to try out for future productions. It also should make clear when and how the child will be notified if he is to be called back for current auditions.

Any children's producing organization should maintain a permanent record of attendance at tryouts and participation in productions. In addition to the tryout card for the individual play, a permanent record card should be made for each child the first time he attends a tryout. On it are recorded the date, title of the play, and subsequently the role or crew position he has been assigned. Similar notations are made each time the child comes to audition for a play. No children's theatre wants to build on the star system, and most organizations conscientiously strive to give opportunities to as many children as possible. A record of consistent interest in the organization certainly should influence casting when final choices are made.

Following mass tryouts the director and his assistants will need to confer to decide which children will be called back for subsequent sessions. From then on, the director works with more manageable numbers, following the same general procedure he uses in casting adults, except for the final call-back session. Adult actors are usually able to understand and accept elimination from consideration for a role, and frequently a number are summoned to the final call-back session only to be eliminated. In selecting a child cast the director must be sensitive to childhood's reactions to false expectations and disappointment, and he should make it a policy never to call back more children than there are roles to fill. A child summoned to the final call-back may then be reasonably certain he will be cast, although he will not know what role he is to play.

Arriving at an ensemble is often more difficult with child actors than with adults, particularly if casting is limited to students on the elementary school level. For example, since discrepancies in size between the sexes are most marked in this group, the director may have difficulty finding a Prince Charming who is proportionately larger than Cinderella. He also may have a real problem finding boys who can play believable adult male roles. Nevertheless, he must exert every effort to find a cast that will be convincing to the audience.

If the children coming to the play cannot believe in the characters in the story they will not be satisfied, and the actors' experience with play production is likely to be less than rewarding. A good rule to follow in casting children is to make certain that each one is given a role in which he has reasonable assurance of success. If the actor does not fit into the ensemble because of his size or his voice, the rule has been violated.

Experience has proved the validity of double casting, at least in major roles, when child actors are used. This does not mean that there are understudies. Both children cast in a given role should have an opportunity to appear in performance. Fortunately, the one-performance run of a children's play is increasingly rare, and several performances permit alternating casts to play. This system allows for the use of more children in the production and, more important, provides insurance against last-minute illness.

To be sure, double casting means double work for the director, and some feel that it is detrimental to the production—an objection that is not necessarily valid. At first the casts rehearse simultaneously and interchangeably, the director taking pains to see that both sets of actors receive equal attention. As rehearsals progress, final casts are set. All members come to each rehearsal, and casts alternate in playing scenes. Competition between casts can prove highly stimulating, and each is likely to adopt the best features of the other's interpretation. At dress rehearsal time, lots are drawn to determine the performances each cast will play.

The problem of relationships between home and theatre is of course unique to working with children. Many parents yield to a child's desire to work in a play without realizing what will be involved. Some view with alarm the demands that are made once the undertaking begins; others minimize the importance of faithful attendance at rehearsal. Some parents push their children into theatrical ventures seeking a showcase for what they regard as remarkable talents. To counteract these tendencies the director, with the support of his producing organization, should carefully interpret to both parents and children the purposes and goals of the group, since the success of their venture will depend to a large degree upon building sound and cooperative home-theatre relationships. Taking time to inform parents in advance of the obligations they and their children are expected to assume during the production period will forestall many difficulties.

When children are called back for the final casting session they should be asked to bring schedules of their outside activities. In turn, the director should send home a notice which includes dates, times, and places for rehearsals, specific information about dress rehearsals and performances, and a reminder of the vital importance of prompt and regular rehearsal attendance. The final cast should not be announced until parents have had an opportunity to decide whether they are willing to allow their children to participate and whether they themselves wish to give the director full cooperation and support. It should be understood that, barring emergencies, every child who accepts a role is expected to remain in the cast and conscientiously meet his rehearsal obligations.

THE IDEAL CAST. It is usually much easier to find adults who can play children's roles than it is to find elementary school children who can portray convincing adult characters. When casting is limited to one or the other group the director is more than likely to be frustrated to some degree in his attempt to assemble an ideal cast. If he is producing children's plays in the high school or on the college campus, his chances of finding actors able to fill both adults' and children's roles are greater than they would be if his choices are limited either to an adult community organization or to young children.

A children's theatre playscript that requires only adult or only child actors is practically nonexistent, for the vast majority of children's plays contain characters of all ages. The director who is able to assemble a mixed company to present his play has a much easier task of assisting the actors in their creation of believable characters. Developing an organization where adults and children act together is a highly commendable goal for any producing group.

BEFORE REHEARSALS BEGIN

The Floor Plan

Assembling the cast is only one step in the director's rehearsal preparation. Before he can begin rehearsals he must carefully determine the arrangement of the stage setting and work it into a floor plan. His general concept of the production will be his reference point as he decides on the type of setting to be used and the scenic elements needed. The relationship and placement of these elements must be established before the first blocking rehearsal. The information given here includes only basic suggestions regarding the placement of set elements to facilitate blocking. The principles of scene design for children's theatre are discussed in Chapter 7.

Ideally, of course, the director is not required to design and execute his own stage settings, but realistically he must often be his own technical director. However, even if he has the services of a designer, the director himself must lay out his floor plan to suit the type of action he wishes to incorporate into the play; the designer then works this scheme into a scale drawing which becomes the working basis for all phases of the production. The director will block action according to it; the setting will be built to conform to it in size, shape, and placement of scenic elements; the lighting technician will use it in designing his light plot.

Even if the director has had no formal training in the theories and techniques of scene design, he will not find it an awesome task to develop an understanding of basic common-sense principles. The playscript itself will specifically require certain set elements and suggest others.

Many published playscripts contain fully worked out floor plans, even to detailed scene designs, light plots, costume sketches, property lists, and other technical information for the producer. Some of this material, particularly suggestions for constructing unusual properties or working out special effects, may be of real value. However, the fact that a setting worked for one director in his unique producing situation is no guarantee that it will be practical for all subsequent productions, and the director probably should ignore these designs and floor plans. Furthermore, rigid adherence to another's ideas imposes needless restrictions and limitations on the director's own creativity. The inexperienced director may be tempted to reject a script which does not provide extensive technical information, but careful analysis of the script—plus a little imagination and ingenuity—usually enables him to evolve a workable floor plan.

Children's plays frequently require exterior scenes in forests, gardens, streets, or village squares. Others take place in palace throne rooms or dining halls. The interior of a rustic cottage or pioneer cabin is the scene of action in many plays. Whatever the environment, the director first conceives it ideally and then adapts his concepts to the practical circumstances in which he must work.

If a play has a number of scenes, the director should not plan full and complete settings for each, but instead arrive at a total scheme which will allow moving from one scene to the next quickly and smoothly. Each setting must lend itself to the action it will contain. Some can be shallow; others will require a larger proportion of the total stage area. The nature of the environment, the number of characters, the relative importance of the scene, and the demands of physical action—all these combined will provide a basis for determining space requirements and floor arrangements for each setting.

In working out his floor plan, the director visualizes the important moments of the play, deciding how he wishes the stage to appear at those times. He also thinks in terms of overall movement patterns. He must decide what kinds of costumes will be worn and provide sufficient space for their manipulation. He must also provide for specialized action such as chases, transformations, magic effects, hiding, dancing, and feats of skill. He should constantly bear in mind that a continuously shifting stage picture and broad, free, fluid movement are vital factors in holding the interest of the child audience.

An acting area which is clear of unnecessary obstructions will make for more interesting visual effects as the actors move about the stage. When he blocks the play the director should plan to use every opening, every piece of furniture in the setting. These points are discussed at greater length in the chapter on scenic design.

Placement of key set properties is critical in evolving action patterns. Although center stage is always an emphatic area, locating a major set piece down center is almost certain to hinder fluidity of movement, just as placing it upstage center imposes unnecessary limitations on blocking. The actors will constantly have to work around a piece of furniture in the down center area. Similarly, if a throne or couch is placed up center, other characters cannot relate well to those sitting on it without facing away from the audience or blocking audience view of the action. But a throne placed down right, raked from down right toward up center and set on a dais, can not only be approached easily, but suggests possibilities for varied and eye-arresting movement and groupings. (See Plate 3.)

Entrances should not be placed upstage center. Even an archway should usually be offset for asymmetrical balance and for more varied movement before, during, and after its use. When a number of characters are in a scene it is often difficult to clear a center arch for an important entrance. Placement of entrances at the sides of the stage or off center on the upstage wall will provide opportunities for stronger focus on an entering or departing character. The opening can be cleared easily; the character can travel a long distance to or from it; and the other characters can easily be grouped to center the attention upon him.

In determining the relationship of entrances to major set properties, the director must remember not to orient all action to any one area of the stage. The units to which important action relates should be separated. The throne in a palace audience chamber should be on the opposite side of the stage from the major entrance through which characters come to pay court to the royal family. Insoluble blocking problems arise when key properties and entrances are crowded together. Fluidity of movement, varied action patterns, interesting groupings, and meaningful stage pictures can be achieved only if the director works out a floor plan which combines artistry with common sense.

Preblocking

Before calling the first rehearsal the director plans the blocking, or movement patterns, he will give to the actors and records it in his playscript. Even the most experienced director should never go into rehearsals without at least a generalized plan for physical action and picturization. Action patterns in children's theatre plays are likely to be complex and involve a number of characters. Furthermore, the child audience demands meaningful and constantly changing stage pictures to hold their attention and interest, as well as to assist them in understanding the story being told. Working out a scheme of movement before the actors assemble for rehearsal will save precious time, eliminate confusion, and contribute to the security of the actors.

The director should plan his original blocking in a way which allows for growth and change as rehearsals progress. However, to expect all blocking to emerge from character motivation without providing some framework is to demand too much from the actors unless they have months to concentrate on preparing the play.

An additional reason for preblocking arises from the desire to present an artistically finished production. Blocking which emerges entirely from the creative impulses of the actors is likely to appear unfinished or to fail in communicating meaning effectively to the child audience. If the director hopes to develop groupings and action patterns which are pictorially sound as well as meaningful to the spectators, he must provide the basic blocking and then spend time helping the actors discover motivations for it. The amount of blocking originally given is usually proportionate to the length of time allowed for preparing the production—the shorter the rehearsal period, the more detailed the director's planning must be.

Many directors find preblocking one of their most difficult tasks. Some aid to visualization may be needed in order to work out movement patterns and stage pictures logically and artistically. A scale floor plan drawn on corrugated paper is one such device. Pins can be used to represent the actors, and a small tab, if possible the same color as the costume to be worn, can be attached to each pin for easy character identification. This device allows the director to block and compose stage pictures according to color balances and harmonies as well as to character relationships.

Working with colored pins or comparable movable objects on a scale drawing of the stage setting is practically the only way the director can assure himself before actually working with the actors that the action patterns he visualizes can be executed smoothly. In addition, it keeps him aware of the presence of all the characters in every scene and reminds him of the forgotten character who is on stage but has no lines to speak.

In preblocking the director may begin at the opening of the play and work out each picture and action pattern as it occurs, or he may compose the climax scene first. In either case he notes all movements in his playscript, which then becomes his working guide as he gives initial blocking to the cast. Every director eventually works out a system of blocking notation that is most practical for him to follow. Most directors divide the stage into fifteen standard areas; and many trace designations of those areas onto the diagram of the floor plan before blocking is begun, so that script notations can be made as specific as possible.

Certain symbols and abbreviations are standard in indicating blocking. Areas of the stage are abbreviated as DR, C, ULC, and so on; an X indicates a cross; an arrow pointing upward means to rise; one pointing downward means to sit; the bodily

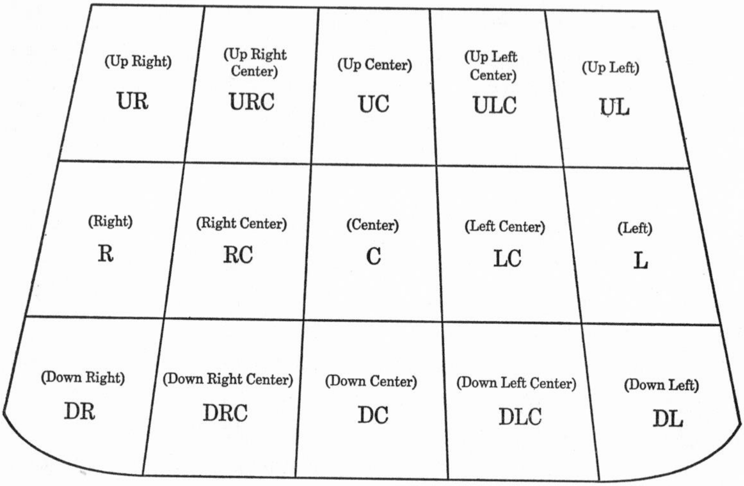

(Up Right) UR	(Up Right Center) URC	(Up Center) UC	(Up Left Center) ULC	(Up Left) UL
(Right) R	(Right Center) RC	(Center) C	(Left Center) LC	(Left) L
(Down Right) DR	(Down Right Center) DRC	(Down Center) DC	(Down Left Center) DLC	(Down Left) DL

Fig. 2. Diagram of the stage with area designations.

position of an actor relative to the audience is often indicated by drawing a circle with an arrow pointing in the direction he should face; "above" indicates position upstage of an actor or a set property; "below" indicates position downstage of an actor or set property; ½ indicates that the actor presents his profile to the audience, ¼ that he faces between full front and profile, ¾ that he faces between profile and full back. Use of these and similar symbols for recording blocking is a quick and concise method of keeping clear notes.

Some directors record their blocking in a series of stage diagrams drawn in the script, using a different colored pencil for each character. Movements are recorded with arrows and dotted lines. Since this plan can become so complicated that one loses track of characters and of the exact moment when a given movement occurs, it is better to use such a diagram only for plotting the positions of characters at the beginning or end of a major shift and to adopt a less confusing system for recording continuing action. One such scheme is to underline and number the word or phrase on which the movement begins, transferring the number of the movement to the margin and writing in the action. These blocking notes are numbered consecutively through each page, and each page is numbered separately. This system is precise and easy to follow.

The director should by all means teach his notation system to his assistant director; then, when blocking rehearsals begin, the assistant records all directions for movement in the script which eventually becomes the production prompt book. His notations should be made in pencil so changes can be made as the action is set. Thus an accurate reference is available throughout rehearsals, and a detailed record of the production is preserved for the organization's files. (See Appendix for sample prompt book pages.)

PRINCIPLES OF BLOCKING

The basic principles of stage composition and picturization have been covered thoroughly in several texts on adult theatre play production; they apply equally to blocking the children's play. Emphasis through visual focus, level, area, and plane is needed to clarify the picture. Stability, sequence, and balance are just as important on the stage of the children's theatre as anywhere else. In planning blocking, the director must recognize that children probably will not comprehend subtle action and gesture—they require broad and definite stage action and business if they are to understand and appreciate the play. The twitch of an eyebrow certainly will enhance a character's total response to a situation, but a mere change of facial expression unsupported by a broad accompanying movement conveys little meaning to the child audience.

A second principle of blocking grows out of the relatively limited attention span of children. Static stage pictures will not hold the attention of energetic youngsters; they demand strong and varied visual appeal in their theatrical entertainment. Auditory appeal alone is never strong enough to hold attention in children's theatre. The visual action must speak clearly in a flow of picturesque movement that appeals to the kinesthetic sense.

The director surely tempts fate if he allows more than four lines of dialogue to elapse without some kind of movement on stage. From the very beginning he is obliged to find means of keeping the stage picture continually shifting. Preferably some change takes place with every line spoken. Broad and definite movements point up meanings and character relationships in a way that line delivery and subtle gesture alone cannot do satisfactorily. From the director's point of view, a movement for the sake of adjusting the stage picture is perfectly valid. Motivation for such movements can be discovered as director and actors work together in rehearsal.

Having worked out a floor plan that allows for freedom of movement, the director thinks of ways he can use every portion of it. Irregular spacing of key properties and scenic units allows the director to orient action to the areas in which they are placed. This irregular spacing provides a basis for determining motivations for movements which otherwise might seem arbitrary. No area of the stage should be slighted in planning blocking, but the various areas should be used in irregular order. The director will often need to check himself to avoid shifting action from one area to another with such regularity that the play takes on the visual aspects of a circus.

As a general rule the downstage areas should be used as much as possible, to establish intimate contact between players and audience. All children's theatre action should be oriented to the spectators and planned for the express purpose of sharing the story directly with them. This is certainly not meant to suggest that the actors stand downstage and declaim—but neither should they hug the upstage wall.

The relative importance of each moment in the unfolding drama determines the portion of the stage to be used for it. The most important scenes should occur close to the audience, and key lines of dialogue should always be delivered from a downstage position. The setting should be so arranged that diagonal crosses, which are stronger and more arresting than parallel crosses, are used to shift the major action from area to area.

In most cases, unless they are of minor importance in a scene, actors should be kept out in the open and free to relate to the audience. Except when the action calls for a character to be hidden, actors should not stand behind furniture. Every character whose presence contributes materially to the forward development of a scene should be clearly visible and preferably in a standing position. As we have remarked before, child audiences respond negatively to a sitting character. Possibly they interpret a sitting position as indicating lack of vitality and readiness to act or a retreat from active participation in the business at hand. Whatever the reason, the child audience is likely to lose interest in a character the moment he sits, and not regain interest until he rises. There is one exception to this rule: in scenes of pageantry, important characters—kings and queens, for example—may be seated on elevated thrones. However, these same personages should not sit on their thrones quietly conversing together in a scene that is primarily one of dialogue between them. If it is necessary to seat a character, he should be placed in an interesting position and not kept there beyond the limits of necessity. Instead of sitting conventionally, actors may arrange themselves in more unusual poses. They may lean, kneel, climb upon a table, stand with one foot on a stool, or rest on the arm of a chair. Certainly the good director of a children's play never seats a group of characters about the stage for a quiet moment of introspective conversation.

Whereas a sitting character loses audience attention, an entering character immediately captures interest. Making an entrance is one of the most important things an actor in a children's play does. Even if a scene is a "wiggle spot" the audience will become quiet to listen and watch for the new strain or concept being introduced into the action by an entering character. In planning blocking the wise director carefully arranges all stage entrances, being especially alert to prepare for the entrances of key characters. Stage pictures should be unbalanced for an expected entrance, characters already on stage being shifted to focus strongly on the incoming character. The character the newcomer is supposed to address following his entrance should be placed away from the doorway to enable the newcomer to travel across the stage to meet him.

The principle of planning a long emphatic cross applies equally to blocking exits. Perhaps a coatrack across the stage from the doorway can motivate movement from one side of the stage to the other, or a character being addressed by the one leaving the scene may stand at some distance from the door. Normally actors should start exit lines as far from the door as possible in order to emphasize the exit cross. If the departing character is in the doorway for his exit line, his going may be practically unnoticed by the audience. Careful planning of decisive movements and of stage pictures to achieve emphatic focus will point up entrances and exits. Attention is thus more strongly held, and perception and understanding increase.

Problems of handling numbers of characters arise regularly in children's theatre plays, since many of them are written with scenes which include persons who have little direct part in the story. Numerous minor characters with small speaking roles, royal entourages and court personages, and throngs of villagers, none of whom have much individual identity, frequently enter the action. Awkward handling of these characters can detract from, even ruin, a scene, and it is a serious mistake to neglect such scenes until late in the rehearsal period. The original blocking should make careful provision for their function whenever they appear. Well directed, they help strengthen the impact of the principal action.

Supernumeraries may either be kept as one group in the stage picture, or they can be ranged about the upstage area and along the sides of the stage. In both cases there is a danger that they will unconsciously arrange themselves in straight lines or semicircles, thus looking more like glee clubs or chorus lines than characters in the drama. Probably it is better to disperse the group into smaller clusters arranged in meaningful positions to focus on the central action. (See Plates 4, 10, and 12.)

Minor characters can add emphasis to the major action, not only through static reaction but through shifting their groups. For example, they can run to each other to discuss something that has occurred and then recongregate in new groups to focus once more upon the ongoing action. Such patterns are not likely to evolve spontaneously. In planning their blocking, the director must clearly determine motivation for minor characters and non-speaking groups so that their movement patterns will be precise and meaningful.

Groups of supernumeraries and minor characters are often brought on stage to serve the practical function of masking the introduction of a special effect, such as the works of magic and the transformation in plays like *Snow White and the Seven Dwarfs* and MacAlvay's *Beauty and the Beast,* or the feats of skill required in such plays as Musil's *Robin Hood*. In blocking action where a crowd is used primarily for masking, the director must find suitable motivation for bringing them on stage and for moving them into positions where they can serve his purposes most effectively.

Scenes of sheer spectacle, such as the Prince's dance in Chorpenning's *Cinderella,* can be materially enhanced by the use of extras dispersed artistically on the stage. In every case where extra characters are used in children's plays they should be considered both as individuals and as groups. Their movements and positions should be interesting and meaningful, not only to the audience, but also to themselves. This is especially true when a child cast is involved—the director must take special precautions to see that extras do more than straggle in, stand in a row, and exit on cue. Unless he is willing to devote time to planning their blocking and to rehearsing them carefully, he should cut out the extra characters.

The majority of children's theatre plays include either a chase or a search which often ends in a chase. In blocking such scenes the director may find it easier first to visualize the moment the pursued character is captured or makes his escape and work back from there, planning each step in the action pattern in minute detail. The capture or escape should occur in full view of the audience. A capture preferably occurs center stage or in an emphatic downstage position. If the pursued character escapes, his exit should be made downstage. There must be no doubt about the outcome of such exciting scenes.

A number of the more romantic children's plays contain duels between the hero and his adversary. Duelling scenes usually occur at a climactic moment when the protagonist and antagonist confront each other in the presence of numerous other characters, thus combining the full panoply of romantic pageantry with the spine-tingling excitement of open conflict. The general principles of utilizing crowds apply to these scenes, though care should be exercised to keep them on the perimeter of the action.

The duel itself may pose a very real problem to the director, and he may be well advised to secure expert advice on both weapons and technique. A physical education teacher frequently will be able to offer advice and assist in training. Every effort should be made to secure weapons suggesting those typical of the period of the play, and the fencing style should be suited to both weapons and period. The combatants should use basic fencing stances and movements with enough variety to suggest actual swordplay.

Except in unusual plays which require a degree of stylization, the director should avoid symmetrical balance in grouping the actors—irregular patterns convey a stronger effect. Straight lines and semicircles are also to be avoided unless they are used for a specific well-calculated effect. (See Plate 8.)

In brief, the director's overall concept of the production, combined with his sensitivity to the peculiar requirements of the children's theatre audience, guides him throughout the process of planning for each play he undertakes. If he wishes to bring the production to artistic fruition for audience and players alike, he will always enter the tryout and rehearsal periods with a carefully conceived scheme, knowing what he wants the characters of the story to become in production. He will have a clear picture of the environment in which the story will come to life and a practical plan for utilizing actors and environment in a manner calculated to present the story vividly, artistically, and with meaning.

6

The Director and Actors Work Together

ONCE THE CAST of the children's play has been assembled, all efforts are directed toward preparing for the opening performance. The rehearsal period is a time of concentrated effort geared to welding the players into a creative ensemble able to bring the play to life for the children's theatre audience.

In this chapter we shall first be concerned with setting up the rehearsal schedule and determining general goals for each phase of the production's growth; later we shall consider in some detail problems of rehearsal discipline and attitude, characterization, acting technique for children's theatre, and final preparations for performance.

REHEARSALS

Though ideally rehearsals should be held on the stage where the production will be presented, few producing groups have that privilege. If we are fortunate we may be able to play on stage a time or two before final technical and dress rehearsals, but most of us find ourselves rehearsing in classrooms, living rooms, basements, garages, or wherever we can find space and a degree of privacy.

To insure rehearsal efficiency the director should exert every effort to get a room large enough to furnish a playing area exactly the size of the stage setting. Action and timing can be completely thrown off and the painstaking work of weeks of rehearsal suffer a serious setback if radical space adjustments must be made at the last minute. In addition to space for accurate blocking, the rehearsal room should be large enough and private enough to permit work on voice projection, as well as to allow the director to get some perspective on the visual effects he is trying to achieve.

Organizing the Rehearsal Schedule

Suggestions for setting up a detailed rehearsal schedule were purposely omitted from our discussion of the director's preparation. The thoughtful director postpones making a final detailed schedule until the cast is assembled. He can then give reasonable consideration to actors with previous commitments and evolve a schedule reflecting a willingness to establish a cooperative working relationship with his company. In the early stages of rehearsal it usually is possible to work around busy days if the director knows of individual problems well in advance. Needless to say, a definite limitation should be placed on such concessions, and last-minute changes certainly are to be avoided.

The overall length of the rehearsal period for a children's theatre play will vary according to the demands of the production and the experience and maturity of the cast. Unless circumstances are unusual, at least four weeks should be devoted to rehearsal. From four to five weeks is adequate for an adult cast, but a six-week rehearsal period is more satisfactory for preparing a child cast for performance. Each session with an adult cast should last about two and one-half hours. Although adults usually rehearse during the evening, the bedtime hours of children must be respected; the child cast therefore rehearses during the day, usually after school, with sessions running about an hour and a half. In scheduling rehearsals for the mixed cast the director should work scenes involving children early in the evening and concentrate on their scenes during daytime rehearsals scheduled for week ends.

After the initial reading and blocking rehearsals, which, for obvious reasons, should follow the order of the play, the script should be divided into small scenes. Each rehearsal then may be planned to cover scenes involving the same group of characters.

Most actors will be attentive and businesslike when they are directly involved in the rehearsal, but only the most unusual of them will escape boredom if they must wait idly for long periods between scenes. Boredom can lead to serious morale and discipline problems. Children will seek their own diversions, frequently creating serious distractions if not chaos. Adults are almost certain to feel resentment if the hours they devote to rehearsal seem unproductive. Certainly the presence of bored and restless onlookers does not contribute to the development of the actors who are receiving the director's attention, and it is just as certain that erratic rehearsal attendance often stems from an impression that too much time is being wasted.

Fortunately, most children's plays lend themselves to division into short segments. If the cast members record the divisions in their scripts and the director prepares a tabular summary of individual scenes and the characters appearing in each, every player knows without question what his rehearsal obligations will be. The chart should be duplicated and distributed with the detailed rehearsal schedule.

In setting up the rehearsal schedule the director first should be certain that every scene gets a fair share of rehearsal time. In addition, he establishes both general and specific goals for each session to insure that rehearsals do not degenerate into dull, unchallenging, mechanical recitations.

General rehearsal goals are usually determined in five stages: reading, blocking, characterization and line, coordination and continuity (polishing), and technical and dress rehearsals. The third phase is the key one, and the largest proportion of time is devoted to developing convincing characterizations. The sample rehearsal schedule shows approximate time allotments for a typical children's theatre play.

Major Divisions of the Rehearsal Schedule

READING REHEARSALS. One or two reading rehearsals should be enough for the average children's play. Here the play is read and discussed, and the director gives cuts and scene divisions. Reading rehearsals also serve as general orientation periods: the director describes his concept of the total production and gives any instructions for the actors to follow through the rehearsal period.

Although the actors' obligations have been outlined at the tryout call-back session, the importance of prompt and regular attendance and of a businesslike attitude during the rehearsal period should be emphasized again. The director's instructions should include a reminder that male cast members should not have their hair cut until after the performance, since the actor's appearance from the stage will be more effective if his hair has been allowed to grow, especially since many children's plays are set in eras when twentieth-century haircuts would look incongruous. Usually the director warns cast members against learning lines until after blocking has been given. As he thinks of details he should mention to the cast, he should write them down. Many of these things are so obvious to the experienced person that they may be forgotten, but a little foresight can do much to prevent annoying problems later on.

Orientation to the child audience, its expectations, demands, and typical responses should begin at the first reading rehearsal. The nature of the children's theatre playscript as a vehicle for bringing a story to life for its audience may well be explained at this time, though we shall discuss it in some detail later.

If sketches or other renderings of settings and costumes are available as early as the first reading rehearsal, the actors should be given an opportunity to examine them. Such aids to visualization are a great help to any cast, but they are of utmost importance to the child or inexperienced adult group. Having a concrete basis for imagining how the completed production will appear to the audience arouses interest and generates such a degree of excitement that it is well worth the effort for the designer to complete drawings before rehearsals begin. Actors can then keep before them a mental image of the environment in which they will be performing. Furthermore, a well-drawn costume sketch often assists an actor in developing his initial concept of the character he will play.

In short, reading rehearsals lay the foundation for a philosophy of children's theatre; they prepare the cast for the unique experience of playing for children; and thus establish the background for character development within a unified scheme.

BLOCKING REHEARSALS.   It is usually good practice to begin blocking rehearsals after one or two readings, though some directors prefer to devote more sessions to reading and discussion. In any case, blocking should begin at the earliest feasible moment. Child casts are composed of energetic youngsters who are anxious to be up and doing; and adults as well as children respond with heightened interest and rapidly developing appreciation of the play as they sense its characters in action.

At least one rehearsal session should be devoted to blocking each act, and more time may be required if the act is unusually long or involves complicated action or large numbers of characters. Blocking rehearsals progress slowly at best. Without doubt they constitute the most tedious phase of the entire production process, and as they get under way the director will appreciate the value of his advance planning. This will enable him to lay out an accurate ground plan, thus permitting the actors to orient themselves to the size of the acting area and to the location of all the set elements. They may begin to discover motivations for each movement pattern the director presents.

Carefully organized, businesslike blocking rehearsals contribute much to the actors' initial understanding of the play, to their confidence in the director, and to their feeling that rehearsals are off to a good start. The director's blocking should in no way hamper the actors' individual creativity but instead contribute to their sense of security. By setting an initial pattern the director frees the actors from technical concerns that may hamper creative development.

As the director gives blocking instructions the assistant director should accurately note each movement and position in the prompt script. Each actor must be responsible for writing his own blocking in his own playbook. The director may need to teach a simple method of notation such as that described in Chapter 5. Certainly he should insist that notes be made. No actor assumes that he knows his lines after reading the script a time or two, but there are many who feel that they can remember blocking without taking it down. This is a fallacy that will become apparent the first time a scene is run.

CHARACTERIZATION AND LINE REHEARSALS. As stated earlier, blocking is by no means completed when rehearsals enter this third phase. As the cast progresses into characterization,

REHEARSAL SCHEDULE

Director's name.
Office and home phone numbers

All rehearsals will be held in (place)

Date	Time	Coverage	Special
T 10/7	7 PM	Reading: cut and edit	
W 10/8	7 PM	Block I-i	*Bring pencils* Alert for costume fittings
Th 10/9	7 PM	Block I-ii	
F 10/10	7 PM	Block II	
S 10/11	8 AM (Special place)		Publicity pictures
M 10/13	7 PM	Block III	
T 10/14	7 PM	**I-i**	LINES Substitute hand props
W 10/15	7 PM	I-ii-1, 3	LINES
Th 10/16	7 PM	II-2; III-4	LINES
F 10/17	7 PM	I-ii-2, 4; II-1; III-2	LINES
S 10/18	9 AM	II-2	
M 10/20	7 PM	II-3; III-1, 3	LINES Sound from now on
T 10/21	7 PM	I-i-1, 3; I-ii-2; III-1	
W 10/22	7 PM	I-ii-3; III-4	
Th 10/23	7 PM	I-i-2; I-ii-1, 4	
F 10/24	7 PM	II-1, 3; II-2, 3	
S 10/25	9 AM	I-ii-3; II-2; III-4	
M 10/27	7 PM	I-i; III	Crews attend
T 10/28	7 PM	I-ii; II	Crews attend
W 10/29	7 PM	II; III	
Th 10/30	7 PM	Whole play	
F 10/31	7 PM	Whole play	
S 11/1 through W 11/5, technical and dress rehearsals on stage with everything.			
Th 11/6	10 AM	First performance	

Figure 3. A sample rehearsal schedule.

Scene Divisions

THE ELVES AND THE SHOEMAKER

Act Scene	I-i			I-ii				II			III			
Division	1	2	3	1	2	3	4	1	2	3	1	2	3	4
Character														
Widget	X	X	X	X	X	X	X	X			X	X	X	X
Gremlo	X	X	X	X	X	X	X	X		X	X	X	X	X
Finella	X	X	X	X	X	X	X	X		X	X	X	X	X
Wife		X		X			X	X	X			X	X	X
Karen		X		X			X	X	X			X	X	X
Heckla		X				X			X	X	X			X
Dame						X			X	X	X			X
Joan				X		X		X						X
Rhoda				X		X		X						X
Meg						X		X						X
Tabitha						X		X						X
Ursula						X		X	X					X
Shoemaker													X	X

Figure 3. (Continued).

new motivations and relationships are certain to develop. Increasing familiarity with the situations of the play and growing identification with its characters will lead the actors to invent additional business, to find better ways of carrying out given actions, or even to alter completely certain movement patterns or character groupings. The sensitive director will notice impulses to move or change position, and he will encourage this type of development.

This does not mean that at a certain point the director should discard all his original plans and allow the actors to reblock the play. However, he should be willing to have them share in the creative process of bringing the play to life, recognizing that their individual actions are an integral part of the imaginative whole. If a change appears necessary to clarify action or meaning, the director can work it out with the actors involved; when it is set, the new arrangement is noted in the prompt script. Needless to say, all stage movement, each grouping, each bit of business must be in harmony with the director's conception of the play and its meaning.

Only as characterizations begin to emerge should lines be learned. Once actors begin to sense their characters they will find carrying books a hindrance to further growth. At this point a definite deadline—preferably after a week of characterization rehearsals—should be set for learning lines. Until the actors are ready to concentrate on details of action and character development they should work with scripts so that lines and movement are learned simultaneously. Lines memorized in isolation may be delivered mechanically with little thought of their meaning, or they may be interpreted in a manner quite out of keeping with the director's concept. Either pattern is difficult to break.

Some directors feel that paraphrasing rather than literal memorization of lines is not only acceptable but may even be preferable, since it often produces greater spontaneity. In our opinion this is a questionable practice. One reason for literal line reading is purely practical. Actors need dependable cues for lines and action, and technical crews rely for the most part on line cues to carry out their functions. Consistency in reading lines is one way to insure a smoothly flowing performance. Furthermore, just as a matter of ethics, if the director has accepted the work of a playwright, he also has assumed an obligation to present it honestly and accurately. Improvisation undoubtedly is a valuable rehearsal technique for enriching characterizations, but ultimately the author's lines should be learned as he wrote them.

This does not mean, however, that no changes must ever be made in a play. Occasionally the director finds it necessary to make minor script changes during his preparatory period. Sometimes during early rehearsals an actor discovers that a given line does not read well, in which case a change is worked out to the mutual satisfaction of the director and actor and is recorded in all the scripts.

As soon as lines are learned, substitute hand properties should be introduced; and it is well to begin using sound effects, including overture, incidental, and between-acts music. Music can be a great aid in building mood and in preparing for smooth act openings. In addition, action must be precisely timed to any background music that may be introduced within scenes. From a practical point of view rehearsals involve habit development as well as creativity. Young Johnny may provide a worthy approximation of the sound of a doorbell during rehearsals, but his unconscious rendering of a vocalized substitute for the real thing in performance can be disconcerting, to say the least. And we all have heard stories of actors who were so conditioned to pantomiming their use of properties that they continued to handle invisible articles in performances although the actual items were clearly in evidence.

If the production requires period costumes or garments which will make unusual demands on the actors, reasonable substitutes should be provided long before dress rehearsal. A noted Broadway director recently deplored the inability of professional actors to work well in period costume. If some of the greatest stars of the professional stage have difficulty adjusting to the garments of past eras, we certainly expect the impossible of young and inexperienced players if we engulf them in long flowing or stiffened gowns or tuck them into tights only at the first dress rehearsal! Moreover, the typical posture and movement of contemporary youth need considerable adaptation if actors are to appear comfortably in character rather than incongruous and ill at ease in a romantic setting. When we introduce costume elements early, security in wearing and handling them will evolve right along with characterizations. More than that, costumes can actually enhance actors' feeling for the period and thus be an aid to character development. We might also add that physical movement is more easily controlled when actors, from blocking rehearsals on, wear shoes comparable to those they will wear in performance.

During characterization rehearsals the director attends to surface details as well as to the more basic problems of building character, setting movement, and learning lines. He knows that a polished, convincing performance will stem from attention to details which are all too often overlooked. His preparation surely has included research into the habits, customs, and conventions of the historical period in which the production is set. He has read about the period and has probably looked at paintings to note typical poses and attitudes. During characterization rehearsals he shares his findings with the cast.

On the other hand, a mass of minute detail is quite unnecessary in children's theatre. Instead, every effort should be made to give a faithful *suggestion* of the period, selecting and incorporating into the performance elements which will satisfy childlike concepts of modes of behavior, movement, gesture, and general demeanor of the period and the types of characters being portrayed. Special rehearsals may be required to master posture, pose, and movement, to perfect bows and curtsies, to develop ease in handling unusual properties, and to work out dances.

Once the general style has been established it should be followed consistently, though here expectations should not be as high with a child cast as when we are working with adults. We try to bring the child cast as far as we can in achieving style and perfecting details, but it is not realistic to demand the level of perfection that adults should reach. It is easy to overemphasize style with child actors, at the expense of sincerity and concentration on characterization, and this is likely to lead to mechanical physical movement and imitative line delivery. The honest, naïve, and genuine quality which children bring to a performance should never be sacrificed to an artificial style.

Characterization rehearsals are a time for discussion of line meanings and motivations, for penetrating study of individual characters, for working out detailed business and timing, and for determining the relationship of each character to the story and to the other persons in it. This is the period of greatest creative growth. Rehearsals can be exciting and stimulating if the director presents a new challenge at each session.

POLISHING REHEARSALS. It is difficult to determine at what point the rehearsal process moves from characterization into the polishing phase. As lines are learned and strong characterizations begin to emerge, attention begins to shift to detail; and as soon as this happens, polishing begins. Actual polishing rehearsals are usually devoted to coordinating the ensemble and to bringing out subtleties in action and interpretation through careful attention to timing and reactions.

Though directors are not likely to permit individual actors to play in a vacuum, a specific effort is needed to integrate the company into a group of believable characters who are meaningfully related to one another and to the dramatic action. There is no place for a star system in children's theatre. Since characters in children's plays exist to serve the primary purpose of bringing a story to life, the ensemble approach is the only suitable means to achieving an effective performance. In this approach, each actor sees his character in terms of the story. He plays with the other actors, relating his character to theirs, always maintaining his perspective.

In polishing rehearsals, scenes which have been rehearsed in isolation are brought together to develop the rhythm and continuity of the entire play. Timing now receives careful attention. Variations of mood and emotional tone develop. Concentration needs to be emphasized. This involves listening and reacting in character, and is essential to achieving both a quality of believability and an essense of spontaneity in performance.

If possible, the director should plan to devote a week of rehearsal to running the entire play, not interrupting the flow of action but reserving his comments for act breaks and post-rehearsal discussions. Technical crews should be present at the final polishing rehearsals to become familiar with the continuity of the play, to get timings, and to set cues.

TECHNICAL AND DRESS REHEARSALS. Technical rehearsals are less harrowing if various technical elements have been introduced from time to time throughout the earlier phases of rehearsal. Frequently these technical rehearsals afford the company its first opportunity to work on stage. There may therefore be minor lapses in characterization, and frequent interruptions may be necessary to solve technical problems and make slight adjustments in blocking. A certain amount of confusion is almost inevitable as all elements of the production are assembled and synchronized. The scenery should be complete by this time, and all properties should be on hand and in place. Lights, sound equipment, and special effects should be ready to function as they will in performance. It is advantageous to have the actors wear full costume for technical rehearsals. Scene shifts should be executed as they will be in performance. If there is to be a curtain call it must be carefully rehearsed.

The director's preliminary planning is an important factor in preventing chaotic technical rehearsals. When all members of the company have been thoroughly briefed regarding their specific functions and responsibilities, and a pattern of organization has been worked out in advance, the technical rehearsal period should proceed without ruffled tempers or undue confusion.

The presence of actors backstage at early technical rehearsals may be a source of confusion which can be avoided if they are allowed to sit in the auditorium when they are not on stage. However, during final dress rehearsals actors should certainly remain backstage, in locations assigned by the stage manager. Child casts should wait in rooms near the stage, in the charge of an adult. An assistant stage manager is assigned to bring them into the wings when it is time for their entrance. Actors must understand that they are not to interfere in any way with members of crews and that full responsibility and authority for backstage operation is in the hands of the stage manager.

Dress rehearsals should approximate performance conditions as closely as possible. Actors wear full costume and make-up. All technical elements are complete. Barring major disasters, the performance should not be interrupted. Some organizations bring in an invited audience for the final dress rehearsal to give the company some suggestion of the type of response the production will receive in performance. If this is done the invited audience should be carefully chosen. Adults alone will not give a true reaction; nor will a small group of children. Some organizations invite students from a school for handicapped children or from a community institution to attend a "dress performance." There is much to recommend this practice.

Dress rehearsal is the time for the director to appraise his work. While he certainly does not withdraw from active participation, he keeps away from backstage once the first act curtain rises. Since it is now too late to make major changes, his post-rehearsal comments should be made with that fact in mind. The play now belongs to the actors and crews. If he has done his work well, his sole responsibility from now on is to remain calm and to assure the company that it is ready for opening day.

DIRECTOR-ACTOR RELATIONSHIPS

Patience and willingness to teach basic stage techniques are essential qualities for any director who works with inexperienced or young actors. Ability to achieve a balance between personal warmth and impersonal authority is equally important. A desirable rapport should grow out of the community of purpose that brought the company together. The director's attitude should be friendly, but he must gain and hold respect. While there is no set formula for this, certain practices may lead to lack of respect: an overly intimate relationship with members of the group, favoritism, extreme permissiveness, unrelenting authoritarianism, loss of composure, or insecurity in his leadership role. Any of these is likely to cause a company to view its director in an unfavorable light.

The director who lets his cast know what is expected of them and what the company may expect of him establishes the type of working relationship which should stimulate everyone to put forth his best effort. As part of this climate, the director needs to retain his sense of perspective as well as his sense of humor, remaining an impartial and consistent leader from first rehearsal through final performance. The effective director is a diplomat as well as an artist-teacher. Sometimes it is difficult to maintain an even disposition and an impartial attitude, because he works under pressure with the wide variety of personalities theatre draws into its ranks. However, he should attempt to understand the unique qualities of every cast member and to discover methods to help each one realize his best potential.

Only in extreme cases should a person ever be dismissed from a children's theatre cast, and then only when his attitude and behavior make his presence a detriment to the production. An actor may not be able to develop his role to the director's satisfaction, but this by itself is not an adequate reason for dismissal. Discipline is another matter. The presence of even a single individual who refuses to take rehearsals seriously can undermine company morale. Such a person should be given fair warning and an opportunity to alter his behavior, but if he continues to be an irritant he should be dismissed.

OBLIGATIONS TO THE CHILD CAST. The director should always attempt to cast children in roles offering them reasonable assurance of success. He has an equal obligation during rehearsals to help child actors achieve the level of proficiency and polish necessary for finished performances. He needs to recognize the natural limitations of immaturity and inexperience, and realize that children want and need the security of direction, of knowing what to do and when to do it, before they can face an audience. The path to success is clearly down the middle road between unreasonable demands, exploitation, or imitation and nondirected creative expression.

A special sort of patience and understanding is required to work successfully with children. Youngsters' motives for being in a play vary, and their behavior patterns are equally diverse. They may include every extreme from the overeager child who demands more than his share of attention to the completely lethargic child who came to tryouts because his friends brought him or his parents sent him. In one case we must help the child achieve perspective regarding his role as a member of an integrated ensemble. In the other, we must work for a high level of interest and enthusiasm among the entire cast, hoping that the resulting spirit will infect the less inspired.

ATTITUDES TOWARD SCRIPT AND AUDIENCE. While an attitude of condescension toward the children's playscript and the child audience is not likely to appear in a child cast, it can easily become a serious obstacle in an adult actor's portrayal. An actor who feels that he is merely taking part in a "kiddies' show" rather than a "major production" is not likely to regard his role as a serious acting assignment. Sometimes this condescension reflects the attitude of a parent producing organization or sponsor, and in that event there is little the director can do to solve the basic problem immediately. Nevertheless he can make strides in this direction by converting the members of his present cast and instilling in them the positive attitudes of challenge and enthusiasm.

Directors should always stress the idea that the child audience presents one of the greatest challenges the theatre artist is called upon to meet. It can be an awesome group, and the actors must be prepared for audience reactions. The director must help them sense the presence of the audience and understand the meaning of their reactions. Only in this way will they be able to play to them and gain from them their frankly overt responses, adjusting to but never exploiting them. The director's own seriousness and sincerity of approach should help him instill a positive attitude in his actors.

One of the most important things children's theatre groups must learn is to distinguish between what is saccharine and patronizing and what is legitimately childlike in quality. While many children's theatre playscripts have been written with little regard for that difference, the better ones are written with child-like simplicity in development of characterizations, dialogue, and story line. Occasionally the first reading of the complete script may suggest to adults that the dramatic complications are solved too neatly and quickly at the end. This is the time to explain children's attitudes toward climax and denouement. In performance the quick ending is far more satisfying than is a fully developed, involved build-up to the final curtain. Once the cast is caught up in the rhythm and dramatic progression of the play and in their developing characterizations, they are likely to realize that writing techniques they questioned at first are valid and essential.

The director helps his cast look beneath the surface simplicity of the script for deeper meanings, just as he helps them develop a sincere attitude toward the child audience. J. M. Barrie once suggested, "Actors in a fairy play should feel that it was written by a child in deadly earnestness and that they are children playing it in the same spirit." This is the approach we should hope to develop when we play for children.

SINCERITY IN PERFORMANCE. Sincerity and convincingness are inseparable. Projection is the first quality to be adversely affected by indifference. However striking an actor may be from a visual point of view, children will pay no attention to him if they cannot hear and understand him. On the other hand, the actor who approaches his role with zest will be vital in physical bearing and movement; his performance will be energetic and arresting; he will almost certainly evoke a desirable response.

Children respond favorably to adults who address them sincerely and directly. Their acceptance of the play and its characters will be joyous and sincere if the actors are having a pleasurable experience with make-believe as they present it. Belief begins with the actors, but the director can do much to inspire them if he is enthusiastic and sincere.

BRINGING CHARACTERS TO LIFE

LOOK BEYOND THE SCRIPT FOR CLUES TO CHARACTER

The uncomplicated characters found in children's plays are relatively easy for child actors to understand and play believably, and in working with them the director concentrates on the more obvious means of building characterizations. However, when an adult cast is involved, characterizations should grow out of a deeper, more penetrating study.

Broadly defined and readily apparent character traits, if approached superficially by adult actors, are likely to lead to portrayals of stereotypes reminiscent of nineteenth-century melodrama—the unflinchingly brave and noble hero, the saccharine heroine, the unrelentingly evil antagonist, the tritely bumptious antagonist, the "cute" elfin character, the bloodless fairy godmother, and so on. An element of condescension is almost certain to creep into such characterizations. To prevent this, the director and actors should study the script together to discover subtle hints that will lead to a fuller understanding of its characters and their motivations.

Logical explanations are not always provided in the script, in which case an acceptable rationale for events or reactions must be devised. Here the sensitive actor finds a real challenge to his art of invention. With the director's encouragement and assistance he should do some independent probing into the various facets of his character.

While the inexperienced director may feel that rehearsal is

not in progress unless the actors are walking through the action of the play, experimenting with the use of discussion will soon reveal the value of allowing time for thoughtful analysis of character motivations, attitudes, actions, reactions, and relationships. Discussion time also should be devoted to filling in details of events immediately preceding the opening of the play and between acts, and of the activity of each character when he is not on stage. Reconstructing these events helps each actor develop logical emotion and reaction patterns. This technique is especially meaningful to the child cast.

Improvisation, too, can help fill in details of character and situation. Using creative dramatics techniques, the director guides the actors in devising and playing scenes which never appear on stage. At times this has proved to be the only means of achieving the emotional tone and reaction patterns the director hopes the actors will project in scenes of the play.

Focus and Balance: The Importance of Minor Characters

Focus and balance are of vital importance in developing characterizations. We have seen that the story is the most important element in children's theatre plays. Each actor should recognize the specific contribution his character makes to the unfolding plot. This understanding is one basis for the integrated ensemble; it also aids in individualizing characters.

Giving a measure of individuality to minor characters probably is a less serious problem than sustaining those characterizations in performance. Minor characters are often brought into the action to serve an immediate purpose; if they are then given no further dialogue or easily discernible function in the scene, they may well have difficulty remaining in character during these lapses. The director should help them find some way to become involved in the scene. Probably the best procedure is to determine character relationships and the effect of the ongoing action upon each character on stage; special attention to nonspeaking characters will encourage them to discover and sustain meaningful reaction patterns.

CROWD SCENES

The directing technique outlined above is equally applicable to members of crowds. We have noted elsewhere that the director should carefully attend to blocking scenes involving nonspeaking characters who have only a collective identity—purely as a technical device to ensure visual appeal. However, even the most attractive groupings are likely to detract from rather than enhance the dramatic action unless the director carries his work one step further. Members of the crowd must know why they enter the scene; they must know what they think, feel, and do while they are on stage. To help them fulfill their function, the director should encourage nonspeaking groups to develop definite attitudes toward the other characters on stage and devise appropriate reaction patterns. Frequently this involves a joint study of the script up to the point of entrance to discover a rationale for these attitudes and reactions. This is not meant to suggest that members of crowds should be strongly individualized or permitted reaction patterns which destroy emphasis, but to stress that if crowds are to be used they must be carefully directed.

CONCENTRATION AND CONSISTENCY

Concentration requires that each actor become fully involved in make-believe, imagining himself to be a character in the situations of the play. He constantly blends into a total picture, responding as a character to the events unfolding around him. He listens and speaks as the character would. He cannot permit himself even a momentary lapse of attention if he is to be believed by the audience. He concentrates only upon the action, not upon his individual lines, his pose and appearance, or upon what he is to do next. Concentration is vital to maintaining the quality of spontaneity that keeps a play exciting for the audience.

As soon as the actors are free of their playscripts the director should begin to check carefully for concentration. He should not permit the actors to relax or break character between lines, trusting that they will become deeply involved in the action once the play goes before the audience. This miracle simply does not occur. The discipline of concentration not only is one of the best methods of ensuring a good performance, but it also provides a strong creative stimulus for enriching characterizations and refining movement and character business.

Concentration can be a real problem with the child cast, regardless of the importance of the role any individual is playing. Children tend to be easily diverted, particularly in the unusual surroundings and circumstances of theatrical production. They do fairly well when they have lines to speak, but between lines they may drop character and look around, become interested in the action, not as characters but as themselves, or, worst of all, stare into the audience.

More than any other single factor, lack of concentration makes performances by children painful to the discerning adult and questionable as a worthy art experience for the child audience. If the director is obliged to emphasize concentration in building discipline among members of an adult cast, he is doubly concerned with it in his work with children. Child actors wish to give believable performances, but they need regular reminders that audience belief stops at the first sign of breaking character.

Characterization and the Playscript

The general principles of characterization apply equally to every type of character found in children's plays, human or animal, realistic or fanciful. The essence of believability should pervade any character portrayed for the child audience.

In contemporary realistic plays the approach to characterization is relatively uncomplicated. As far as the audience is concerned, characters in realistic plays should be acceptable as real people they might one day meet. In realistic period dramas characterizations are more romanticized, and their development necessarily involves an understanding of the customs and attitudes of the era in which the play is set.

Characters in fairy tales and fantasies generally fall into two groups—those with a more or less realistic orientation and those that are entirely imaginary. Even elfin or ethereal characters are endowed with some human traits, making them recognizable as something more than abstractions. In fanciful plays all the characters should be developed somewhat more broadly than characters in realistic dramas. Children in the audience believe in and identify with fairy tale characters, but on a less literal level. The actors should bring these characters to life in a manner that will be in keeping with the essentially unrealistic quality of the story and its environment.

Plays demanding stylization present another problem in character development. The most common example of this type of drama is one with animal characters. A great deal of sophisticated comment is implied in stylized theatrical fare, and this type of comment is essentially adult rather than childlike in quality. It is hard to say to what degree stylization should be carried in children's theatre. Certainly it cannot be carried so far that the audience refuses to accept the characters as believable. For example, animal characters in plays stem from human reference. In developing animal characterizations actors should avoid a tendency toward coyness or cuteness, finding motivations for these characters just as carefully as they do for the most realistically conceived characters.

Actually the basic approach to characterization is essentially the same for all children's plays. Characters will differ in their presentation according to the style of the production as a whole, but they must emerge as understandable and believable individuals, exhibiting traits that will convey a sense of artistic reality to the child audience.

PRESENTING THE CHARACTERS TO THE AUDIENCE

Thus far our discussion of the actor has emphasized characterization, the ensemble, and style as it applies to historical periods and character types. Developing a suitable and unified acting style also is an integral part of the rehearsal process.

The following discussion of acting style applies primarily to the adult cast. Recognizing the perfectly normal limitations of children, we should be satisfied when the child cast is able to master basic acting techniques, to play sincerely, and to develop an acceptable degree of historical accuracy and polish in their performances. The adult company, however, should be expected to develop technical proficiency in acting style.

Acting style is determined by two factors: the nature of the material to be communicated and the nature of the audience to whom it is addressed.

THE PLAYSCRIPT AND STYLE

In sharp contrast to popular adult dramas, children's plays idealize life. As we have seen, they fall into categories ranging from realism to pure fantasy. Realism in children's theatre differs from realism in the adult theatre, for a high degree of romanticism and idealism is inherent in even the most realistic children's play. The dramatic action is based upon wondrous adventures children dream about, and the ending inevitably is a happy one. While the characters are essentially realistic, the playwright deliberately exercises selectivity in delineation so that they emerge not as complex psychological studies but rather as people individualized by dominant traits.

As we have seen, by far the largest number of children's plays are fairy tales and fantasies, and neither the characters nor the events are therefore essentially realistic in conception. While a child might in unusual circumstances experience an adventure similar to those in the more realistic plays, he will never have direct contact with a fairy godmother, a cruel giant, or a bevy of elves; nor is he likely to encounter animals who behave and talk like human beings.

Essentially, the typical modern adult drama is illusionistic in nature, and performances tend to be stage centered. The actors represent the characters they portray and convey a sense of actual life to the spectator. In children's plays, on the other hand, the events, the characters, and the physical action are likely to have little meaning if conveyed to the audience by representational, illusionistic acting. To find a style which lends itself to children's theatre we must turn to the romantic acting of the presentational, frankly theatrical, audience-centered theatre.

Presentational style is frankly acting. It allows the actor to remain part actor, part character; it permits him to select only those facets of his character's personality which will most clearly define the character for the audience; it lets him comment upon his character, be aware of the audience and its responses, play openly, and engage in honest make-believe.

The Audience and Style

A child reading a children's theatre playscript might or might not experience aesthetic satisfaction from it. Probably he will need to have the play brought to life in production to experience true satisfaction. The very nature of the script suggests the style of presentation that is likely to assure an aesthetic response.

Children come to the theatre to share in its make-believe; we should not wish to delude them into believing they are viewing actuality.

What constitutes an aesthetic experience in the theatre? How do we make certain that such an experience will be provided? To a large extent the answer to these questions lies in establishing a proper actor-audience relationship when we bring the carefully rehearsed play before the audience. Preparation for this relationship is just as essential a part of the rehearsal process as is the development of believable characterizations.

EMPATHY AND AESTHETIC DISTANCE. The concepts of empathy and aesthetic distance usually enter any discussion of the spectator's experience with an art form. For our purposes, empathy may be considered synonymous with identification, and aesthetic distance with the spectator's awareness of the non-actual nature of the art form. To have an aesthetic experience in the theatre the audience must believe in the events and characters on the stage, but in an imaginative rather than a literal sense. In other words, they respond emotionally while remaining aware that they are viewing a play.

We can be certain that children will experience a strong sense of participation in a sincerely presented theatrical performance. Arousing empathic response is much less difficult than is maintaining the necessary degree of aesthetic distance. Actors who understand the nature of the child audience and are trained to sense its presence during performances are more likely to create an aesthetic experience for children than are actors whose portrayals are largely stage centered.

ACHIEVING PRESENTATIONAL STYLE

Sincerity and belief are essential to good presentational style. The rest is largely a matter of technique.

On the purely mechanical level the broad, free stage movement given by the director in blocking rehearsals establishes a physical framework for presenting the story. Direct sharing is further enhanced if the players maintain open positions on stage. There is a practical as well as an artistic reason for this more frank relationship with the audience. Many children's plays are presented in large auditoriums to audiences of a thousand or more. If the actors remain open to the audience, facing them and directing their lines to the front, projection problems are considerably lessened. (See Plates 6, 8, 9, and 12.)

Quite apart from purely physical means of achieving presentational style, there are subtle means of accomplishing it. One involves striking a balance between the actor as a character and the actor as an actor. In other words, presentational acting requires that the actor remain sincerely in character, concentrating on the dramatic action, while a part of him remains outside the character, fully aware that he is acting and equally aware of his audience and its responses. The director must help his actors learn to combine a sense of real life with a sense of the theatrical in their portrayals. Selectivity and comment, two factors inherent in the presentational acting concept, will assist the actors as they work for this balance.

SELECTIVITY IN CHARACTERIZATION. Although the playwright's selectivity in character delineation may pose problems as actors work to develop an initial approach to their roles, it can also be advantageous as they near the final phases of rehearsal.

After the players have arrived at a well-rounded conception of their characters, each one should return to the playscript and consider his role in relation to the story. Is he the protagonist? The antagonist? If not, to which side of the conflict is he allied, and what is his role in relation to the force with which he is identified? Is he comic or serious, realistic or fantastic in conception?

Remembering that every character in a children's play must be justified in terms of his contribution to the unfolding plot, each actor selects the dominant personality traits which best serve to reveal his character. These are the ones he emphasizes in his portrayal. He is concerned not with representing a many-faceted personality but with presenting a character whose motivations and actions will be readily understood.

THE ACTOR'S COMMENT. Emphasis on personality traits will also assist the actor in commenting upon his character. As he identifies with the character, the part of him remaining outside the characterization has an opinion about the character. To some extent this opinion comes through in performance, combining with emphasis to constitute the actor's comment.

Comment should not be confused with caricature—undue emphasis on any personality trait may cause a character to appear ridiculous. Nor should comment be made condescendingly, with the actor suggesting through a knowing wink or other overt sign that he is giving the children an extra treat by sharing his secrets with them. Good taste defines the limits to which comment should be carried.

Comment may be made through posture, pose, movement, gestural pattern, and to some extent, even through facial expression. Costume in itself frequently makes a comment upon a character, and the actor can take cues from it in devising means to make his own comment. The modes of behavior typical of the various social classes of the period in which the play is set suggest additional devices that may be adopted. For example, the snuffbox and lace handkerchief of the eighteenth-century fop, the walk affected by the dandy of a given era, the lady's fan, the stance of the tomboy, and many other typical personal mannerisms and accessories may be used to advantage.

Achieving the proper degree of subtlety and consistency in comment is important to its effectiveness. Actors should avoid the repeated use of any single mannerism or gestural pattern to the point where it becomes obtrusive and loses effectiveness. Since they sometimes overuse devices without being aware of it, the director should be alert to check such tendencies, as well as to see that each character's behavior is consistent.

Through selectivity and comment, actors in children's theatre plays can do much to ensure audience understanding of the story. Through comment each actor consistently brings a clear-cut portrayal to the audience.

By remaining partially outside their characters, actors help maintain aesthetic distance. This is particularly true in scenes of suspense or strong conflict where the emotional response of the child audience is likely to get out of hand if aesthetic distance is not maintained. Three factors of presentational acting help maintain this balance: it is frankly make-believe; it allows actors to comment on their characters; and it permits them to control response by remaining aware of the audience.

CONTROLLING AUDIENCE RESPONSE

In actual performance the players alone are responsible for holding attention, preventing boredom, relieving fatigue, and controlling tension. The experienced director knows how impossible it is to predict audience response with any degree of accuracy. However, he should thoughtfully analyze the play to determine which scenes may pose problems, planning his direction to help the actors maintain audience control. He must decide what kind of response he wants to each scene and direct the actors accordingly.

Before they go into performance the director needs to prepare the actors for the overt nature of typical child audience reaction. There will be few moments of awed silence in playing to an audience of uninhibited youngsters. Unrestrained reactions are normal and natural, and audience response will range from restlessness and undercurrent of conversation, indicating boredom or inattention, to the squeals and shouted warnings of tense involvement in exciting sequences.

Although each scene has a specific reponse goal, actors should always be prepared for the unexpected from the audience. For example, certain lines or action sequences which do not appear amusing to them may prove to be hilariously funny to children. On the other hand, a scene they intend to be comic may be received with deadly seriousness. Something which provokes gales of laughter during one performance may not arouse the slightest chuckle in the next. This unpredictability of children should keep the actors "on their toes," ready to hold for a laugh at any point in the play, unflustered if expected responses do not occur. The actors work to arouse desirable responses, using every legitimate means at their command to prevent undesirable responses. At the same time they should be able to remain composed even in the face of apparently meaningless confusion.

TENSION AND CONFLICT. Children become deeply involved in the tense sequences of a play. When the hero is in direct conflict with the antagonist or someone is hiding or being chased or the antagonist seems to be besting the hero, they will squeal, shout warnings or suggestions, jump up and down, or even be reduced to tears. We have commented on this tendency before.

It is impossible to know in advance the exact point at which pleasurable spine-tingling fear is going to become undesirable terror; good taste alone can dictate the degree to which any tension response should be prolonged. The actor should sense the moment when tension should be relaxed, resisting any temptation to carry it to the point of exploitation—which is simply violation of the faith which children give to the performers. The excitement generated within the audience (and the audible evidence thereof) may become so gratifying to the actor that he will seek to prolong it unnecessarily, even to incite it where it is not intended. Such a practice is very dangerous. The border line between stimulation and exploitation is thin indeed.

Scenes of direct conflict between opposing forces are usually played at a fairly rapid pace, and there is frequently considerable dialogue in these sequences. The problem of making lines heard increases, once the audience response has been triggered. While the players should hold for laughter, topping the response with the next line of dialogue just after the laugh reaches its peak, they should not worry about lines during a fear response. At that point the audience is far more interested in observable action, and holding dialogue will only prolong the scene. The high point should be reached quickly and tension released before audience control is lost.

Through comment, actors can try to avoid presenting frighteningly harsh portrayals of antagonistic characters; but sometimes, in performance, audience response may show the need for further modification. However, basic characterization never changes, and the performance must never be watered down to the point where it loses strength and meaning. Audiences enjoy disliking and fearing antagonistic characters, but they find little pleasure in being terrified.

RELAXATION VS. BOREDOM.   Tense scenes in children's plays are usually followed by quiet moments, to allow the audience to relax before it is taken to the next high point in the action. The actors may notice that the audience is restless at these times. Up to a point this is a perfectly normal and desirable reaction and does not indicate a loss of interest in the play. However, tension-relieving scenes are prolonged in some scripts, continuing on a low level of emotion and interest beyond the point where they serve their function. Invariably such scenes contain more dialogue than action, and in a children's play any scene which is primarily conversational is a potential problem. The director should warn the actors which scenes are likely to lose the audience if tension is relaxed more than necessary. In blocking such conversational scenes he should attempt to retain visual attention through interesting movement patterns. In addition he may employ changes in lighting or have music underneath the dialogue, thus making a sensory appeal to attention. However, the ultimate responsibility for controlling restlessness and preventing boredom rests with the actors.

Again there is no set formula for determining the moment when restlessness, the natural accompaniment to relaxing tension, becomes boredom. The actors simply must sense intuitively when they are losing the audience. The amount of restlessness and conversation is their guide.

There are some specific techniques which can be employed to hold the audience through the less exciting scenes of the play. First, the actors should not be distracted by rustling movement but should continue to play sincerely and with increased vitality. They should be very definite in executing stage movement and business. While the tempo of a quiet scene written to release tension should be slower than the exciting moments which precede it, the pace should not be relaxed to the point where the scene seems to drag, and it should be stepped up again once the quieter mood has been established.

Since nothing is more disconcerting to actors than the sensation that the audience has lost interest in the play, they sometimes thoughtlessly resort to tricks in an effort to recapture attention, such as inventing new action solely for effect. Frequently actions of this type are superimposed, completely irrelevant to the play, and therefore dishonest. When an actor builds expectations that are not going to be satisfied he unfairly misleads the audience and risks losing them even further. If the audience is disappointed by being prepared for an action which never occurs, it is likely to reject the next effort to arouse attention, however legitimate it may be.

Strangely enough, restlessness in itself does not necessarily indicate that the audience has missed the significance of a scene. Frequently actors have been pleasantly surprised to discover an element of interest or inherent tension in scenes they dreaded most.

PERFORMANCE

Before the Curtain Opens

The director should always retain control over any plans that are made to introduce the play to the audience. The matter of preperformance and between-acts audience management probably is one of the greatest concerns of children's theatre producing organizations, and a wide variety of techniques has been developed to keep the audience under control and prepare them for viewing the play.

Producers always face the problem of deciding how long to wait beyond scheduled curtain time for the arrival of late comers. The director should be the one who decides the precise moment when the curtain will rise. Ringing up the curtain while a number of children are still lined up at the box office or before all the busses bringing groups of children to the theatre have arrived is unfair to both actors and audience. On the other hand, bedlam is invited if early arrivals are made to wait for the isolated straggler. Recorded music may be played to maintain a measure of order during the waiting period.

As soon as the last large group is seated, the house lights should be dimmed and the director or his assistant should come out to make a brief curtain speech. This should be a cordial, sincere presentation to make the audience feel welcome. It should include an introduction to the play, an explanation of act and scene divisions, and a statement that there will not be time between scenes to leave the auditorium, but that time will be allowed to stand and stretch before the next act begins. This type of forthright introduction orients the audience to the experience they will have, and it is usually surprisingly effective in discouraging a mass exodus to the drinking fountain the minute an act ends.

Following the curtain speech the house lights remain dim while the overture is played. The music used in children's theatre should be selected with great care and should be limited to orchestral compositions in keeping with the spirit and period of the play. The overture should run approximately three minutes, bridging the gap between the reality of the auditorium and the make-believe of the play. The point at which the house lights go out and the curtain opens should be carefully predetermined, and the music should carry under the opening moment of the action.

PREPERFORMANCE ENTERTAINMENT. One of the strong arguments advanced in favor of live theatre for children is that such entertainment gives them an experience that differs from their regular exposures to the mass media. Another is that attendance at children's theatre productions provides valuable training for future adult audiences. Those who accept these two principles are also likely to hold the opinion that preperformance entertainment which is not relevant to the play has no place in children's theatre. Certainly a motion picture never should be shown as a prelude to a live dramatic performance. Some children's theatre groups have brought into existence a veritable menagerie of mascot characters as devices for explaining what it means to be a member of the theatre audience. Such figures commonly appear prior to the opening of the curtain to address the audience by means of poems or songs dealing with audience behavior, or they conduct a contrived interview with a child who supposedly has been selected at random from the audience. Such presentations are often condescending and moralistic in tone, and they are not likely to have much ethical appeal to the child audience. While the youngest children may find animal or clown characters intriguing, their response to the sermons presented will usually be negative. Older children may even reject the characters themselves with jeering discourtesy.

If a group considers a mascot figure necessary to establish identification with the theatre during publicity campaigns, that same figure may logically be present in the lobby the day of performance to welcome the children and answer their questions. However, this figure should not introduce the performance, particularly if the techniques noted above are employed.

The introduction to the children's play should begin to set the mood for the performance. This function properly belongs to a mature adult who is capable of making a sincere, matter-of-fact curtain speech.

Between the Acts

Intermissions are commonly regarded as trouble spots in children's theatre. If intermissions are not carefully arranged and controlled the audience may be completely lost and their attention never fully regained. Knowing the potential problems, many producing organizations spend an unwarranted amount of time and energy devising between-acts entertainment or activities. These diversions include having the mascot character or a minor character from the play come out to teach a song, a game, or even a dance; organized calisthenics; community singing; or, on occasion, a narrative or scene having to do with what is happening in the story.

As a rule these devices are of the same questionable value as preperformance entertainment. Except for scenes or narratives which bridge the action, between-scenes activities usually are not relevant to the play. At their worst they suggest a patronizing, even fearful attitude toward the audience. A reasonably brief intermission permits children to relax, momentarily finding necessary relief from tension and emotional involvement. Cramming such a moment with organized activity is likely to cause the audience to stray too far from the play and its story.

Plays requiring only one setting should pose no intermission problems. At the end of each act the curtain remains closed for no more than one minute, which is quite long enough to allow the children to stand, stretch, and relax for a moment. In a show requiring several settings, however, technical considerations dictate the length of intermissions. In such cases control of the time element begins when the settings are designed. No insurmountable problems should arise if settings are designed and built to shift easily and quickly and if the stage crew is carefully organized and rehearsed. Frequently the director must modify his technical demands to ensure that scene shifts will not cause undue delays.

Music should be used in performance to punctuate act endings, bridge the time lapse between scenes, and lead forward to the opening of the next sequence. Keeping the house lights at minimum intensity also seems to have a controlling effect on confusion in the auditorium.

The cover scene is probably the best way to bridge scene shifts. As we indicated in Chapter 4, a number of plays are written with such scenes, and often the director will add them. When they are employed they should be directed with the same careful attention that is paid to on-stage action. Frequently the audience can be involved to some extent in these scenes. A procession of characters through the audience to the stage can be delightful. Any audience involvement should be carefully controlled and in keeping with the play itself. (See Plate 12.)

THE CURTAIN CALL

Children's plays usually end on a note of spectacle with most of the characters on stage. If the director decides to have a curtain call, it should be taken in character and grow out of the last event in the play. The curtain opens on what appears to be an extension of the final sequence of action. Only a single curtain call should be taken, and it should be very short. The curtain call should be carefully planned and rehearsed and executed smoothly. If the actors are then to meet the audience in the lobby, the procession through the auditorium begins immediately after the actors acknowledge audience applause.

The adult company should by all means take a curtain call. Acquaintance with this convention of the theatre is an integral part of children's audience training. However, additional factors should be considered before the director decides to have the child cast take a curtain call.

Most children's producing organizations usually emphasize that the actors are only one of several groups responsible for bringing the play to the audience and are no more important than the crews. When we teach this philosophy the final curtain should remain closed. Since the curtain call frankly brings credit to the actors alone, it may tend to break down attitudes which the director has taken great pains to instill in the whole producing group.

Some children's producing organizations take curtain calls because they consider audience training important enough to risk the possible sacrifice of other values. These curtain calls should be limited to a straight company front formation, and every effort should be made to avoid singling out any individual actor.

MEETING THE AUDIENCE

Adult actors frequently meet the audience in the lobby after performances. This experience can be valuable to them as actors because children will frankly share with them their reactions to the play as a whole and to individual characters. They crowd around sympathetic characters, but often avoid the antagonistic characters, staring at them from a distance and hesitating to approach them directly. They will speak to the actors as characters, giving little indication that they regard them as having an identity separate from their roles.

From the point of view of children, lobby receptions may break down identification and destroy illusion, at least for the younger group. They will notice make-up and become aware of the falseness of wigs and exaggerated facial features. They may be disillusioned to discover that weapons which seemed dangerously real in performance are only wood and plastic after all. To modify this breakdown of illusion the actors should be prepared for the reactions and questions typical of children and should plan to converse in character, relating their answers to the play.

Older children delight in unmasking theatrical secrets. They take real pleasure in exposing the techniques of illusion, and, having done so, they feel that they have truly shared in the make-believe. Discovering explanations for special effects does not appear to destroy the quality of illusion for older children— it may even increase their appreciation. Makers of stage magic may feel genuinely complimented when a fourth grader glowingly admits, "Boy, you really had me fooled!"

THE CHILD CAST AND THE AUDIENCE. Casts composed entirely of children have less audience identification with performances than characters played by adults. Bringing the child cast out to meet the audience may destroy any illusion that has been created on the stage. Child actors step out of character as soon as they leave the stage. Furthermore, their lack of maturity and experience makes them ill equipped to cope with the reactions and questions they will receive.

The fact that in postperformance interviews children pay a great deal of attention to some characters and shun others is another argument for keeping the child cast backstage. The young actors are not likely to understand that the attention they receive from audience members reflects attitudes towards characters in the play, but are more apt to interpret it in personal terms. The sensitive director will immediately recognize that this can be detrimental to child actors.

Children who play in a mixed cast usually are well integrated with the adult group, taking their cues from them. These children meet the audience with poise and control. It is interesting to note that child actors who play with adults arouse a dual identification among members of the audience. During the play they have high interest value as characters, but when the audience meets them after the play they talk to them as actors, often expressing great interest in the fact that a child like themselves has been in the show.

SUPERVISING THE CHILD CAST

The child cast must be carefully prepared to meet the pressures and excitement of performance. However, under the stress of the moment even the best-disciplined group requires the support of adult supervision. Children should not be left to their own devices at any time while in the theatre. If they are allowed complete freedom there will be running through the halls; curious faces will appear through the stage curtain to survey the arriving audience; crowds in the wings will hamper the work of the technicians, block passageways and sight lines, interfere with scene shifts, and create unwarranted noise and confusion backstage.

Calmly authoritative adults should make sure that child actors report directly to the locations assigned for make-up and dressing. Immediately prior to the opening curtain the children should be assembled in the room where they are to remain throughout the performance except when they are on stage. Actors should never be permitted to stray into areas where the audience may see them in costumes and make-up.

Adult chaperons should always remain in the room where child actors wait. Perhaps the director will arrange to have a skilled storyteller entertain the children. Some groups encourage them to bring quiet games or reading material. Crew members in charge of costumes and make-up should have emergency supplies on hand to take care of last-minute repairs.

The director should assign a highly reliable assistant stage manager to call the actors for entrances, and this should be his only backstage assignment. When confined to a room away from the acting area, children feel uneasy unless they can be certain they will receive dependable entrance warnings.

The Director's Role in Performance

The director has no place backstage during the run of the play. From the beginning the company must understand that they will be on their own during performances. They will have no prompter to help them with lines. The play belongs to them, and the stage manager is in complete charge from now on. If the director has done his work well the company will be prepared to assume responsibility and to cope with any difficult situation that may arise.

Since he is likely to be as tense as any of the actors, the director's presence backstage would probably be more irritating than reassuring. The production is now out of his hands, and if he continually comes backstage he gives the impression that he has little confidence in the company.

During performances the director's place is in the auditorium, where he observes the play and notes audience reactions, devoting his energies toward increasing his understanding of the child audience and arriving at an objective evaluation of the production as a whole.

Following each performance the director should interpret his observations to the cast, challenging them to strive for greater effectiveness each time they play. Sometimes he needs to call additional rehearsals to work out solutions to problems arising in performance.

It is certainly to be hoped that an increasing number of directors will attempt to systematize their study of the child audience. Recorded observations, postperformance interviews, as well as yet untried techniques should be employed to supply facts usable for raising production standards in children's theatre.

PROBLEMS OF THE LONG RUN

Most organizations present several performances of each children's play they produce, some playing daily in a continuous run while others space performances over several weekends. Either system may give rise to problems.

During a continuous run, the director is not concerned with keeping the show together from one performance to the next, but when four or five days elapse between performances this is a problem. Usually, however, a cast meeting and line rehearsal the day before the play resumes will suffice to bring it back to performance quality.

Retaining spontaneity and freshness is probably the greatest problem of the long run. Unless concentration and sincerity remain at a high level, line readings and reaction patterns become mechanical and uninspired. The actors may not be aware that their performances are developing these qualities. Reminding them of their responsibility to every audience is the job of the director.

Fatigue usually does not operate to the detriment of performances—often a company gives its best performance when the actors are tired. Apparently they sense that they do not feel at their best and exert additional efforts to remain vital and alert. The director can do little to control the fatigue factor except to warn the company that a long series of performances is energy consuming and to insist that they get as much rest as possible. He should avoid making unreasonable demands on company time and energy for extra rehearsals or technical work, and he should discourage continuous partying.

Fatigue is actually less likely to have an adverse effect on performances than is the relaxed feeling of well-being that comes with overconfidence. The director should be alert to notice signs of indifference and to check for loss of vitality. The minute he senses overconfidence he should present the company with some new challenges to keep them alert.

The director also should notice any tendency to alter characterizations. Actors sometimes decide to make changes in their portrayals without consulting the director. If these changes are not stopped the entire play can be thrown out of balance. Actors must realize that there is a difference between modifying a portrayal to temper audience response and changing a characterization to satisfy a personal whim.

Company discipline includes maintaining respect for the audience and for every member of the producing group. As a long run nears its end, adult actors frequently begin to engage in practical jokes. In extreme cases they seem to compete to see how far they can go with their backstage tricks, and they devise some alarming schemes in their attempts to test each other. Many a final performance has been all but ruined as a result of trickery that sometimes includes on-stage jokes. Usually a company does not engage in practical jokes with malicious intent, but even the most reliable groups have been known to succumb to them. Apparently they feel that the child audience cannot detect that things are going wrong on the stage. Every cast should be forewarned that backstage or on-stage behavior detrimental to the production will not be tolerated.

Throughout a long run the director must maintain high company morale and enthusiasm for the production. He should remain calm and impartial in his dealings with the group. He should sense the proper moments to make suggestions and phrase them in an acceptable way. He should know when to be firm and when to relieve tension with humor and understanding. He should encourage each member of the company to respect the talents and responsibilities of co-workers, and he scrupulously avoids any suggestion of favoritism or rejection in his dealings with individual members of the company.

The professional attitude held by members of a children's theatre cast is the direct result of the training they have received through long hours of rehearsal and conferences, or even in moments of relaxation. A director sets the tone of serious intention and expectation at the first gathering of his company. His dedication will be contagious, and the actors will come to know that their very best efforts will be needed until the final curtain comes down.

7 &

The Production Is Designed

THE CURIOUS, effervescent, expectant nature of the child audience makes it inevitable that a large share of responsibility for the effectiveness of any children's play will rest upon the staging. With what delight each change of setting, of lighting, of costume is greeted! What an immediate effect suitably chosen music has upon this acutely sensitive audience! What gasps and delighted wriggling greet each effect of stage magic! With what accuracy each child in the crowd can describe key properties down to the most minute detail!

Surely the slipshod methods of the past—scenery left over from previous productions, crepe paper foliage, and cambric costumes—are unworthy of the belief children give to the imaginary happenings on the stage. The varied aspects of staging the children's play deserve the same careful thought, the same imaginative planning accorded the selection and rehearsing of the play.

Beginners in the field of children's theatre are frequently appalled at the apparently limitless demands which even the most modest of the popular plays seem to make on technical facilities and ingenuity. There are few "single set" children's plays. More often three or four settings are required, and occasionally as many as fifteen scenes are called for by the action. Large casts moving through historical or "romantic past" periods need a sizable allotment of both time and money for costumes. The effectiveness of dream sequences, visions, magical appearances, weather conditions, as well as the unreal atmosphere necessary for extraordinary happenings—all these will depend upon carefully contrived and flexibly controlled lighting. Unusual makeups for animals, witches, fantastic characters of all kinds, cannot be managed with the customary "dash of lipstick and spot of rouge." Most of the properties probably will not be found in the homes of cast members or friends of the theatre. These and other technical problems may well worry even the most seasoned producer, but upon their solution may actually hinge the success of the play.

In Chapter 5 we outlined the principles the director follows in constructing his floor plan, since the use of the available stage space must be decided before rehearsals can begin. The position of entrances, approximate distances between points on the set, placement of set properties, and the possible use of levels will probably be decided by the director and explained to the designer. At this point the director either turns responsibility for the visual aspects of production over to the designer or continues to assume it himself. The present chapter is intended for the person who assumes the function of the designer, whether this is a director who carries out his own plans for staging or a full staff of scene designer, costumer, and lighting designer.

VISUAL ELEMENTS IN THE TOTAL PRODUCTION SCHEME

Since the visual elements of a children's production contribute so vitally to the total impression a child receives from the play, the nature of that contribution should be kept clearly in mind as plans are made. These visual elements should make four contributions to the production, as discussed in the following pages.

First, the flavor, line, and details of setting, costumes, and properties will help the children understand *where, when, and under what circumstances the action is taking place*. What children see is far more meaningful to them than what they hear. For this reason, a producer cannot rely on the words of the actor to tell the circumstances of the play. The moment the curtain opens the audience should be able to sense the romantic past in a far-off country, the historical past at Boonesborough, Kentucky, or Concord, Massachusetts, or the present day in suburban New York. The fact that children are unable to date scenes accurately or place them geographically in anything other than general terms imposes upon the designer even more obligation to present an accurate picture, consistent in all details, insofar as accuracy is important for an understanding of the story. Documentation of social station is particularly important, since so many children's plays make a commentary upon the contrast between apparent and true worth of characters. The cottage must be truly humble, the palace truly magnificent. The lighting should help further to tell the circumstances of the play —the weather, the time of day, or the season of the year.

Second, the visual elements of production should work dynamically to *help the actors tell the story*. Scenery which provides only a "background" to the action contributes little to the play, regardless of how pretty or elaborate it may be. Beautiful and expensive costumes which do not delineate character are a waste of money. Properties not used by the actors contribute nothing but confusion as far as children are concerned and should be eliminated from the stage.

Sets, properties, and costumes should be recognized solely for the part they play in the action. An examination of a few children's theatre scripts will show how closely the story and the technical elements are interrelated. Beanstalks and vines are climbed, roofs fly off houses, secret panels and doors open, spinning wheels turn by themselves, sets change before our eyes as action continues, magic vistas open up, trap doors in the floor are used for concealment. Properties such as treasure chests, caskets, couches, stoves, ovens, swords, pumpkins, and cages figure prominently in the action.

Even though great attention may be given to these specific demands of staging, equal attention should also be given to the more aesthetic uses of spectacle. Designers need to provide for the movement patterns of the actors—vantage points for important speeches, focal areas for specific scenes, levels for emphasis, space for chases, dances, and sword fights, a physical framework for hiding, scenes of pageantry, and the many other kinds of specialized action which characterize children's plays. Lighting should be utilized to reveal the elements of the stage picture as they are needed, to direct youngsters' attention to important happenings, and to integrate the plastic elements of the stage picture with the movements of the actor.

Variety in stage levels has been found especially useful in children's plays to help the actors tell the story. Not only do they make the movements of actors more meaningful and varied, but the movements can be seen much better by small viewers. And they are almost essential for scenes involving many characters or pageantry sequences, in order to keep groups separated as forces and yet provide for focus upon the principals. The floor then becomes a valuable additional playing space which can be used by the director for variety in the sequence of stage pictures. There are few scenes in which varied levels cannot logically be a part of the floor plan.

The third function of the visual elements of a production is to *arouse ideas and emotions relevant to the themes being ex-*

pressed by the playwright. His script must be the point of departure for all the artists who work to bring a play to life. The scene designer works with the director to discover the themes inherent in the drama and the methods by which they will be projected to the youthful audience. A scenic artist who works without a clear understanding of *what the play means* on the allegorical and anagogical levels is like a man constructing a skyscraper from unseen plans—his work may be beautiful, but has no relationship to the original dreams.

An example may serve to clarify the point. One of the main themes of Corinne Rickert and Frank M. Whiting's *Huckleberry Finn* is that freedom is worth any sacrifice. Huck opens the play by sawing himself out of the cabin in which he is imprisoned. Jim, the slave who has run away from his mistress, joins him, and together the two escapees embark on their journey in search of freedom. Designs for the five exteriors and one interior scene of this play would be quite unsatisfying if they did not project this desire for freedom. A formal outline of the straight proscenium frame would be quite out of keeping for this play, since straight lines suggest strict and conventional discipline. The irregular lines of Mississippi River foliage can be employed all through the stage picture to suggest this thematic element—one which is necessary for both an intellectual understanding of the action and a sympathy for the plight of the main characters. (See Plate 16.)

Little has been said or written about symbolism in children's theatre, though it exists in the plays themselves and in the stories upon which much of the current repertoire is based. Ideas are conveyed to the child audience by means of symbols—words, music, settings, action—all of which are symbolic because they stand for something; they represent a conventionalization of the actual thing which is interpreted and understood. True, young children are still in the process of developing ability to generalize from examples, of developing concepts upon which to base generalities. Nevertheless, we cannot assume that they are unable to comprehend any symbolism just because a vast knowledge and experience are needed to grasp the import of advanced forms.

In both children's and adult theatre, ideas and emotions pertinent to the drama must be aroused by means of symbols. The fact that the symbols used must be kept quite literal should not discourage us from trying to find just the right ones to project a given theme, those which will mean what they are intended to mean for children of a certain age.

Intellect and emotions work together on the interpretation of a play. Intellectually, children should perceive the lush furnishings of the Black Brothers' home in Marjorie Evernden's *The King of the Golden River*. It should appear rich and prosperous. But emotionally they should feel that love is absent, that happiness is gone, and that Gluck, the hero, is really a prisoner within those walls. Capturing essential atmosphere goes beyond documentation of the country or the historical period. The designer reaches into the mind and heart of the child with his carefully selected details to plant the seeds of deeper meaning, to arouse emotions consistent with the intentions of the playwright.

The fourth function of the visual elements of production in children's plays is to *compensate for children's uncertain comprehension of language, for their unmet psychological needs, and even for child actors' relatively unskilled technique.*

The natural limitations of running time and attention spans which govern the children's theatre playwright make it almost imperative that the stage picture be immediately comprehensible, understood and recognized for what it is without further word. Long explanations of the physical environment should be unnecessary. If matters of spectacle are handled properly by the designer, all that needs to be known will be comprehended soon after the opening curtain.

Children long to see the pictures built up in their minds come to life upon the stage, and they expect to experience the sense of achievement which comes as formidable obstacles, concretely presented on the stage, are overcome. Hansel and Gretel's forest, Tom Sawyer's cave, and the broken trestle in Chorpenning's *Radio Rescue* hold the promise of danger, even death; but the fortitude of the heroes is sufficient to conquer them all. Settlement house children, children of the slums and crowded industrial centers, are especially gratified when the visual elements of production provide them with a glimpse of unworldly beauty— a beauty which is sadly lacking in their everyday lives. Here is one of the most sacred obligations of the children's theatre designer.

Child actors, with their smaller stature, voices limited in carrying power, and relatively unskilled technique, need the help of visual elements even more than adult actors in communicating the thoughts and emotions of the characters to the child audience. Settings which focus and elevate these youthful performers should be provided. Costumes which not only project character but which help the actor *feel* more like the character he is playing are a sound investment. Lighting which constantly interprets the intended mood of the progressing action increases the effectiveness of the performance by working on actors and audience alike. Properties scaled down in proportions lend convincingness to stage pictures inhabited by less-than-full-sized people.

In a word, organizations which use child actors should stress high technical theatre standards by way of support for the players.

EVOLVING THE SCENIC DESIGN

Understanding in a general way what the visual elements should contribute to the production, the designer begins evolving his plans. At first he will pay no attention to stock sets or units he may have in storage. He will even ignore his budget or the fact that the play must tour. He will try to make this a period of dreaming, allowing his imagination to soar and visualizing the ideal, not the inevitable compromise. That can come later. At the beginning he needs an ideal vision from which the practical design will eventually emerge. At each major decision he reaches, he should check with the director, since a clear understanding between the two during this entire process is most important for the eventual unity of the production.

Consider the Child Vision

Children probably have their own mental image of the locale in which a story ought to take place. It will matter little to them that palaces and castles at the time of *Snow White* were actually cold, dark, and unbelievably filthy—memories of the Walt Disney picture of the Wicked Queen's palace will seem far more factual to them. Other palaces have appeared on home television screens—decidedly romanticized versions, reflecting the romantic nature of the stories themselves.

To a child, palace throne rooms are huge in proportion. People are dwarfed beneath graceful Gothic arches, immense tapestries, and gigantic fireplaces. The woodcutter's cottage is generally warm and friendly, intimate in its dimensions, with all things oriented to the stone fireplace which furnishes heat against the north wind's chilling blast. A cave is filled with strange irregular shapes, sheer walls, and narrow ledges to walk on. The palace garden has marble steps, balustrades, and fountains bathed in moonlight, while the farm or cottage yard

PLATE 9

Above. *A "plastic stage" setting by Richard Corson for* Alice in Wonderland, *University of North Carolina Woman's College production, 1945.*

Below. *A setting under sculptured light.* The Emperor's New Clothes, *Michigan State University Youtheatre production, designed by Edward Andreasen, directed by Jed H. Davis, 1960.*

PLATE 10

Above. *Ramps, levels, and a bridge provide for varied heights in the stage picture.
An adaptation of formalism that works well even in a basically romantic setting.* The
Emperor's New Clothes, *Michigan State University Youtheatre production, designed
by Edward Andreasen, directed by Jed H. Davis, 1960.*

Below. *Decorative formalism in J. Morton Walker's design for* The Blue Bird,
*University of Minnesota Young People's Theatre production, directed by Kenneth L.
Graham, 1952.*

PLATE II

Above. *A modified box setting designed by James Bronner and Patton Lockwood for Chorpenning and Tully's* The Elves and the Shoemaker, *Michigan State University Children's Theatre production, directed by Jed H. Davis, 1958.*

Below. *Another modified box setting designed by Erwin Feher for Mitchell's* The Utah Trail, *Michigan State University Children's Theatre production, directed by Mary Jane Larson Watkins, 1959.*

Merlin's narratives before the presentation curtain.

PLATE 12

A unit set designed by J. Morton Walker for Engar's Arthur and the Magic Sword, *University of Minnesota Young People's Theatre production, directed by Kenneth L. Graham, 1949.*

The old king's throne room.

A castle courtyard.

Before the cathedral.

PLATE 13

A horizontal simultaneous setting designed by Lee Mitchell for Barrie's Peter Pan, Cain Park Theatre production, directed by Kenneth L. Graham, 1942.

PLATE 14

A vertical simultaneous setting by Edith King for Aucassin *and Nicolette,* King-Coit School *production, directed by Dorothy Coit, New
York, 1955.*

The Wizard's garden.

PLATE 15

An adaptation of the drop-wing-border setting designed by Jed H. Davis for Gray's Beauty and the Beast, *Michigan State University Children's Theatre production, directed by Margaret Paton, 1955. The background remained throughout, while props and set units changed the locale.*

Beauty's home.

Outside the Beast's castle.

is little more than an open space surrounded by a wooden fence with perhaps a stone well curb near the doorstep. Such concepts as these have been used to justify stock settings—a "palace interior," a "cottage," a "rustic exterior," a "woodland glade," and many theatres in the United States still have and use a few of these relics. Obviously such stock settings cannot reflect any of the individual qualities of a given play. They can serve only as a "background" against which the action is performed.

Designers today recognize that each setting, regardless of similarity of general location, has its own unique requirements, its own distinctive atmosphere. The qualities to be projected to the child audience differ in each play according to the intention of the playwright and the plan of the director. One cottage may need to project a weird sort of chaos, as in Meigs' *Helga and the White Peacock*. In Maeterlinck's *The Blue Bird* the atmosphere of poverty in the cottage is subordinated to a feeling of love and family happiness. The individual flavor of each locale in the children's theatre repertoire thus precludes the use of stock settings. The designer is successful in his task only as he is able to project the essential qualities of each setting and provide for the action which takes place within it.

Children's concepts of locale are based on the very special view the child has of the world about him. From his low vantage point objects tend to appear larger than they are. Proportion, to children, is largely a matter of relative importance in the action. Drawings which children frequently submit following a production tell what scenic units, which properties, which details are most important to them, for these will be enlarged beyond their realistic size. A designer needs to make use of this fact, considering the size of the actors who are to perform as well as the tendency of children to exaggerate size according to importance—a tendency which decreases with advancing age.

CONSIDER THE INTERMISSIONS

Before proceeding beyond rough sketches, the designer and director should decide upon their scheme for handling intermissions. As explained in Chapter 6, many producers prefer to keep children in their seats during act breaks, and several methods have been devised to do this. The designer's concern with intermissions is, of course, obvious: he must provide swift methods of shifting sets so that the audience will not be kept waiting. Children are anxious to get on with the story and are not interested in mundane reasons for delay.

Intermission devices frequently complicate basic designs and staging plans. Director and designer may decide to shift sets within view of the audience. Some extremely interesting "magic-appearing" changes are possible as the lights dim out at the end of a scene, leaving only black silhouettes of walls or arches against lighted blue sky. Miraculously, without visible means of propulsion, these shapes begin to move, to the accompaniment of appropriate music. Gradually, rhythmically, they re-form into a new pattern, and the lights return to normal for the next scene. Essentially the same effect can take place behind a scrim on which a changing pattern of lights, moving clouds, or falling snow is projected. Incidentally, when methods of this sort are used, scene shifters must be rehearsed as carefully as the cast.

As we have noted, some plays provide their own between-scenes narratives in which a character from the play explains interim happenings, talks to the audience, or supplies additional information about the play. The staging of these scenes often requires special attention by the designer: additions to the apron or forestage may have to be planned; small side stages with entrances may be needed in front of the main curtain. Sometimes a special "presentation" curtain situated somewhat further upstage than the regular act curtain may be the best way to give more space for these cover scenes. (See Plate 12 for use of the presentation curtain.) Any number of special lighting effects may be required. If the actor is to contact the audience directly, there will be a need for steps down to the auditorium floor.

The designer must integrate these special devices with the total production design so that they will not stand apart or be distracting when not in use, and the director should plan to use those special areas through other portions of the play as well as between scenes. Every effort should be made to unify the production to prevent intermissions from being so spectacular they distract from the major action of the play.

INVESTIGATE SOURCES

Early in the preparation period the designer should devote hours to careful investigation of source material in the library. This ought to give him the satisfaction of knowing that the scheme he eventually comes up with is sound and worthy of the attention it will receive from the children. He will then start his work with a clear picture of historical detail for settings, properties, and costumes. Most children's stories can be located in time and place, either through descriptive passages within the stories or from the occupations of the characters. If other means fail, reference to a history of children's literature may provide the story's background. It is well for the designer to fix at least approximately the period of the action, even though he may have decided on a basically imaginative scheme rather than one which is historically realistic. When details of a given period are chosen as the basis for an imaginative design, this period should be used consistently throughout all of the visual elements—sets, properties, costumes, perhaps even the music. Mixtures of periods in the visual scheme violate the educational purposes of children's theatre and are difficult to defend on any ground. True, children "may not know the difference," but we are nevertheless obligated to present a consistent picture for them so that they will reach maturity with less cluttered visions than so many of their elders possess.

At this time it will undoubtedly help the designer to locate as many versions of the story on which the play is based as he can find, comparing them for thematic implications. At the same time he may gain a helpful knowledge of how various illustrators have visualized the story's characters and environment. This should not be taken to imply a literal carry-over of any illustrator's scheme to the special conditions of the stage: nevertheless, the designer is bound to be helped by recognizing the kinds of pictures children may have in their minds, probably derived at least partially from illustrated versions of the story. From such illustrations the designer may get an idea, a detail, a period, or a suggestion which will become the basis for all of his subsequent visualization.

DECIDE THE STYLE OF PRODUCTION

The style of the production is the most important decision the designer and director make together. Too frequently style is thought of as concerning only the stage setting or costumes or both. Actually style should be thought of as a point of view toward the production as a whole, carried all the way through, from acting to properties. Style determines the consistency of the impression the production makes. Its contribution to the story itself is comprehensive. It satisfies not only the artistic sensibilities of the people responsible for the production but also the need of the children to comprehend the essential qualities of the script.

Precedent—the fact that a play "is usually done" in this or that manner—has little validity in children's theatre. A designer has no more obligation or need to copy the sketches or plans in the printed copy of the playbook than the director has to follow the suggested blocking. It is equally a mistake for a designer to sit down with the express purpose of planning a set in any given style, regardless of its popularity, even if that style is "recommended" as best for children's theatre.

Actually, several factors should govern the choice of style. The script itself is the point of departure. Its general classification or the kind of dialogue, characters, and action may suggest the need for at least a limited range of styles. The abstraction ability of the age group for which the production is intended will obviously have much to do with the area of choice. Preferences of the children themselves should also be considered, though the recognized educational purposes of children's theatre activity suggests that we must also be concerned with children's artistic growth. To a certain extent available lighting facilities limit the choice of style.

Nevertheless, designers usually have a rather extensive range of possibilities from which to select a style. Just the photographs included here demonstrate that almost all known styles have been used for children's theatre productions—and surely no one believes that the limits have been reached as to future possibilities. It is interesting to note that Russian children's theatres have already gone beyond recognized dramatic styles to produce combinations of several theatre forms—puppetry, movies, animated cartoons—in their search for methods of projecting specific themes. The demands of children's theatre repertoire tend to compel imaginative designers to evolve a dynamic approach to the staging of plays—not a quiet acceptance of prevailing fashions in the theatre.

The various styles of production discussed below form a continuous progression from the most *representational* to the most *presentational,* that is, from *naturalism* to *formalism.*

Styles close to the middle of this scale may possess both representational and presentational aspects. Advantages and limitations of each are suggested, with reference to both the current repertoire of plays and the child audience.

NATURALISM.   A style purporting to depict reality, an actual locale in every detail, is known as *naturalism*. This style is photographically exact, permitting little or no selection to the designer. If possible, actual objects are used rather than stage representations of those objects. Obviously, naturalism is more effective for interiors than for exteriors. The proscenium frame itself tends to reduce the convincingness of the naturalistic picture, especially when the sky is involved.

Naturalism requires the least sophistication on the part of the audience because it puts the fewest demands on their interpretative powers. The production as a whole can be taken for just what it appears to be. Regardless of his age, maturity level, or training, a child may see in a naturalistic setting the very life he knows intimately. For this reason, it has a certain validity in children's theatre production, though there are also serious limitations to its use. (See Plate 5.)

Because it requires least from the child viewer, it also contributes the least of any style to his artistic growth. Furthermore, the cluttered appearance which inevitably accompanies a nonselective stage setting is likely to destroy the focus on *important* elements which the child needs for clarity and ease in following the action. Practical limitations exist as well, such as the elaborate facilities required to construct and shift rapidly several absolutely complete settings.

True naturalism in art is considered something of a historical oddity today and is in rather universal disrepute. Even in its heyday, during the first quarter of this century, it was used mostly in modified form for children's theatre. Perhaps the chief reason it is not used more extensively today is that there are practically no truly naturalistic children's plays. Their "slice-of-life" characteristic is too confusing to children, who require a strong story line and plot structure to maintain their interest.

REALISM. Any modification of the photographic quality of naturalism is likely to change the style to *realism*. Here the designer attempts to give the *illusion* of an actual locale rather than the locale itself. He selects details which will give this impression and incorporates them into the design; he does not put in everything that would be found in life but includes only those details which are pertinent to the play. This selective process makes realism a higher artistic achievement than naturalism—and hence it contributes somewhat to a child's artistic growth. On the other hand it demands only a reasonable amount of interpretation on his part and is consequently easy to comprehend. Exteriors done in this style can be more consistent with interiors than they are in naturalism, since a certain amount of stage convention is automatically assumed.

A rather large number of children's plays fit loosely into the category of realism, and the style has much to recommend it for children's theatre. Many studies have shown that children themselves prefer realistic treatment above other styles in their art works and usually list real, natural, or lifelike qualities as the basis for choosing one picture over another. From the earliest age, children's own drawings are attempts to depict reality. They feel secure with it. There is no confusion. They can see and recognize familiar forms without having to interpret their meaning extensively in order to figure out how they contribute to the action on the stage. Clearly, realism answers the children's own demands upon the visual elements of the production. (See Plate 5.)

However, in many plays demanding more than one setting,

complete realism is just as much out of the question as naturalism. From a practical point of view, realism often requires
a lot of scenery to be constructed, painted, and shifted quickly.
When the physical plant is adequate, several realistic settings
can be handled efficiently; but when serious limitations of time,
space, manpower, and money enter into the problem, the com-
promises that must be made can make the designer wish he had
decided on a less demanding plan of production.

Nevertheless, when the audience is to be composed largely
of younger children, designers should not stray too far from
realism if they would put their message across.

SIMPLIFIED REALISM. When a designer keeps on eliminating nonessentials from a realistic setting he eventually arrives at *simplified realism*. This style of setting is characterized
by the presence of a minimum number of the realistic elements
which give, in general, the feeling of a complete locale. The
few units which remain are as complete as possible in themselves, frequently with constructed three-dimensional details.

Since it is much easier to load a setting with elements than
it is to reduce them to a minimum, simplified realism is a much
higher artistic achievement on the part of the designer than
either realism or naturalism. Furthermore, if the essential
atmosphere of the locale is conveyed, if there is enough to
support the actor in his telling of the story, and if the desired
mood is projected, there is no reason why simplified realism
cannot be fully as satisfying to children as realism. Properly
handled, this style can contribute greatly to children's artistic
growth, since it requires some interpretation and completion
from them. (See Plates 6 and 11.)

Some designers, unfortunately, carried away with the obvious
practical advantages of ease of constructing and shifting sets
done in this style, have eliminated so much that the very func-

tions of the setting vanish from the stage. Furthermore, this and all the remaining styles of design depend for their effectiveness largely upon a flexibly controlled arrangement of specific lighting instruments (spotlights) which keep illumination where the setting is, not where it has been eliminated. The impression the designer sets out to create with this style is of a complete locale, not one cut down to the level of abject poverty.

IMPRESSIONISM. The style which has probably been most frequently misunderstood and misinterpreted in children's theatre over the past quarter-century is *impressionism*. Here the same process of elimination of superfluous details and selection of the most representative elements is carried out as in simplified realism, but the difference shows up in the treatment of the scenic elements that remain. Whereas the artist working in selective realism makes every effort to bring about the appearance of actuality in what elements he uses, the impressionist works in a nondetailed way, giving to the objects he uses an *atmospheric* rather than a realistic quality. His purpose to heighten the mood of the scene usually extends beyond the setting to include very atmospheric lighting, scrims and transparencies, and perhaps even light projections.

A barren stage is no more impressionism than it is selective realism. An artist does not become impressionistic simply by reducing the setting to a minimum. Impressionism demands that the *feeling or flavor* of the locale and the attending situation be clearly conveyed. In other words, the style makes a distinct comment upon the situation, often imbuing it with a haziness, a nebulousness, which in extreme forms can prove distinctly irritating to children, who generally prefer clarity.

True impressionism is a distinctive artistic achievement on the part of the designer. If children could be trained to accept it they would make a significant advance in their artistic growth. Unfortunately, however, the extreme moodiness which often accompanies this style is apt to prove frightening to the younger children who somehow get into the audience. Older children, however, can not only tolerate, but actually enjoy, the heightened mood which impressionism conveys.

Only a limited number of plays or scenes in the contemporary children's theatre repertoire could be effective or even suitably presented in impressionism. The very nature of the children's play demands contrast in moods rather than a single emotional response throughout the play. Some of the techniques of the impressionists, however, if incorporated in settings of other styles, could well increase the degree of involvement when such a response is desirable.

SYMBOLISM.   The symbolist approach to stage settings is also a modification of selective realism. The difference here is one of purpose. The symbolist deliberately sets out to symbolize the essence of the locale with as few partially constructed units as possible. In general, symbolic settings are sparsely decorated scenes in which a single unit is made to stand for an entire locale—a Gothic arch for a cathedral, a tree for a forest, a water wheel for a mill.

While symbolism in the adult theatre has been extremely popular, designers must recognize that children will interpret the style literally. If a single tree is all there is on the stage, they are more likely to see a yard than a forest. Unless the lighting is well handled, confining attention to the portion of the stage where the unit of setting is located, visual focus may be disturbed and attention wander.

Abstract symbolism in design contains another inherent danger for children's theatre. In setting Burnett's *The Little Princess,* for example, we cannot expect children to interpret the decline in Sara Crewe's social station from seeing an arrangement of cobwebs on the stage. Such a setting requires a measure of translation beyond children until they reach a relatively advanced age. In the adult theatre, connections with a locale can be much more remote.

There could not be much objection to a *literally symbolic* setting for children's theatre, provided the general demands made upon settings are fulfilled. Literal symbolism is, in fact, often difficult to distinguish from selective realism. Good sense and a recognition that children are realistically oriented should guide the designer in his use of this as well as other styles of production.

In all of the styles discussed thus far, the shape of objects is represented more or less as they exist in nature. While the children in the audience may be required to "fill in" varying amounts from their imaginations, little interpretation or translation is asked of them. Abstract symbolism, however, begins to introduce these processes, requiring the children to extend what they see on the stage to include a comment upon the situation, the locale, or the play itself. In the styles which remain to be discussed, the shape of objects is still further distorted to reflect a point of view of the designer. The flavor or atmosphere of a locale is *presented* rather than *represented*. Each style named moves farther and farther away from literal indication of a place of action. Each requires more and more of the child audience to comprehend its meaning or relation to the story. Each makes progressively greater demands on the lighting to compose the stage picture.

STYLIZATION. Strictly speaking, *stylization* is simply a designer's individualistic approach to a stage setting; it therefore differs from the approach of any other designer. We have come, however, to regard stylization as a style in itself, possessing rather clearly defined and easily recognized characteristics. Forms are basically unrealistic in order to emphasize a particular quality of the script. Compositional elements of line, form, or color are exaggerated or distorted; perspective may be forced. Spectators are aware of the designer's hand in the appearance of things on the stage. (See Plates 6, 8, 9, 10, 14, 15, and 16.)

Storybook illustrators have for many years used stylization as a method of projecting the elements of humor, satire, or fantasy. The popularity of this style for children's theatre has increased steadily over the years, probably because of the recognition that unusual happenings such as those found in the children's play call for unusual scenery.

Stylization which effectively captures the spirit of a children's play is a high artistic achievement. Nevertheless, we must proceed cautiously in our use of it in children's theatre, since the comment it makes is essentially an adult one. Adults have come to regard stylization almost patronizingly, exclaiming over its "cuteness." Older children may consider it suitable for younger children only, drawing on their knowledge of children's book illustrations to support the observation. Younger children have difficulty grasping the conventions which usually accompany the style, and the middle age range really prefers the more realistic styles.

If stylization is used, the whole production must be keyed to its characteristics. Properties must usually be constructed to harmonize in line with the background. Costumes must possess a similar exaggeration of line or color. Even the acting must be of a kind which brings it into harmony with its environment. There is, furthermore, a danger that the visual elements will attract more attention than they deserve. Designers must make sure that the comment made is not too adult, the degree of translation demanded not too great.

If the stylization reflects qualities inherent in the script, it can account well for the general functions of the visual elements. Its very purpose is one of projecting the mood and theme of the story. It can be decorative enough to satisfy children's need for beauty on the stage. It can provide rather arbitrarily for the focal points and levels the actors need to help them tell the story effectively to the child audience. Designers can frequently select a historical or geographical detail of the actual time or place of the story as the motif for stylization. If objects can be recognized and the degree of abstraction is not too pronounced, the stylized method should serve many children's plays in a way which will satisfy both the audience's present need to comprehend and their eventual artistic growth.

EXPRESSIONISM. The expressionist depicts objects not as they are normally seen but as their inner essence might be conceived in the mind of one of the play's characters. This could mean that perhaps very little about the setting depicts the place of action; all its elements contribute only to an understanding of a character's mental or emotional state. Items which remain in the set are usually distorted in line and decorative treatment.

If expressionism were carried to an extreme, it is easy to imagine the confusion that would result in the children's theatre. (See Plate 7.) Actually, however, when the style is coupled with good sense and a knowledge of children's abstracting limitations, there is a place for expressionism even here. This apparent paradox stems from the fact that there is a strong emotional component of weirdness or capriciousness attending the strange shapes, lines, and forms, and this can be of real help in conveying the right atmosphere, especially for "unworldly" scenes or dream sequences. To be of greatest value, however, expressionism will continue for some time to be combined with other styles in the children's theatre as well as in the adult theatre. Elements should remain recognizable in spite of their distortion if they would satisfy children.

THEATRICALISM. As a style of setting *theatricalism* makes no attempt to depict reality but instead presents a background of some sort in recognized terms of the theatre. It is highly artificial in mood, frankly decorative, and usually humorous. Paint and canvas substitute obviously for any realistic forms. Theatrical settings may take the form of drop and wing, of a segment of a wall or corner of a room, of draped swags, of bare outlines of houses or rooms—any kind of background which does not pretend to be the real thing but is only a bare suggestion, decorative in itself. Settings or costumes designed after some famous illustrator or painter are usually theatrical in style. Such is the case, for example, in countless productions of *Alice in Wonderland* whose designs are based upon Sir John Tenniel's drawings.

There is always a danger in literal transference from one art form to another. While attention may be diverted by the device of copying a famous manner, and some irrelevant pleasure may be taken in seeing the designs which come close to the original model, actors will often have trouble carrying through the illusion. It is quite pointless to try to bring a storybook literally to life on the stage. It would seem far wiser to try to contribute something new and fresh to an interpretation of an ageless story rather than to invite a continual comparison with preconceived pictures and concepts. Surely a designer should know what illustrators have done with specific material; but this does not mean that he should copy those illustrations literally. (See Plate 8.)

However, the limits of theatricalism, especially for older children, have certainly not been reached as yet. Designers are limited only by their imaginations in discovering new and interesting variations of this style of production. The cautions are the usual ones: the designer should make sure the comments made upon the place or the script are not too adult, that his forms are not too sophisticated for the child audience, that he does not get carried away with the decorative element of the style, and that the set retains its proper place in the scheme of production. (See Plate 15.)

FORMALISM.   On a scale which extends from the most to the least representational settings, *formalism* will fall at the extreme presentational end. Indeed, so neutral is this style of setting that it could be used with no changes for play after play. It presents a completely abstract locale. The term itself is applied to several variations of the basic concept, though it usually implies a completely bare stage, flat and unadorned, surrounded by neutral drapes. As levels and ramps and steps are added, modifying the stage floor, the designation is changed to a "plastic stage." As suggestions of place are added to these levels, such as a column, an arch, or a segment of a wall, the setting is more accurately designated as symbolism, impressionism, or simplified realism, depending on the treatment of those elements. "Space stage" is another name for any of the above variations, since it establishes the symbolic relationship between characters in terms of stage space. (See Plate 9.)

With so completely neutral a background, we can readily see why lighting is the principal means of focusing an actor in a formal setting. Color is provided principally through costumes.

The principal disadvantage of this type of staging for children's theatre is that children need more of an indication of place than pure formalism allows. Not only is place unimportant in the style, but the mood of dignified sedateness which accompanies it is out of key with the average children's play.

Nevertheless, the steps and levels associated with the plastic stage can be adapted for children's theatre. Many palace scenes in children's plays could well be staged in modifications of formal style. Fantasies done "in the Oriental manner" could often benefit from simple levels and steps coupled with decorative scenic units to relieve the austerity and gloom of black drapes.

The chief advantage of the formal style is that it allows the actor to dominate the play and greatly extends his possibilities of movement. If this aspect of formalism can be effectively combined with scenic elements which satisfy the other demands made upon the visual elements of production in children's play, the style will be successful. (See Plate 10.)

DECIDE THE SCENIC FORM

As the designer considers the various styles of production in relation to the script at hand, he may also think in terms of the *form* which the style will take on the stage. Some of the scenic forms described below are strongly associated with specific styles, while others can be adapted to several.

The scenic form finally chosen must obviously be directly related to the facilities available for staging the children's play, though, as the discussion so far has suggested, the designer should first assume a more or less ideal producing situation in order to visualize the most appropriate setting for the script at hand. It is far better to modify an ideal setting to fit a particular stage than it is to start with a vast array of limitations and expect an artistic setting to emerge. The challenge of "finding a way" may lead to an entirely new and dynamic concept of staging which will fit even the poorest facilities.

The forms discussed here are just a few of the possibilities a designer might consider. Each has proved relatively successful in production, but they are certainly not the last to be devised by ingenious men and women of the children's theatre.

THE BOX SET.   So common is the box set, with its three walls of a room and the fourth wall open, that it hardly needs explanation. Plays which call for a realistic shop, kitchen, living room, or other interior usually assume a conventional or at least a modified box. (See Plates 5, 11, and 18.)

The straight back and side walls usually associated with box settings make an arrangement which is both artistically unimaginative and impractical and should therefore be avoided. A rear wall that is raked (that is, on a diagonal to the sides) provides better visual focus and interest as well as more space. If both side and rear walls contain small jogs at strategic points near windows, or a fireplace, or a door, the setting will be better supported and swaying will be minimized. Levels introduced in doorways, alcoves, stairways, and patios provide vertical emphasis of the actors.

To be completely realistic, the box set requires a ceiling piece suspended overhead. Modifications of the box occur as soon as the ceiling is omitted. Replacing the ceiling by "ceiling borders" is seldom successful. These are pieces of cloth suspended horizontally above the stage and painted to match the walls. If a ceiling piece is impractical it is better not to pretend that it is there. Such an element of theatricalism or stylization injected into the design helps to assert frankly that the walls are not quite complete and that a ceiling isn't really necessary. The walls, instead of being straight across the top, might terminate in a sweeping line, a jagged line, or perhaps even a cutout design which capitalizes on some decorative motif of the period or locale of the play.

When more than one setting must be used in the play, the full box setting is usually difficult to handle and takes too long to shift, unless it can be handled by a revolving stage, an elevator stage, or complete wagon stages. Occasionally an ingenious designer conceives a plan whereby various small units, each on its own wagon (small platforms with casters), combine to form a box setting; then on cue the box formation is broken and recombined rapidly into the next set.

Most producing organizations would prefer, however, to work in less complete forms of scenery than the box setting when more than one locale is required.

UNIT SETS. For children's plays that require one or more changes of setting, an attractive and practical *unit* may be devised which accommodates the physical requirements of all the locations. The unit may be planned in any of several styles— basically realistic, stylized, formal, or theatrical—depending upon the quality of the script the designer wishes to emphasize.

The unit set stands throughout the play. It may remain essentially unchanged, or it may be constructed to receive slight individual modifications for each scene. For example, a series of arches may be devised to remain throughout, various "plugs" being inserted into or withdrawn from them to satisfy each scene's requirements. Such an arch unit can serve as either an exterior garden background or an interior palace, kitchen, or cathedral. Similarly, steps and levels can be incorporated into the unit and used in various ways throughout the play. A large single arch structure can readily serve several purposes: it can be completely open to an inner vista, partly closed by drapes or flat structures, or completely closed off by stairways, lattice windows, entrance ways, or balconies. There are almost unlimited possibilities open to the ingenious designer. (See Plate 12.)

One caution should be observed with the unit setting: it is conceivable that children as well as adults will, at about the third shift of the unit, sit there wondering what will be made out of the basic structure next time, a distraction that may prove somewhat detrimental to enjoyment of the play. However, the advantages of shifting small plugs instead of complete settings are certain to keep the unit set popular with children's theatre producers for some time to come. Designers should make every effort to satisfy the children's need for change in the aspect of scenes with *significant,* if not extensive, variations in the unit.

THE SIMULTANEOUS SET. An occasional play offers the possibility of setting all the needed locations at once, each area on the stage indicating a separate locale. The setting is then called *simultaneous,* and the actors simply move from one area to another. Little or no shifting is involved. Depending upon the space available for the setting, it may be executed in basically realistic, stylized, or theatrical styles. To avoid confusion for the child audience, lighting must be concentrated on the specific area being used at any moment, with no general illumination of the entire stage. (See Plates 13 and 14.)

DROP-WING-BORDER SETS. New uses have been found in recent years for the old faithful drop-wing-border setting. The form consists of a painted backdrop across the upstage plane, with two or three wing pieces at the sides of the acting area, seemingly joined overhead by cloth borders painted to match or complement the other scenic units. In old-time theatres these wings and borders were arranged so that the vista of diminishing perspective was helped by literally decreasing both the height and width of the arch formed by wings and borders; and the backdrop was cleverly painted to complete the illusion. Over the years the style of painting these forms has undergone an interesting evolution, from magnificent and detailed grandeur to "naturalism," from wildly stylized color splashes to facsimiles of Currier and Ives prints. (See Plates 3 and 15.)

Designers in the modern children's theatre have come to recognize that this form is unconvincing as realism and have therefore exploited its *theatricalism* instead. The only essential for the flexible manipulation of this kind of setting, is a fly loft into which a drop can be raised while another is lowered. If the wings must be changed during the play, they are usually arranged together in order and each one is successively drawn aside revealing the next one behind it.

Other scenic forms offer little opportunity for a realistic approach. All of those discussed below assume acceptance of conventions of the theatre on the part of the audience. As children become more and more artistically sophisticated through repeated exposures to settings like these, they may learn the conventions on which they are based, accepting them more readily then than on first contact. At best, though, these settings will probably never be as satisfying to children, or as readily accepted by them, as the various realistic forms. Nevertheless, they represent a highly artistic yet essentially practical solution to the many problems of staging the multiset play, far more satisfactory from several points of view than a lonely property making a valiant effort to "suggest" a setting on an otherwise bare stage, or a small "set piece" amid neutral drapes.

THE SCREEN SET. There are as many kinds, shapes, and sizes of *screen sets* as there are people who design them. Basically they are composed of two or three less-than-full sized flats hinged together, which makes little pretense of being complete walls. They may even be covered on both sides and reversed for two different scenic effects. They are usually decorative, and serve as a point of focus among surrounding neutral drapes. Their arrangements are infinite in number, and their chief virtues are that they can be easily shifted and they stand without bracing. (See Plate 16.)

OUTLINE SETS. Pieces of rope, strips of material, or even flats painted the same color as the neutral background except for their edges are sometimes used to form an *outline* of the scenic unit suggested by the play. The effect is one of a drawing in space, with the actual structure omitted. This is a far cry from realism. If the outline is made with something other than the edge of flats, shifting methods may have to be specially contrived. The simplest way to shift such sets is to lower the entire outline down from the flies, the various parts being suspended by piano wire. Sometimes the outline can be "erected" by characters in the play who attach the various sections to vertical supports prepared for them. The outline set has one serious disadvantage, especially if rope or material strips are used: the setting has no masking qualities. Entrances, exits, and the manipulation of special magic effects can become a problem when the view extends beyond the limits of the "setting." (See Plate 16.)

THE BOOK SETTING. A frankly theatrical and arbitrary background for the action of a few children's plays uses the principle of the life-sized storybook whose pages—wide flats painted on both sides in a decorative and nonrealistic manner— are opened by costumed scene shifters. This sort of thing works best on short plays, during which the audience is not likely to tire of the trick device, or on plays in which the setting does not participate directly in the action or the telling of the story. A rigid vertical support for the "spine" of the book will be one technical problem for the stage carpenter to solve. He also must make sure that the pages turn smoothly without scraping and sticking on the stage floor.

MINIMUM SETS. A scheme for reducing the height of wall flats to a three- or four-foot level except around window, door, or fireplace units, is known as a *minimum set*. The walls usually continue all the way around the room at low height, and the effect is one of a series of larger, more important focal units connected at the base. This kind of setting is sometimes used for an interior of a living room or kitchen, the details which are included being treated quite realistically. Such settings are usually backed by neutral drapes which thus comprise the greatest mass of the visual composition. Children will probably not accept it as realism at all.

Unfortunately, this form of setting requires a considerable amount of construction, some of it quite special and hardly reusable. Its chief advantage is the reduction of weight when it comes time to shift. A cleverly contrived minimum set can be assembled or struck in much less time than it would take to assemble a complete box from individual units.

THE FRAGMENTARY SET. When the stage proportions are quite small and lighting facilities are good, a designer sometimes plans to center visual interest on a single scenic unit—a corner of a room, an entrance way, or an arch. Such a setting is called *fragmentary*, for it presents only a fragment of a complete locale. The unit itself may be designed in realism, stylization, impressionism, expressionism, or theatricalism. Unfortunately, however, unless the fragment is well designed, the artist risks an unimpressive, unsatisfying barrenness reminiscent of the blackest days of the depression. The unit should not appear lonely on the stage. It is expected to fulfill the same functions as any other setting in children's theatre. The fragmentary set is not, therefore, the automatic answer to the multiset play. (See Plate 18.)

LIMITS TO SIMPLIFICATION

Simplifying settings is a highly artistic process and one which children's theatres find necessary to accommodate the usual large number of locales. There are, however, limits beyond which it is not wise to go. For example, simplification of settings should not surpass the audience's ability to accept the conventions involved in reductions from realism. This will depend on the age, maturity, and artistic sophistication of its members.

Simplification of settings should not be extended beyond the point where a clear indication of the place of action is established. Settings that merely "suggest" place, that rely heavily on the children to "fill in details" from their imaginations, belie the nature of childhood perception which proceeds from the general picture to the details. The details are extremely important to children. Nor should simplification proceed beyond the point where the setting lends an effective support to the actor's dialogue and movement in telling the story. If settings are reduced excessively, the burden is placed upon the actor to tell the story using his skill alone.

Simplification of settings should certainly not be carried beyond the point where a fair amount of visual interest and beauty, traditional ingredients of theatrical experience, are supplied for the enjoyment of the child audience. Through pleasurable exposure to the magic and wonder of the theatre, children should continue to find satisfaction in beauty, harmony, and imaginative staging for years to come.

Finally, simplification requires for its effectiveness a lighting system that confines attention to the elements of the setting which remain intact. Great lighted voids destroy focus and emphasize only the lack of scenery.

An understanding of the principles of simplifying scenery

and a clear knowledge of its limits should guide the children's theatre designer as he plans a production. Because excessive simplification ignores the best interests of the child audience, it has no place on the stage of the children's theatre.

We must avoid rationalizing that children can fill in from their imaginations the scenic details we leave out, and we cannot justify oversimplification by saying that the actor is the one who must be emphasized and the setting should not attract attention anyway. Herein lies one of the major differences between adults' and children's productions. Children need more help from visual elements than do adults. All simplification must be carried out from this point of view.

DESIGNING THE COSTUMES

While occasionally costumes are planned before settings, the person responsible for costume design usually plans them with a clear mental picture of the environment in which they will be seen. Though the basic production scheme is established more through the scene than through the costumes, the costumes must certainly be an extension of the same plan in order to appear consistent. A scheme of historical accuracy or of basically imaginative design in the sets will establish the keynote for the costumes as well.

Since the costumes are a part of the visual scheme of production, the basic principles stated earlier apply here. Costumes can help children sense the country and period of time in which the action takes place, if either consideration is important to an understanding of the story. They aid the delineation of character by enhancing an actor's stage appearance, by reflecting his outstanding traits, and by contributing to the effectiveness of his movement. While they should not be merely decorative, they supply an element of beauty through rhythmic line, form, and color projected as emphatic elements against a reticent background. Costumes can help both actor and director to project a character's symbolic purpose, his deeper significance in the drama, his place in the theme. A well-recognized function of costumes is to help actors, both young and old, feel more like the characters they are portraying, thus strengthening their interpretations.

HISTORICAL ACCURACY

The educational purposes of children's theatre dictate that when characters of known historical period are being portrayed their costumes will exemplify that period as closely as good stage practice will allow. As any text on costuming will state, *absolute* adherence to historical line, detail, or material is seldom desirable because of what such treatment would do both to the comfort of the actor and to his ability to move effectively. Small details of any kind, while they may be the very essence of an era in history, are likely to be completely lost on the stage. The *line* or *silhouette* of the historical costume is the element that contributes a sense of period.

A mixture of period costumes in the same play is especially bad, since children need a consistent picture in order to form an accurate concept. In adult plays this kind of costume treatment may be considered extremely clever and, indeed, may actually be a most telling "comment" upon both the characters and the play, but it has little validity in children's theatre. Such "comments" are far too adult to be interpreted accurately by children.

Many plays do not really require details of any particular era for an understanding of the story. Even so, a historical period is frequently chosen. The producer simply states that the action *could* have happened at a given time, and the choice of period then makes it possible to focus designs around known facts. Even in the most imaginative costuming, a historical detail or characteristic is often used throughout the production as the stylized motif. This approach, if not carried too far, allows the costumer a freedom that strict historical costuming would not permit.

Every effort should be made by the costumer to acquaint children with correct and accurate pictures of the past. Every artist concerned with children's theatre functions as a teacher just as surely as if he were in a classroom.

CHARACTER DELINEATION

The projection of a clear-cut character who performs a specific function in the story can be aided greatly by the proper costume. Children should recognize the essential quality of a character the moment he enters, before he says a single word. The line, weight, and color of the costume will contribute a large part to that first impression.

The "semidimensional" concept of characterization in children's theatre has led to a similar concept of easily recognized childlike qualities in costumes. Thus we have difficulty visualizing Daniel Boone in anything but his traditional outfit of fringed buckskin and coonskin cap. His long rifle is always with him. We see Abraham Lincoln in his frock coat and black cravat. Peter Pan is visualized in the traditional outfit made popular by Maude Adams in 1905 and carried out practically the same way by Walt Disney decades later. Many of the popular characters of children's literature appear in the mind's eye completely outfitted in the manner of illustrators who have carried out a traditional treatment.

Whether for better or for worse, children have deeply rooted ideas of what certain kinds of characters look like. Fairy godmothers are usually wispy and filmy beings with flowing gowns; the dashing prince wears doublet and hose; the stern governess wears a floor-length dress of dark hues and straight vertical lines; the king is decked out in an ermine robe and crown, whether he is engaged in affairs of state or personal business.

While the costumer may take a chance in deviating at all from these firmly established pictures, he should feel free to do so if he has a good reason. In his enthusiasm, however, he must be sure to supply an acceptable substitute, one which will not take long to recognize. He will make an effort to capitalize on the emotional component of lines and colors as far as they can be determined. Curved lines will continue to denote freedom and nonconformity; straight lines will suggest rigidity, unfriendliness, and tension; zigzag and irregular lines will convey capriciousness and humor.

Colors help characterization, too, probably reflecting the natural associations children have established with them, such as the warmth or heat of yellow sunlight, the earthiness of brown, the gaiety of red and orange flowers. Cool colors, the blues and greens, are also associated in the child's consciousness with the gloom of approaching night or the vividness of grass and leaves. Obviously, advanced color symbolism is pointless for the child audience, though it may help adult actors or even the director in formulating his production scheme.

Since a large part of an actor's effectiveness in conveying a character rests upon his movement, his costume should facilitate his movements. How a costume drapes and flows will depend upon the weight of the materials from which it is made. Where a costume that clings closely to the body suggests a quality of restraint, one that seems to drift on currents of air conveys the idea of etherealness. Cloaks can be used effectively to emphasize the romantic nature of both characters and script.

Costumes can also help in establishing characters' relationships to one another. Children should have no trouble seeing a connection between a prince and his prospective bride, between members of a family, between principals and minor characters, or between two or three characters who operate as one. Relationship may be suggested by repeating a color in the costumes, or various tints or shades of one color may be used. Frequently a decorative pattern or motif can be used to show a connection between characters, provided the pattern is large enough to be seen easily. A repetition of the line and form of a costume in contrasting colors will sometimes work.

Once the connection is established in the audience's mind it is unwise to disturb it by introducing more changes in costume than absolutely necessary. If a long period of time is supposed to elapse between scenes, characters need not change their basic costumes, but new detail may be added such as a cloak, a hat, or an overskirt revealing the established costume underneath. In the third act children should not have to ask a neighbor, "Who's that?"

Compositional Focus

Costumes can be a great help to the director in focusing attention on the part of the stage picture to be emphasized at any given moment of the play. The eye of child or adult centers on a moving object, one more vivid in color than its surroundings, one lighter in value than the rest of the stage picture. All these qualities can be exploited by the costumer who plans his color scheme around the director's plan for movement patterns and stage pictures.

Materials and Workmanship

The age of crepe paper and cambric costumes for children's theatre is happily behind us, as costumers have discovered the lasting value of good material, well put together. Economy-minded costumers no longer skimp on the quality of the cloth they work with, since they realize it takes no more work to make good costumes than shoddy ones. Any outfit made of substantial materials can be reworked, added to, or altered in size for future productions, whereas one of flimsy stuff will probably have a short life. A good stock of flexibly built items —sleeves, bodices, collars, capes, skirts—will save many hours of work by providing a ready basis for imaginative modification. Wide seams, hook and eye attachments, and variety in textures and colors of materials allow for year to year use of the same basic items without monotony or extensive new construction.

Costumes of many periods should be readily available for an active children's theatre group. Play selection should not have to be based on what costumes can be contrived or assembled from attics.

CHOOSING THE COLOR SCHEME

The compositional element of color deserves special attention in all aspects of children's theatre design, for it is a more noticeable design element than line or mass as far as children are concerned.

Color is used in children's theatre design to achieve three kinds of responses: to seize and focus attention, to satisfy the need for beauty, and to convey the proper mood and emotions.

As we have seen in the case of costumes, the eye will travel to the brightest color, the lightest color, or the shiniest surface within the total stage picture. We must therefore be careful not to use too many bright colors in a single composition, or attention will wander. As a rule the brightest or lightest colors are reserved for costumes; the next most emphatic elements —and hence the next brightest, lightest, or shiniest—are the key properties and important scenic units; and peripheral scenic units are generally the darkest, or the least bright, within the stage picture.

Designers must take into account in their planning the fact that the painted colors of sets and properties, as well as the dyes in fabrics, are modified by the color of the light that hits them. Any pigment color can be enhanced, changed, or neutralized (grayed) by the use of light. Through subtly changing the lighting over portions of the stage picture the designer can change emphasis as the action progresses. The chart on page 191, while it is subject to several variables, gives some indication of how colored light affects pigment.

In the children's theatre attention is at least partly determined by the extent to which children's sense of beauty is satisfied. Obviously we cannot drown the stage in unearthly splendor independent of the play; yet we must also realize that the characters are living a heightened existence, beyond the bounds of mere living. We can, without undue caution, try to satisfy the child's desire for the new, the unusual, the beautiful, remembering, however, that a child's sense of what is beautiful is not necessarily what adults consider beautiful.

Several studies of children's color preferences suggest there is a pattern of change which accompanies increasing age. For example, red and orange are the favorites at early ages, and blue increases in popularity as children grow older. These color "favorites" are in isolation, however, and not as meaningful to the designer as favorite combinations. Third through eighth graders prefer yellow as one of a two-color combination, that is, with red-violet or blue. Generally speaking, they prefer the warm combinations to the cool ones; and they prefer complementary and constrasting colors (those opposite or several colors away from each other on a color wheel) to analagous (adjacent) colors.[1] Not until well into adolescence do their preferences conform to existing principles of color harmony

[1] Based on Ann VanNice Gale, *Children's Preferences for Colors, Color Combinations, and Color Arrangements*, University of Chicago Press, 1933.

CHART SHOWING THE EFFECTS OF COLORED GELATIN IN LIGHT ON COLORED PIGMENT

Gelatin Colors (Roscoe Series)

Pigment	#71 Bastard Amber	#11 Golden Amber	#110 Fire Red	#114 DuBarry Pink	#22 Medium Magenta	#25 Violet	#120 Special Lavender	#28M Medium Purple	#29 Daylite Blue	#32 Moonlite Blue	#40 Medium Green
Yellow	yellow	orange	red	peach	red	lavender	lavender	purple	blue-green	blue-green	green
Orange	orange	orange	red	orange	orange	red	rose	fuchia	red	black	brown
Red	red	red	red	red	red	red	purple	fuchia	rose	black	brown
Purple	rose purple	red	purple	rose	purple	purple	purple	purple	violet	blue	gray
Violet	lavender	gray	dark gray	purple	purple	blue	violet	violet	blue	blue	green
Blue	lavender	gray	gray	lavender	purple	blue	blue	blue	blue	blue-green	green
Green	gray-green	brown	dark gray	gray	black	blue-green	blue-green	gray	blue-green	blue-green	green
Gray	pink-gray	dull orange	red	pink	purple	blue-gray	lavender	violet	blue	blue-green	green
Brown	brown	gray	dark gray	purple	purple	blue	violet	violet	blue	blue	green

—a fact which designers should remember when planning color schemes.

All this does not mean that designers should throw their own knowledge and experience to the winds. We have an educational function to perform, and just because children attend to violent color combinations does not mean that the stages of the children's theatre should be uncontrolled riots of color. What does seem indicated is this: the range of colors which children consider beautiful is very broad. While preferences in color combinations may not conform to accepted theories of color harmony, children's sensitivity to this mature concept develops as they develop in other ways. A relatively free use of bright color is justified in staging plays for the very young. For the intermediate ages a realistic relationship between colors and objects should exist in productions. Only the older children will appreciate subtle color effects. In general, warm, contrasting combinations will be more satisfying than monochromatic schemes.

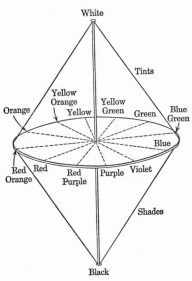

Fig. 4. Two color cones with a color wheel in the center, showing complementaries connected by dotted lines and analagous colors next to each other on the perimeter. Mixing complementaries gives gray.

The use of color to arouse mood and emotion should be based on children's probable experience in color association. As in the case of costumes, highly saturated warm colors are gay and happy, while grayed and dark colors seem more gloomy. We must not expect children to be acquainted with any conventional use of colors on the stage, although we can certainly guide them toward an appreciation of the standard associations common in the adult theatre. Since mood in children's plays is a rhythmic matter, built upon the idea of contrasts and attention spans, changing light colors on pigments can do a great deal to guide children into tensions and releases which augment the established rhythmic pattern. Successive scenes in a multiset play should be of contrasting color schemes, even though the style of the total production remains consistent.

RECORDING THE PLANS

Complete plans for a children's theatre production include the same items required for any theatrical venture: floor plans, color plates or sketches of sets and costumes, working drawings such as elevations and detail drawings, and light plot.

The Floor Plans

The director is primarily responsible for establishing the use that will be made of the stage space; but it is the designer's responsibility to work out the floor plans accurately and to distribute them to the others who will need them in their particular phases of the operation. Many people rely on the floor plans for their proper functioning—the lighting designer, the assistant director who sets the rehearsal area, the stage manager who arranges the stage, the scene builder and stage crew heads, the property master who must know where each item is to be located, and the director who must know exact dimensions to work out his blocking.

Floor plans are the first things established in the production schedule. They usually are worked out in a scale of one-half

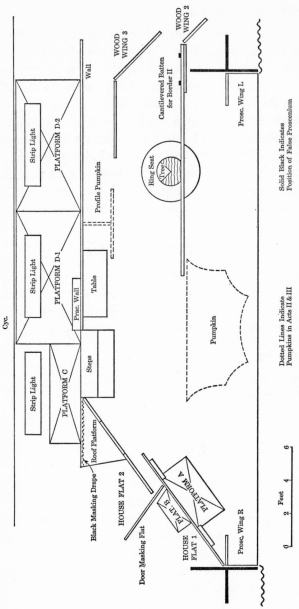

Fig. 5. *A floor plan, designed by Merlin E. Bement for King's* Peter, Peter, Pumpkin Eater. *Note that the location of each element is indicated.*

inch to one foot, preferably in blueprint form or duplicated by the newer "ozalid" process which is easier to read. Any changes made during rehearsals should be recorded on all copies so that no one concerned with them is left uninformed. The floor plan is one item which is not discarded until the final curtain of the last performance is down.

In formulating the floor plans, the designer confers constantly not only with the director but also with the lighting designer, if he is a separate person. The plan may be seriously affected by the need for providing mounting positions for lighting instruments. Sky pieces may have to be moved upstage to allow room for striplights at the base. Ceilings may have to be raised and moved upstage from the lighting pipes to allow for adequate coverage of the area underneath. Side walls may have to be shortened in height or narrowed in width to provide for tormentor tower lighting. Other walls may need extra bracing to support equipment to be mounted on them.

The location of all scenic and property units is indicated on the floor plans, as well as the position of magical contrivances both on and off stage. The storage position of each unit after a shift is also clearly shown.

THE COLOR PLATES

Color plates of each scene in the play are a great help to the director. With this complete visualization of the scene before him, he is able to arrange his stage pictures with relation to the scenic units involved and to foresee movement possibilities which might not otherwise be apparent until the actual setting is completed. Furthermore, he has a chance to verify the existence of an artistic composition, one which exemplifies the standard principles of unity, variety, emphasis, balance, and harmony. He can tell whether the plan exemplifies the desirable qualities and features of a setting for children's theatre as outlined throughout this chapter. Preferably the director has the color plates before tryouts, since they can help immeasurably in explaining the concept of the production to aspiring actors.

The color scheme of the setting must be determined before the costumer can proceed with his plans. If costumes are to contrast or blend with the background as the situation requires, the exact nature of that background—the colored pigment *as it will appear under colored light*—must be known by the costumer as soon as possible. The property master will also find these sketches useful in choosing upholstery and drapery fabrics, in building and painting the various pieces of furniture and set dressings. The color plates cannot be left till the last minute on the assumption that they will be used only for lobby displays.

Costume Sketches

Costume plates or sketches of each character in the play should be submitted to the director for approval early in the production schedule. Each change of costume should be recorded separately, but modifications of a basic costume may be indicated on a single plate. Preferably, the costumer attaches a swatch of material directly to the plate so that the element of texture may be understood more clearly. If several characters are costumed in the same manner it is not necessary to have a separate plate for each—all that is needed is a notation of the colors or a swatch of material to indicate whatever variations are planned for them. Special instructions for cutting, draping, or sewing the costume are usually noted lightly in pencil, with arrows to the exact area involved. (See Plate 17.)

Working Drawings

Front, rear and side elevations, and scale drawings of scenic and property units to be constructed are necessary if the scene builder is to avoid costly mistakes. As large a scale as the paper will permit, at least one-half inch to one foot, is advisable, even larger if possible. Elevations may be of a single flat or an assembled wall unit consisting of several flats. All details of construction are indicated, including size of lumber, kind of covering material, method of joining, placement of hardware, and every dimension needed by the carpenter. If the scene builder is experienced in the methods of standard theatrical construction, only unusual details need be noted, as he will assume standard methods elsewhere. Only the necessary elevations will be drawn. Complete front, rear, and side elevations would be needed only for very unusual units such as rocks, furniture, tree trunks, and the like.

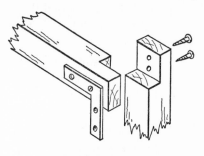

**CORNER DETAIL
EXPLODED VIEW**

Fig. 6. A detail drawing of a special joint, showing method of cutting and assembling.

Detail drawings of all kinds are sometimes needed to show precisely how a particular joint, a stencil pattern, or a special attachment is to be made. These are frequently drawn to actual size and are really a "close-up" view of a marked segment of an elevation or plan.

THE LIGHT PLOT

A light plot is the complete plan for the setting up and operation of lights. It consists of a master layout, a connection schedule, an instrument schedule, a control board layout, and a cue sheet or marked script. How extensively each part of the light plot is drawn up in advance depends on how much time there is for setting up and rehearsing this highly technical phase of production. Most children's theatre directors operate without access to their stages far in advance of performance, and there is therefore not sufficient time to let the lighting scheme evolve in rehearsals. Careful advance preparation for the mounting, connecting, and manipulation of the lights is necessary if they are to contribute their full share to the total production.

The detailed philosophy, techniques, instrumentation, and control of light are beyond the scope of this book. However, we urge students of children's theatre to become well acquainted with the possibilities offered by this living medium of dramatic expression. A number of excellent books on the subject are included in the Bibliography, and a sample light plot will be found in the Appendix.

If the children's theatre designer is to take his place as a full-fledged member of the producing team, he needs training in all the aspects of technical theatre. He must be a thorough craftsman and a dedicated artist. He must see the production as the children will see it, aware that his vision must match the soaring flights of children's imagination. His is an important role in bringing about a full and exciting theatre experience for his audience.

8

The Production Is Mounted

THE EFFECTIVE STAGING of a children's play calls for much careful thought, a great amount of study and preparation, the concerted efforts of many people, and the highest degree of artistry on everyone's part. There is no room here for the choreographer who wants to display the talents of her class in ballet dancing, but a warm welcome for the one who understands the contribution of both the dance and graceful movement to the drama. There is no place for the scene designer or costumer who insists on displaying his particular specialty at the expense of the story.

It is the function of the director to indicate the approach for all the artists working under him. He must insist that all phases of the production contribute to the unified concept he has developed. Should he fail in this important administrative duty, he can blame only himself for the ensuing artistic fiasco, in which he may find himself with a production in which the acting is romantic, the sets realistic, and the costumes stylized. The ability to encourage the creative efforts and contributions of all the production workers without compromising the unity of con-

cept is one of the most important talents a children's theatre
director should try to develop.

IDEAL AND ACTUAL PRODUCING CONDITIONS

Some theatres in the United States today are admirably
equipped to handle the elaborate technical requirements of
children's plays. The auditorium is planned to permit intimate
contact between actors and audience, the stage is well propor-
tioned, the seating space accommodates no more than six hundred children, and acoustics are perfect throughout this area.
Sight lines are excellent, affording an uninterrupted view of the
acting area from every seat in the house. Lighting is controlled
from a soundproofed enclosure which commands a clear view
of the stage. Amplified sound, centrally controlled from a
similar booth out in the house, can be fed to any one or any
combination of speakers spaced throughout the auditorium and
the acting area. An intercommunication system connects the
light and sound booths with the stage manager's position backstage.

Ideally the stage has a proscenium opening no more than
32 feet wide, with a proscenium height of 15 feet, though both
dimensions can be reduced without damaging the sight lines
from the house. Behind the proscenium frame the stage stretches
to a width of 75 feet or more, with equal off-stage space on
both sides of the proscenium arch. From curtain line to rear
wall the depth is 50 feet, and the stage space is clear of obstructions of any sort.

On this ideal stage provision is made for the use of all
standard scene shifting devices. A revolving turntable is recessed in the stage floor. Wagon stages can roll in and out of
view. Sixty feet above the stage floor is the gridiron with sets
of counterweighted lines placed every two feet from the
proscenium to the rear wall.

Ample electrical outlets which terminate flexibly at the control board are placed around the stage and the ceiling of the auditorium to accommodate lighting instruments mounted in almost any conceivable position. Several traps in the floor of the stage can take care of various "magic" effects and disappearances.

Adjoining the stage, behind a large soundproof door, are the quarters of the designer and his staff of technicians. A well-equipped shop for construction and painting of scenery and properties, a costume shop with plenty of work tables and sewing machines, make-up and dressing rooms well supplied with mirrors, as well as plenty of storage space make the work of these technicians efficient and economical.

This, as we said in the beginning, is the ideal theatre for children's plays. Unfortunately, most children's theatre work is done under conditions not quite so ideal. The "staff" of technicians frequently consists of one or two enthusiastic but untrained volunteers, and the director must do much active supervision of every technical phase of production, since he may be the only one with experience. The "scene shop" may be someone's unused garage, the basement of a home, or the stage itself. The "costume shop" may be someone's living room or a momentarily vacant classroom. Make-up and dressing facilities may be temporarily rigged in a school storage closet, the band room, or even a screened-off portion of a hallway.

More often than not the house seats between one and two thousand children, this large seating capacity made possible by the addition of a balcony beneath which the acoustics are almost completely dead. Incorrectly calculated proscenium splays and decorative froufrou further reduce the number of seats from which small ears may hear the dialogue comfortably. Sight lines are often poor, especially when an attempt is made to reduce the proportions of a huge proscenium opening.

There is no "beam" light mounting position above the seating space; an inflexible control board is often located backstage behind every possible obstruction to a clear view of the acting area; and an elaborate installation of footlights and borderlights is permanently connected to a few red, white, and blue dimmer circuits. One or two floor pockets are supposed to take care of "any special effects" needed. If a sound system exists, the speakers are mounted behind microphone positions so that there is constant feedback and squealing.

The stage itself is frequently unavailable until one or two days before the performance. The highly polished surface of its hardwood floor must not be marred by inserting stage screws to hold up scenery. It has no traps. There are probably two or three feet of off-stage space to one side and maybe none at all on the other. A ventilator duct traverses the rear wall. Two feet above the top of the proscenium arch there is a cement ceiling into which have been chained a minimum of cloth borders to conceal the overhead borderlights. There are no spare fly lines, no extra mounting positions for lights. One ordinary door opens into the main hallway, down which the school children trample loudly as they change classes; and the band, practicing diligently directly behind the stage, provides a forceful accompaniment to both the tramping school children and the play in progress.

Admittedly, the above description is a composite of most of the theatre construction faults one is likely to encounter. Only rarely will a producer be cursed with all of them. Even so, it has taken ingenious designers and indefatigable technicians endless hours of dreaming, planning, and experimenting to circumvent these obstructions to artistic production. Ever since the beginnings of the children's theatre movement these workers have improvised, modified, cajoled, and broken fire laws to mount their multiset plays on hopelessly inadequate stages. The amazing thing is that the standard of production can be held so high in spite of what seems almost like a conspiracy on the part of the theatre planners!

These are the conditions we can expect as we move the production from the drawing boards to the construction shops and finally to the stage. With luck, we will have planned adequately for them and will have produced an artistically valid plan in the bargain!

THE PRODUCTION ORGANIZATION

A closely knit production organization with a clearly established chain of command is one of the surest ways to achieve success. Ideally, each person in the pattern understands his job thoroughly, but actually producers are fortunate indeed if their supervisors are acquainted with standard theatre practices and are able to instruct those under them in the ways of backstage operation.

The production staff may be organized in this manner:

Whatever variations occur in the organizational structure from group to group, the *director* has at least three distinct functions in this plan: he trains the cast, he oversees all the production designs, and he supervises the execution of all plans. In each of these functions he certainly should have the help of at least one other person.

The *assistant director* functions chiefly during the rehearsal period. He can relieve the director of many administrative details, such as contacting cast members for a multitude of rehearsal instructions and handling publicity matters and special sessions of all kinds. Before each session he sets up the rehearsal area according to the floor plan. He records all blocking and business in the prompt book and keeps a constant check on the cast as they familiarize themselves with movement and lines. He can help conduct drill sessions called for only one or

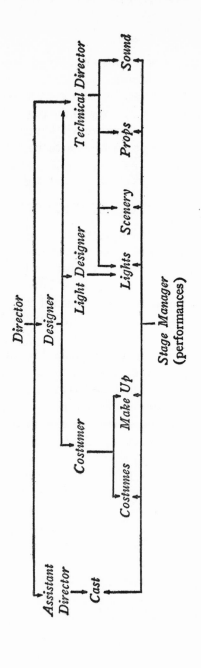

two cast members. Occasionally he may be in complete charge of a rehearsal when the director is absent, and it is in these experiences that he will find his greatest satisfaction.

When technical and dress rehearsals begin, the assistant director's job is almost over. He usually sits in the house with the director, taking notes on anything which must be attended to before the next run-through. During performances, instead of acting as book holder or prompter, he will usually be found out in the house with the director, checking constantly on the quality of the performance; later he can convey to cast members the director's notes for improvement. An assistant director who can do all these things and yet keep the respect and friendship of the cast is an invaluable aid to the director and an indispensable part of the producing organization.

A *designer* is sometimes versatile enough to handle as many as four of the positions indicated on the production diagram: He may not only design the settings but also build them— normally the *technical director's* job. He may also design the costumes, thus eliminating the need for a *costumer,* though a good seamstress may still be needed. He may also act as *lighting designer.* Just which of these responsibilities are assumed by a given individual will depend upon his talents, and the organizational pattern must then be adjusted to be sure that each aspect of the production process is provided for.

In general, the designer's job is to plan and supervise the mounting of the production in all its visual aspects except the training of the actors. In a fully staffed organization he will have three people under him, each of whom is responsible for one phase of the planning or execution of designs, though the designer himself keeps in constant touch with all phases of preparation.

The *technical director* actively supervises the scene construction and painting crews, the property crew which collects and builds all the stage paraphernalia classified under "set" or "hand" properties, and the sound crew. He may also take an active hand in carrying out the *lighting designer's* plans for the mounting and control of lights when the production "goes on stage."

The *costumer,* too, works under the general plan of the designer, preparing costume sketches, assembling the needed materials, constructing and fitting the costumes with the help of a crew, and advising on accessories, to the extent of working with the actors on the entire costume's proper display and use. Usually the costumer also has at least nominal charge of the make-up of the actors, since this is a reasonable extension of the costume. A make-up crew may be selected from the costume crew or be completely separate in its organization.

When a production goes on stage for the final phase of rehearsals the *stage manager* comes into action. Up to this point he has been quietly observing rehearsals to familiarize himself with the play and its manner of presentation. While he watches the design evolve he should be conferring with the technical director on matters affecting the manipulation of scenic devices, lighting operations, sound cues, and property changes, and with the director on the coordination of sound, lights, and curtain openings and closings. When the final rehearsals begin, everything should be entirely familiar to him, since his stage manager's script should by then have every cue marked.

Frequently before the first technical rehearsal the director makes a little ceremony of handing over the production reins to the stage manager, and from that moment the stage manager should be in complete command of the backstage area, both actors and crew heads taking their orders from him. A wise director is meticulous about not going over the head of this key person and giving orders directly to crew members. If the stage manager is to maintain his organization backstage his position must be respected, especially by the director whose representative he has now become. If the director is conscientious about making the organization self-sustaining when he takes his spot in the house during performances, he must do all he can to foster respect for the stage manager.

During the last rehearsals, the stage manager should work out each scene and property shift methodically, using all crews as they are needed, and noting any problems of construction, painting, assembly, repair, or changes which need to be pointed out to the designer or technical director. It is his responsibility to work out in detail his own cuing system for lights, sound, curtain, shifters, and special effects personnel, by means of an "intercom system," hand signals, blinker lights, or other consecutive cues.

Under certain conditions a stage manager can delegate some of his cuing responsibilities. For example, if the light control is so located that it has a clear view of the stage, most internal cues for changes of light—that is, those not at the beginning or end of a scene—may be taken directly from the action itself by the crew member in charge. This may also be true of internal sound cues, if the operator has a clear view of the acting area. Or lights may need to be changed at a certain place in the music. The curtain may close when the music reaches a certain point, or when the lights are completely out. Such cues may be taken directly by the crew member concerned without waiting for a signal from the stage manager, provided there is no danger that he will get confused and receive some cues in one way and some in another. It is also the stage manager's job to see that all entrances are made on time, that all cues are taken, and that the production runs smoothly.

Responsibilities for running the production may be still further delegated if the stage manager has one or more assistants. Each of these should have clearly defined duties, such as calling the cast from the green room in time for entrances, or cuing certain light or sound changes from vantage points not accessible to the stage manager. If the production is extremely elaborate two or three assistants may be needed.

The technical director usually supervises the work of most crews, though certain exceptions are common. The director himself often prefers to work personally with the head of the sound crew, since sound effects and music must correlate closely with the action and therefore need to be introduced early in the production schedule. At the same time, the technical director is quite likely to have charge of setting up the actual sound equipment to be used in performance. Costume and make-up crews are usually supervised by the costumer, sometimes by the designer— rarely by the technical director.

Each crew in the organizational structure is managed by a *crew head,* sometimes called a "committee chairman." Preferably this is someone who has worked previously on a similar aspect of production. All crew heads function directly under a staff member during the preparation time and under the stage manager during technical and dress rehearsals and performances. Crew heads are frequently included in the designing and planning phase and hence are well acquainted with the job to be done. They supervise crew sessions, delegate responsibilties, and in general organize and schedule work so that it will be completed on time. Their role is one of active leadership and frequently of teaching the techniques of standard stage procedure. They are directly responsible for setting the standard of work for the crew.

CHILD CREWS

One of the most valuable experiences a child of fifth grade age or older can have comes from useful participation with others in a children's theatre crew. Organizations structured to include this aspect of theatre training for the children usually try to emphasize the importance of the backstage operation to the success of the performance, being careful not to assign crew work as a salve to disappointed uncast actors. A regular scheme of alternation in acting parts and crew responsibilities is a good way to establish crew work as a rewarding and valuable part of theatre activity.

Children are usually more successful in certain phases of production than in others, but they need to be carefully supervised in all their crew work. Wardrobe management is a job they can handle well, but few girls or boys younger than junior high school or high school age are able to construct costumes with much skill. Ten- or eleven-year-olds will work diligently applying base or powder in a make-up job, but usually the more detailed make-up work has to be done by older children. If the units are not too big or heavy, scenery or property shifting can be handled successfully by sixth grade or junior high boys. At this age they are not likely to have much skill with hammer and screw driver for set construction, but they may be able to manipulate dimmers and take light cues from the stage manager. Children under thirteen or fourteen should never be asked to mount lighting equipment or string electrical cable. The assignment of crew responsibilities must necessarily take into account the physical limitations of children of different ages.

When using child or youth crews, a director or technical director should try to make sure that the most mature and most respected member of the group is selected as stage manager. He should also try to be sure that each crew includes some children with experience and some without. If possible, an adult should be on hand at each crew session to help with advice and active guidance, to make sure the job is well and safely done, and to keep the crew work a learning experience for the youngsters.

It is assumed, of course, that the actual planning of the production is done by adults, though in some cases precocious children have been able to contribute meaningful and workable designs with only a minimum of help.

Persons who set up children's theatre production organizations, whether these are self-perpetuating or exist for a single play only, should be careful not to overstaff the crews. If the size of each job is determined before assignments are made, each crew can be planned to have enough but not too many hands to accomplish the work. Judicious use of valuable time should be the goal in organizing crews, just as it is in planning rehearsals. This principle holds true for either adults or children.

THE PRODUCTION SCHEDULE

Just as a good cook times the various courses of a meal to be ready when they are needed, so does the director of a children's play begin each phase in sufficient time so that the entire production arrives intact on the stage with only the final coordination and polishing to be done. There is no place in children's theatre production for a frantic last-minute search for a neglected property, the nerve-wracking process of completing the set minutes before the opening curtain, or the disappointing failure of the magic effect which never got rehearsed. While changes in plans are bound to occur despite all we can do, a logical schedule of production, based upon a clear knowledge of what is involved in each phase, will go a long way toward assuring that the performance will turn out to be as it was originally conceived.

The size and kind of production, the number and extent of technical elements involved, and the exact producing situation will determine the order of starting the various phases and planning their completion dates. All staff, cast, and crew members should focus their sights on the first dress rehearsal as the last possible moment to introduce any new production element. Child casts and crews need time to learn their jobs when all the actual material is finally at hand.

The following schedule suggests a logical and practical order for planning the steps in a production. Here nine weeks are allowed from selection of play to performance. There may of course be many variations in this schedule for any given play, but at least it will suggest, especially to the inexperienced director, how much time is usually allowed to accomplish each production phase. Note that the schedule does not include any of the director's responsibilities in business and house management. These are discussed in Chapter 9.

TECHNICAL PROBLEMS

Comprehensive coverage of stage techniques is beyond the scope of this book. Books treating the various elements of theatrical production in detail are listed in the Bibliography. However, a number of problems involving these elements usually arise during both planning and mounting phases of staging the children's play, and the remainder of this chapter is therefore devoted to a brief discussion of such special problems which involve scenery, costumes and make-up, lighting, properties, sound, and special effects. These are problems which affect the designer in his planning, the technical director and costumer in construction, and the crews in their operation.

The "production notes" frequently included in the text of a children's play sometimes suggest ways of solving specific staging problems. As we have said before, these notes may be useful to some extent, but there is really no substitute for each director's tackling the problems in his own way and arriving at solutions which fit his particular situation. If the playbook has

TYPICAL PRODUCTION SCHEDULE FOR A CHILDREN'S PLAY

WEEK PRIOR TO PERFORMANCE	DIRECTOR	DESIGNER/TECHNICAL DIRECTOR	CREW
9	Choose play; send to publisher for scripts or permission to duplicate text.	Order stock of standard materials.	
8	Study script; begin to develop general concept of production. Give scripts to key staff members.	Study script.	
7	Confer with designer on general plan; work out floor plans, and give them to designer.	Begin to design sets and costumes. Order special materials.	
6	Prepare materials for distribution at tryouts. Conduct tryout. Choose cast. Confer with designer on staging. Preblock play.	Finish color plates, and get to director for tryout. Assign crews. Finish working drawings.	
5	Rehearse regularly. Choose sound; make preparations to record sound cues in sequence on tape.	Begin scenery and costume building. Plan lighting in time to order special material.	Scenery, costumes, on regular schedule.

4	Record sound. Introduce it at rehearsals. Substitute hand props at rehearsals. Rehearse with costume items that affect movement. Arrange publicity pictures.	Properties should be designed. Plan make-up. Enough costumes should be finished for publicity pictures. Adequate set should be ready for publicity pictures.	Sound, at rehearsals. Props, begin locating and assembling set and hand props.
3	Stage manager begins to attend some rehearsals. Schedule make-up practice.	Light plot should be completed and crew briefed.	Props, at rehearsals. Stage manager at rehearsals. Make-up session.
2	All crew heads attend some rehearsals; confer with each. All crew members attend one rehearsal.		Crew heads and members at rehearsals. Sets, props, costumes completed; lights, sound equipment assembled.
1	Production on stage now run by stage manager. Check on outcome of production concept. Rehearse all cues. Complete uninterrupted run-throughs.	Mount production on stage. Check outcome of design; make necessary corrections. Check on costumes and make-up. Post make-up calls.	Assembly of all elements on stage. Small details corrected. Assure proper operation of all elements, rehearse each adequately. Costumes and make-up organized.

no production notes the director is obliged to fall back on his own ingenuity and experience. Some of the general problems considered in the following pages may suggest methods of solving still others the producer may encounter.

SCENERY

SHIFTING DEVICES

A number of the scenic forms described in Chapter 7 suggest their own methods of shifting—the drops in the drop-wing-border setting are flown in and out on sets of lines; the book setting unfolds its pages one by one; the unit set receives plugs which fill in the arches or modify the basic aspect of the set. The simultaneous set eliminates the need for shifting. Before the designer can complete his plans, he must decide the exact system to be used in getting the sets into and out of position.

Running is the most primitive method of shifting flat scenery, but it is very commonly used since it requires nothing but manpower. One person, grasping the edge of a flat as high and as low as he can comfortably reach, can quickly "run" a flat into or out of position. Lash lines attached to flats provide a simple method of joining them, but unfortunately this makes no provision for covering the cracks between flats. Unless such lashed flats can form a corner, it is better to compose the setting of two-fold or three-fold flat sections which have joints covered with strips of muslin called dutchmen. These can also be "run," but with somewhat more difficulty than single flats. Generally speaking, shifting a setting by the running method is quite cumbersome and can be recommended for the swift scene changes required in children's theatre only when the flats are small and few in number.

Wagons of almost any size, ranging from one as small as

two feet square to one the size of the acting area, offer the technical director a solution to many shifting problems. Wagons are low platforms on large rubber casters concealed by a facing which just clears the floor. They can be used to carry anything from a single cumbersome property to an entire set. Rocks, ovens, or a pumpkin house can be rolled easily and swiftly into place on specially shaped wagons. "Vista shifts"—those taking place within view of the audience—can proceed with a minimum of distraction as the silent wagons are pulled into position by concealed stagehands.

Casters can be added at the base of almost any scenic unit to facilitate shifting. For example, such a method can be used to remove the outside wall of a house or garden to reveal the inside while action continues.

Revolving stages or *turntables* can likewise be built in any size. While we tend to think that this method of shifting is possible only with elaborate built-in motor-driven turntables, it can be managed quite easily by making use of one or two smaller manually operated tables. There is no doubt that it is an advantage to have the tracks for such revolving stages recessed in the stage floor; but where the floor has not been constructed this way the designer can provide small ground rises which remain fixed throughout the production to mask the edge or thickness of the turntable. The designer must likewise provide for the off-stage masking of small sets or parts of sets which are revolved by the table.

Revolving stages of modest dimensions (probably not more than eight feet in diameter) can be constructed of $2'' \times 4''$ lumber. Eight segments, each in the shape of a piece of pie, are bolted together and attached to a free-turning metal pivot mounted on the floor. Heavy rubber casters are arranged around the outer edge of the table so that the whole "pie" will revolve noiselessly. Either two or three settings are arranged on the table, and a pull on the control rope brings a new set into place.

Sliding small units on "gliders" is a common practice when the weight is not sufficient to mar the floor of the stage. Occasionally flats can be slid along grooves formed by two thin boards laid parallel to each other with a space equal to the thickness of the flat between them. A similarly grooved structure supports the tops of the flats. The grooves are usually "lubricated" with graphite. Such a system is sometimes used to pull aside a backing, perhaps one that splits in the middle, to reveal an inner area while action continues.

Some productions may need to use several systems of shifting in order to make changes as swiftly as possible. One or another method may be impractical because of lack of space, but the designer can usually find a method that will work in the conditions he must contend with. A stock of standard-size wagons or a collapsible revolving stage is usually a sound investment for a children's theatre.

TRANSPARENCIES

Some of the most interesting effects used in staging children's plays are achieved with the use of transparencies. Magic vistas, magic mirrors, dream sequences, and visions fall into this category. To be truly effective, such devices require the most careful coordination between the planning and operation of scenery, lighting, properties, and sound.

The *scrim* is the basic ingredient for all transparencies. Whether the effect is to cover the entire stage, a section of a wall, a framed arch, a window, an oversized mirror frame, or a cupboard door through which we see a hazy vision, some wide-mesh material, hung taut or in draped folds, is necessary. Its form will depend on its use—whether it must open to admit characters or objects. (See Plate 18.)

The audience can see through scrim materials when light strikes the objects *behind* it. The lights in front are then usually dimmed for the best effect. However, the area behind the scrim is not completely opaque as long as the area *in front* of it is lighted at all—spectators can usually detect moving figures or those dressed in light clothes behind the scrim. If absolute blackout behind the scrim is necessary until a critical moment, a black velour drape hung immediately behind the scrim will prevent any light leaks from illuminating the subject too soon. Or the direct beam of a spotlight can be focused at an angle on either side of the scrim to increase the effect of haziness. Sometimes the shaft of light thus created gives exactly the effect desired, though usually it only serves to increase the opacity of the scrim. In general, the light crew should be cautioned to keep the beams both in front of and behind a scrim but not *on* it. Each area must be controlled separately.

If any design, decoration, or motif must appear on the scrim —such as bricks, trees, foliage, architectural details, or castles— it can be brushed or sprayed on with analine dye. Paint of any kind stiffens the material and is likely to clog the mesh, making it opaque. Designs brushed on it will be visible only when the front of the scrim is lighted, disappearing when the light is taken away in front and brought up behind. Light projections, either still scenes or moving effects, are often used in preference to a dyed design, since they may be manipulated at the control board dimmer.

Sharkstooth scrim is best for the scrim curtain, especially if a wide section is needed. It is readily available from theatrical fabric houses. Sometimes organdy or other material available locally can be used satisfactorily if seams make little difference. White, dyed a suitable color for each use, is probably the wisest choice, though a light blue or even a black scrim has many uses. Cheesecloth has too little body to make a satisfactory scrim. It hangs unevenly, snarls easily, and lasts only a few performances at best.

All wide-meshed materials are rather fragile and easily

snagged. Shifters should therefore exercise special care in moving units which contain scrim sections. If the production tours, all scrim sections should be stacked together and suitably protected with heavy canvas. Nothing can destroy an illusion faster than a "magic vista" with a hole or rip in it!

SLIDING PANELS

Many children's theatre scripts call for secret entrances and sliding panels. Their size and shape is often irregular, conforming to the architectural forms which comprise the rest of the setting. Such panels should appear exactly like the surrounding walls. They should not be recessed unless other paneling is also recessed. Since cracks surrounding the panel are almost inevitable, and cracks in a broad plain surface are almost certain to be detected, a scenic design which incorporates strong and definite architectural features throughout will help disguise the opening. Designers should also keep in mind the bulk of the costume as well as the size of the actor who must go through the secret entrance, or the size or quantity of any props that must go through the panel.

A panel door may either be hinged so that it swings off stage or rigged to slide in grooved tracks—up, down, or to one side. Usually either kind is manually operated by stagehands, but if necessary a piece of strong fishline can be attached to open or close the door from a remote position. Careful construction and ample practice in operation should assure complete closure and silent functioning of sliding doors.

COSTUMES

Quite apart from the usual problems of design and construction of period and modern stage costumes—formidible enough in themselves—a children's theatre costumer is faced with many special requirements that must be solved to the satisfaction of both actors and child audience.

Animals

A veritable zoo of animals abounds in children's theatre plays —dogs, cats, horses, cows, wolves, ostriches, peacocks, hens, cockerels, lions, tigers, owls, penguins, dragons, crocodiles, and monkeys, to name a few. Most animal characters are played by a single actor, but a few, such as cows, horses, and an occasional dragon, must be played by two actors.

Any costumer recognizes that none of these—least of all the two-actor animal—can be completely convincing as realism. However, children accept animal portrayals as simply a happy convention, and since they are generally found in the fantasy plays, there is little point in striving for a realistic effect.

A full animal costume usually consists of a headpiece and a body covering, usually built as separate units, especially if the head is at all bulky. The attachment is made with a loose fold of material on the body which snaps or hooks to the head on the inside.

An animal head is first shaped roughly in outline with heavy wire. The neck portion must be large enough to permit the head of the actor to go through easily, and the inside wires are padded to hold the structure in place and to make it comfortable to wear. A screen mesh is then molded over the wire outline to complete the form. Papier maché strips or celastic pieces are used to cover the mesh and to add appendages such as ears, teeth, molded scales, or spines. The part of the head through which the actor sees must be kept clear through all stages of construction. When the structure is dry it is painted according to the design, and its attachment to the body is provided.

Some types of animal heads will have to be almost form-fitting. For certain dogs, cats, or "The Beast," a kind of mask may be built which makes use of the actor's own eyes and mouth. Layers of liquid latex, a rubber material, are spread over a plaster form of the actor's head leaving holes for the eyes, nostrils, and mouth. When the layers are built up sufficiently to give the mask strength, a final coating of latex is given, and the hair (either crepe or nylon saran) and other appendages such as ears and any special modelings are added. When the hair is suitably trimmed the actor has a flexible, form-fitting animal head which will stand many performances.

In some plays, such as Kristin Sergel's *Winnie-the-Pooh,* almost all the characters are animals. In such cases, treating the heads as elaborately as just described is probably out of keeping. Simple costumes of outing flannel can be constructed in the form of children's "sleepers," complete with feet; open-face heads can be attached directly to the bodies. Ears would be the only suggestion of the actual animal, the rest of the impression being completed by make-up. (See Plate 19.)

Animal bodies should conform in style to the head. Cotton batting between layers of muslin serves well for padding basic heavy muslin or canvas cover garments in strategic places. Tails must be attached to the bodies as securely as possible; if the tail is heavy, precautions may have to be taken to make sure it does not rip off in violent action. Painting is the usual method of finishing an animal body, though in some cases a furry or plushy cloth covering gives a more convincing texture. Unfortunately, painted animal costumes do not clean well, and their reuse is somewhat doubtful.

At best, both head and body of animal costumes are hot and uncomfortable to wear. It is always advisable to have at least the head available well in advance of performance date so that the actor can get used to expressing himself by manipulating the head as a whole instead of relying on facial expressions, which will not be seen.

TRANSFORMATIONS

An effective transformation in costume needs the cooperative efforts of costumer, scene designer, lighting technician, sound man, actor, director, and several crew members. The magic of the miraculous change from beast to human form, from witch to beautiful woman, from evil creature to a melted mass on the floor, from ogre to inanimate property, or from a statue to a living being should appear wondrous indeed to the children in the audience. Such transformations, which compel the actor to make a quick sloughing of one costume and a sudden appearance in another, are the responsibility of the costumer.

An actor must *underdress* his final costume—that is, he must wear it underneath the one which is first seen. The overgarment is preferably made in one piece and must completely cover the other costume. It is closed down its entire length with snaps, which release quickly when a ripping movement is applied. The operation of a long zipper is too precarious to risk in the cramped quarters in which such action is usually carried out. If a mask is worn in the first part, it may simply be removed and hidden along with the costume. But if make-up must do the job for both characters it should not be extreme in either direction. In such cases, the actor will have to rely principally on his facial expression to exaggerate the change in his personality. Sometimes a change of wigs can be managed in the moment of transition; however, unless the actor has help in the process, he risks a bad job of fitting which is likely to be almost worse than no wig at all.

In addition to the costumer, the designer is also concerned with such moments in a play, since he must provide the place for the transformation to occur. The director, too, can help by providing a barricade of other characters or some distracting business (which must be very cleverly handled to be successful) to conceal the critical change. The lighting and sound men can provide special effects to enhance the magic moment, thus momentarily distracting attention from the mundane side of the business at hand.

A "melting" character usually moves close to a break in the scenery or a split drape, behind which off-stage helpers can unfasten the costume from behind. This permits the actor to slip down and out of it, leaving the costume in a heap on the floor. The cries of the melting character can combine with magical music and flashing lights to complete the illusion.

A costumer for a children's play sometimes becomes so engrossed in providing all manner of fantastic costumes—overgrown feet; large ears; trick noses that grow, shrink, or change color; and countless other irregular features—that he may neglect some of the most obvious essentials. Many children's productions have been spoiled by oversights such as saddle shoes with tights or Elizabethan gowns, sweat socks or argyles with medieval peasant dress, or eighteenth-century court costumes without wigs, leaving modern crew cuts ludicrously exposed. Such details may contradict the production standards which an organization professes; its stage picture speaks much more loudly than its printed constitution. And never think that "children will never know the difference."

PROPERTIES

Properties consist of that rather broad category of set dressings, furniture, articles that the actors use and handle, and any other paraphernalia which cannot be classed as scenery. *Set* and *hand* props are distinguished according to the size and use of the article. In children's theatre work a third category is not uncommon: *special properties*. If these are at all extensive in any production, a special crew is often assigned to construct or manipulate them. For instance, in a production of Charlotte Chorpenning's *Cinderella* it would be wise to designate several people as a "pumpkin crew" because of the number of ordinary pumpkins and the two coaches required by the action.

The problems of a property crew are centered principally around the three aspects of construction, assembly, and running. Because each one involves a number of important details, careful organization by the crew head and active supervision by the technical director are absolute essentials.

A complete property list should be compiled by the crew head as early in the production schedule as possible. Playscripts often contain such a list, but it is seldom complete. The director will usually point out certain necessary additions; the property crew head can scrutinize the book for others which have been omitted; and both the director and designer should add specifications on the kinds of articles to be assembled. The designer needs to include in his planning the designs and working drawings for any properties which must be specially constructed. Since the need for some props or for certain specifications on an article may not become apparent until well into the rehearsal period, a continuing liaison between the director and the property head is advisable. During early rehearsals, the assistant director might well make a point of checking whether each property mentioned by the actors is actually on the prop list.

Constructing Properties

One aspect of children's theatre production frequently noted is the fact that properties are of such an unusual nature that special construction is the standard procedure rather than the exceptional one. Many items will be good for only one production, but a few should be built to last since there will be occasions to use them over and over.

A *spinning wheel* is one of the familiar properties in many children's plays. If the construction is fairly rugged, it can be converted from a foot-pedal wheel to one which operates electrically by a hidden motor, making the magic of a "self-spinning" wheel amazingly convincing. Scene paint, gilt or silver paint, and glitter can be used to convert it from the wheel of a peasant's wife to one found in a fairy castle.

Figure 7 shows a spinning wheel with a detachable wheel

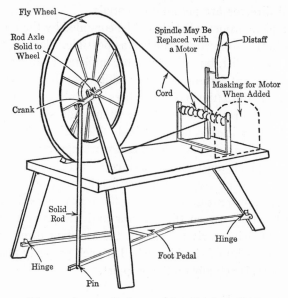

Fig. 7. A versatile homemade spinning wheel.

for touring. This wheel consists of three thicknesses of ¼" plywood glued together, the center layer being slightly smaller to form a groove around the wheel. A continuous cord is run through the groove and around the shaft of a motor mounted in the spindle position. To operate it manually the large flywheel is spun by means of a crank which also serves as the axle; to

PLATE 16

Above. *Short disconnected flats or screens designed by Virgil Godfrey for Whiting and Rickert's* Huckleberry Finn, *Michigan State University Children's Theatre production, directed by Jed H. Davis, 1954. Note the use of the portal.*

Below. *An outline set for Chorpenning's* The Emperor's New Clothes, *Federal Theatre Project of the Works Progress Administration, New York, 1936.*

"Billy Bones."

PLATE 17

Two costume plates designed by Herbert L. Camburn for Drew's Treasure Island, *University of Kansas Theatre production, directed by Bee Harvey, 1959.*

"Blind Pew."

PLATE 18

Above. *A fragmentary set by Richard Graham for McGrew's* Raggedy Ann and Andy, *Michigan State University Junior Players production, directed by Anna M. Clark, 1953.*

Below. *A dream sequence shown through a scrim. Virgil Godfrey's design for Chorpenning's* Cinderella, *Michigan State University Children's Theatre production, directed by Jed H. Davis. Note the specific lighting of the scene.*

PLATE 19

One kind of animal costume with head attached. The material is outing flannel. Costumes designed by Ronald Grow for the Michigan State University Junior Players production of Sergel's Winnie-the-Pooh, *directed by Jed H. Davis, 1957.*

PLATE **20**

Above. *The cast meets the audience. (Michigan State University Children's Theatre)*

Left. *Children press in on their favorite character after a performance of Heidi. (Robert Darling, San Francisco State College Children's Theatre)*

PLATE 21

Above. *Operating lights on tour.*
Below. *Assembling a collapsible portal for tour. Designed by Virgil Godfrey for the Michigan State University Children's Theatre.*

PLATE 22

*Strong directional light emphasizes dramatic qualities. A scene
from Siks'* The Sandalwood Box, *Macalester College Children's
Theatre production, directed by Jed H. Davis, 1951.*

this is attached a solid rod which goes to the foot pedal. Both legs and spokes can be made from turned chair spindles, but dowels and tapered pieces of plywood function equally well and are easier to work with. There are several possible methods of bringing electric current to the upstage side of the wheel and lighting varicolored Christmas bulbs for a spectacular effect.

A *pumpkin* is made quite simply by forming the basic contour out of small-mesh chicken wire and covering it with papier maché strips or scraps of scene muslin soaked in "dope" (a mixture of one part melted glue to five parts water, thickened with wheat paste). A stem of the same material is added, and the contours are emphasized in the painting after it has dried.

A *pumpkin coach* is constructed in the same way, except that an opening can be left for a small window. A light which glows inside the coach will add a touch of magic as the carriage glides across the stage drawn by the mice. Toy buggy wheels and chassis work quite well as a support for the pumpkin; the profile-board mice are attached to strap iron rods and bolted to the chassis so that they do not actually touch the floor. To make sure that the coach does not swerve on its trip across the stage, a thin black guy wire is run through eyelets under the chassis and is attached to supports off stage at both sides. A fish line is also attached to the coach waiting off stage, and as a pull is exerted on the line the coach appears on stage, guided along by the wire.

Vines, flowers, and *flowering bushes* are required properties in many plays. They are not difficult to make, but the property crew should consider the style of the production before beginning. A vine is usually made of clothesline with the desired kind of leaves attached. Leaves are best made of carefully cut pieces of scene muslin or canvas, painted, and attached with black stovepipe wire. Tendrils may also be added to give it additional thickness.

A vine which grows across the stage will require two crew members to help it along, one to "feed" it out of its storage position and the other to pull it by means of a strong fish line. A vine or beanstalk that grows upward requires pulleys mounted in the loft through which is run a length of piano wire attached to the vine. Piano wire treated with gun bluing to minimize the reflection of stage lights cannot be seen by the audience. Of course if the vine is Jack's beanstalk which must be climbed, the base will have to be a substantial rope. Actually, most producers prefer to use a real rope ladder for this type of vine, making sure that its ladder construction is disguised by the leaves and tendrils.

Depending on the exact variety, flowers are made from many kinds of materials. Milk filters, obtainable from any creamery, make excellent white roses when wound and bound with florist wire. Quick-drying "spray can" paint can transform them into red or pink roses. Crepe paper is frequently used for flowers, though it rustles loudly when handled and generally looks just like crepe paper. If its stiffness makes no difference, painted muslin models easily and tends to curl in a natural way. Very large stylized flowers can be cut from thin profile board or ¼" plywood and attached at the base to a narrow batten.

Flowering bushes must usually be constructed by standard methods according to the total production design. Real bushes are sometimes dug up from the yard or built up with natural foliage, but they never look lifelike under stage lights, since natural green usually turns gray on stage. Bare natural branches are readily used as the basis for a bush, with muslin foliage and flowers added by the prop crew. If one blossom is to be picked, it should be the same as all the rest and identifiable only by position.

Excellent, detailed, and natural-looking artificial flowers are available at most florist shops. While they are initially quite

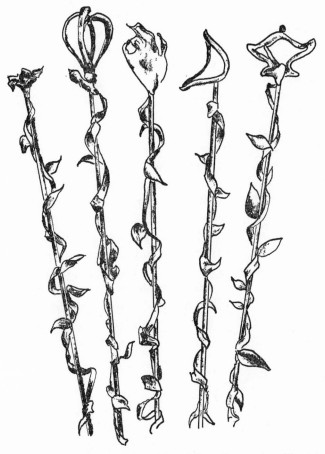

Fig. 8. Five wands designed by Albert Senter for Chorpenning's The Sleeping Beauty. *Each represents the kind of magic wielded by its user. These are made from doweling and celastic.*

expensive, with reasonable care they will last for many seasons.

Parchment scrolls get so much use that it is advisable to keep on hand a variety of sizes, lengths, and degrees of ornateness to satisfy different requirements. Doweling, obtainable in several sizes, makes excellent rollers for parchment rolls, and white shelf paper treated with strong tea simulates parchment. Knobs, moldings, and other motifs can be added to the exposed ends of the dowels for decoration.

Wands, too, are often needed. Imaginative variations in the traditional design of a rod which ends in a glittering star can be worked out with papier maché or celastic to emphasize the particular brand of magic called for. The wands described in children's literature sometimes suggest a completely fresh approach, like the godmother's staff in *The Little Lame Prince.*

The problems of constructing properties for children's plays are of such infinite variety that only a few are mentioned here. In general, standard scene building techniques, or modifications of them, are used whenever possible for lightness, strength, and ease of assembling. When standard construction does not suffice, designers, technicians, and ingenious crew members must figure a new way to get the job done.

Assembling Properties

Properties are gathered from a wide variety of sources. Producers who do not operate in or near metropolitan areas which boast property rental establishments must keep constantly alert in travels about town and the surrounding countryside to note fresh sources of supply. The acquisition of a usable stock of standard props should be a goal; even between plays we keep our eyes open for possible additions.

With the exception of simple benches and stools, furniture is difficult if not impossible to construct except in a well-equipped scene shop. For this reason producing organizations should have a number of versatile pieces on hand, especially pieces with interesting line and rather indefinite period characteristics. Chairs, tables, divans, and desks which can be altered in appearance with simple additions of profile board painted to match the *décor* should be available without long searching. Used-article shops, secondhand stores, the Salvation Army and Goodwill Industries centers, as well as retail furniture stores are often willing to lend or rent pieces when special furnishings are needed. Antique shops are often an excellent source of unusual items; and if the producing group has a reputation for careful handling of sometimes valuable or irreplaceable articles, a shop manager may be quite willing to help the cause in return for a program acknowledgment.

An occasional property-gathering campaign may yield some useful items from attics and garages—such as old cooking and eating utensils, a genuine churn, articles that could become a buried treasure, picture and mirror frames, clocks, and perhaps even an old loom or spinning wheel. These items soon begin to cut down the list of items which must be built or specially procured.

Running Properties

Not later than the third week before performance members of the property crew begin attending rehearsals and noting the location of every property to be used in each act and scene of the play. Regardless of how clever or unfailing his memory is, the crew head should make out a check list for each act and scene and have it verified by the director. He should note on a floor plan the position of each article of furniture, each set prop, and all hand props on the set at the beginning of every scene; whether doors or windows are to be open or closed; whether each item to be carried on by characters should be located off right or left. During the performance it is his job to see that no actor goes on stage without the properties he is suppose to have.

When a shift in properties must be made, each crew member should be supplied with a list of those for which he is responsible. Since catastrophe can result if even one prop is omitted or misplaced at a shift, crew members should be in position well in advance of the shift cue, ready to go to work the instant the curtain is down, in order to provide the maximum time for a final check before the curtain opens again.

Shifting during a stage blackout presents other problems. When this is necessary the positions for props should be clearly marked with luminous tape or paint, using different colors for each act. If crew members cover their eyes about a minute before the shift cue they are able to see well enough in the dark to locate the glowing tapes. Counting steps from the off-stage position is sometimes necessary as well. Obviously a considerable amount of rehearsal is necessary to enable the crew to shift both accurately and quietly.

The secret of successful operation of properties is to have them in the charge of conscientious crew members, people who learn the job thoroughly and early and who keep well ahead of deadlines so that when the inevitable additions and changes come up in the final rehearsals they are set to cope with them.

LIGHTING

As we pointed out all through our discussion of scenic styles and forms, a system of keeping illumination where it should be and away from areas where it does not belong is essential for the effectiveness of the total stage picture.

In the standard method of lighting, the acting area is divided into six or more light areas, depending on the size and shape of the floor plan. Each of these light areas is usually covered by two spotlights mounted so that their beams converge at an angle of 45° on the horizontal plane and strike the face of a standing actor at a vertical angle of 38°. These angles give the actor the three-dimensional aspect which needs to be emphasized in the theatre.

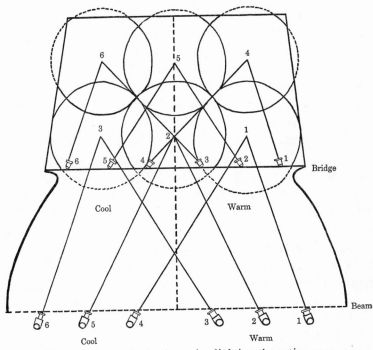

Fig. 9. The standard scheme for lighting the acting area.

In order to establish these angles, two mounting positions for spotlights are normally assumed: the "beam" position over the heads of the audience and the "first pipe" immediately behind the proscenium. Unfortunately, as these positions do not always exist in auditoriums where children's plays are presented, they must often be improvised.

Towers which can extend about 15 feet into the air and which are fitted with crossbars near the top substitute reasonably well for any position not provided by the building's architect. Two of these towers, each containing from three to six spotlights, can be placed in the auditorium—where, however, they must be suitably protected from inquisitive hands. Two more can be placed just off stage to the right and left of the procenium arch so that the lights can be focused over the top of the setting into the acting area. While these angles are certainly not ideal, they are far superior to general illumination provided by the customary footlights and borderlights. The false proscenium described in Chapter 10 is better for mounting the first pipe spotlights, since the angle is then much closer to the ideal.

These positions, as well as several others, can be used in children's plays to mount special effects instruments which are needed in addition to the acting area instruments. Such requirements are many. Sunshine or moonlight may stream through windows or doors or may flood the entire playing space. Sky drops need an even coverage. Fireplace fires, campfires, the play of colored lights during a magical sequence, shafts and pools of light for transformations and sudden appearances, storm and lightning effects, dawn rising across the base of the sky—all these need careful planning and execution if they are to delight the child audience. (See Plates 9 and 22.)

BATTERY-OPERATED EFFECTS

The basis for many special lighting items is shown in Figure 10. With slight variations in arrangement, this electrical scheme serves for candles, lanterns and small lamps, torches, eyes or noses that must light up, or any other item that is carried around so that an electric cable cannot be attached off stage. It is unwise ever to use real fire on any stage. In fact, many cities have specific regulations prohibiting its use. Flame-shaped lamps usually can be used just as effectively without endangering life and property.

BLACK LIGHT

Black light effects (ultraviolet) are increasing in popularity because of their spectacular nature. Black lighting requires a strong source of ultraviolet rays, usually a mercury vapor lamp or, if it can be mounted close enough, a "sun lamp" fitted with a UV filter. Carbon arc spotlights with UV filters, commercially available, are necessary if a long distance or throw is involved or a broad area must be covered. All properties, set units, costumes, or make-up which are to glow under the black light must be treated with special fluorescent paint, which is available in many colors from any stage lighting concern.

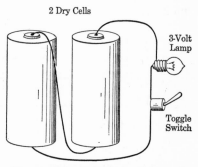

Fig. 10. Standard wiring scheme for all dry-cell lighting effects.

The lamps must be lighted well in advance of the cue in order to warm up sufficiently to emit ultraviolet rays, and there can be no other light of any kind on the stage at the same time. A good deal of experimentation is needed to work out black light effects. When these are skillfully done they can be absolutely breathtaking in beauty and a source of great wonder to the children.

PYROTECHNICS

Smoke effects range from puffs emitted from cone-shaped caps to surges from braziers to smoke from a fire filtering through cracks in cabin walls. Each of these probably will be handled in a different way. Since chemical smoke powders give off extremely offensive and toxic odors, their use should be avoided unless there is no other way to produce the effect. If they must be used, a heating cone containing a small amount of the powder is inserted in a socket mounted inside a property or masking device. Current must be turned on at the control board well in advance of the moment when the smoke is needed. Moreover, since the smoke does not stop when the current is turned off, a mechanical trap must be devised to release and to stop the smoke on cue.

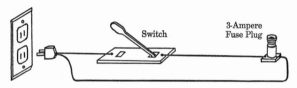

Fig. 11. A simple flash pot wiring scheme.

Dry ice makes the least offensive "smoke." Actually it produces a visible gas rather than smoke when hot water is poured over it. The flow can be controlled by regulating the amount of hot water. Caution should be observed in handling dry ice, for its extreme cold can easily burn the skin.

Flashes of light often accompany the magical appearances of articles or characters or emphasize a supernatural phenomenon. The electrical basis for a "flash pot" is shown in Figure 11. The plastic top of a three-ampere fuse plug is removed and flash powder is put into the cavity of the fuse. When the switch is closed, a short circuit is created which blows the fuse and ignites the flash. To be sure of blowing the treated fuse, it must be lower in amperage than any other fuse in the whole electrical circuit. Instead of a fuse a single strand of thin copper wire attached between two small alligator clips may be used to ignite the flash, but this is not as sure a method as the other. Common sense dictates that any such device be kept away from inflammable materials of any sort and that nearby characters are not so close that they are burned or momentarily blinded.

MOVING PROJECTIONS

Children's plays occasionally have need for moving effects such as flying bluebirds, storm clouds, falling snow, or rippling water. A sciopticon is the instrument best adapted for these effects. This is an arrangement of lenses and a motor-driven "effects head" which attaches to the front of an ordinary large spotlight. It is quite bulky and sometimes difficult to place so that the effect appears where it is wanted. Usually sciopticon effects are projected against either a scrim or a sky cyclorama. A wide variety of these instruments is available from most stage lighting companies. The lenses can of course be used over and over, but each effect called for requires a separate effects head. If the organization budget does not permit the purchase of this instrument, a rental arrangement can sometimes be made.

Rippling water can be simulated by aiming a small spotlight at a piece of corrugated or wrinkled shiny metal. The light shines on the metal and is then reflected onto some scenic or property unit which would normally receive this reflection—perhaps the wall of a pool, a marble archway nearby, or table and chairs alongside the stream. The sheet of metal must be kept moving slightly to keep the "water" rippling. A concealed stagehand or a rocker arrangement controlled by fish lines off stage are the usual methods.

The effect of falling snow can be projected against scrim or sky by means of the condensing and objective lenses of the sciopticon, using a homemade motor-driven disk of black cardboard punctured with tiny pinholes instead of an effects head. Other light will have to be quite dim for any of these projections to be seen easily, and only by experiment can the instrument be located to its best advantage.

Lighting Control

As we noted when we were discussing actual producing conditions, a complete and flexible system for the control of lights is the exception rather than the rule. Producers who work without an adequate system of light control are severely handicapped, and in many cases they would be better off to ignore the existing control board and concentrate on procuring small, flexible control units.

Small dimmers of the autotransformer type, from 500 to 1000 watts, are far more useful for children's theatre work than the larger and more expensive units. Multiples of six should be the goal, since six dimmers make it possible to control each of the six light areas separately. (See Figure 9, p. 231.) If there are only six dimmers, they should be at least of 1000-watt size, capable of controlling two 500-watt spotlights on each area. A number of excellent and inexpensive portable control boards, each containing six dimmers, are now available. As funds become available, additional units can be bought to increase the intricacy of control.

Portable individual 1000-watt dimmers can also be purchased separately. These may be used to augment an existing control system which permits the use of only those instruments permanently hooked to the board. Portable dimmers are plugged directly into any wall outlet, and the lighting instruments are plugged into the dimmer.

Occasionally, with a bit of extra trouble and labor, an existing board may be made more useful by removing the bulbs from the circuits of foots or borders which are permanently connected into it and replacing them with female plugs into which the instruments to be controlled can be plugged. While this method is definitely an improvisation and should be replaced as soon as possible with a standard system, it has the advantage of providing for the control of spotlights where no provision is otherwise possible.

SOUND

The use made of the tremendous potential of sound in a children's production will vary from director to director. Some prefer to incorporate a minimum number of cues; others use it very extensively. The nature of the production will have some bearing on the demands of sound effects and music; but in most cases how much the director uses sound and music in his productions will depend on his ability to search out possible applications and to recognize the emotional impact of suitably chosen background sound, as well as on his own personal repertoire and experience with music.

Playscripts often suggest a minimum sound plot. For example, when thunder is to be heard, when a bell tinkles or a clock strikes as a critical cue in the progress of the story, the script will usually indicate it at the proper place. Dogs barking, guns shooting, gongs striking, and other such sound cues usually work integrally with the plot and constitute a minimum of sound.

Playwrights have long recognized the positive effect of music on children, and they often season their plays liberally with songs, dances, and stylized movement to musical accompaniment. When these are required the melodic line of the music is usually given somewhere in the text. The director, however, must decide what treatment it is to be given—whether the song will be sung without accompaniment, with live piano in the wings or orchestra pit, or to recorded orchestral accompaniment. With productions requiring a fairly extensive use of music—a specific piece, a repeated theme, an integral melody— a director may begin to explore the maximum use of sound to accompany the drama. Such plays as Evernden's *Greensleeves' Magic,* which calls for repeated focus on the Elizabethan "Greensleeves" theme; Groff's *The Christmas Nightingale,* with its emphasis upon a Polish lullaby which finally leads the lost boy to his home; or even Walker's *The Birthday of the Infanta,* which features the little hunchback's "Song of the Autumn Leaves," seem to call for the assistance of a talented composer who can sense the emotional impact of variations on the basic theme and work them out to accompany key portions of the drama.

While music specially composed and recorded by symphonic artists for a particular production is almost always out of the question, directors can certainly explore less expensive methods of interpreting a given play in terms of music. Recorded music usually offers the best solution, in spite of the long hours that must be spent locating just the right portion to do each job.

Music serves many purposes in children's productions. It can be used to concentrate the audience's attention at the beginning of the performance and to lead the children into the opening action with the desired frame of mind. It can be used to underline scenes of emotion which might be missed or disregarded were it not for the air of specialness which reinforcing music gives them. It can suggest what audience response is expected in a situation. It can bridge the time-span between the end of one scene and the beginning of the next; in this case it does not end abruptly with the opening of the curtain but continues on under the action for a smooth transition. Music to function in these various ways must be carefully chosen for its rhythmic beat, emotional tone, consistency in style from cue to cue, and for its quality of being "just right" for the play and the production as a whole.

MANUAL EFFECTS

Because of the cuing problems or the tone quality desired, certain kinds of sounds are better produced manually than by recording. Light tinkly bells can be quite convincingly produced with a toy xylophone, and the operator has a choice of tone to suit each occasion when the effect is needed. Gongs produced by striking a suspended brake drum with a rubber hammer have just the right length of reverberation to make the sound convincing. Gunshots are best produced with a blank pistol fired backstage. Doorbells, buzzers, and telephone bells are best produced with actual equipment kept as stock items in almost all theatres. Bird calls, special whistles obtainable from music stores, can be cued in better live than recorded.

RECORDED EFFECTS

Commercial manufacturers now produce almost a limitless range of recorded sound effects, from crowds cheering to railroad trains approaching, from the tolling chimes of Big Ben to chirping crickets and barnyard sounds. Recorded thunder is more convincing than the traditional thunder sheet, and a whistling wind from a recording is steadier than one produced on a wind machine. However, there is a wide variation in different recordings of the same basic effect, and a director must frequently search to find the right one.

OPERATING SOUND

There are various methods of handling sound effects and music in performance. The director may prefer to control them through a set of dual turntables which feed into an amplifier and then to speakers. In this case the crew must practice until the procedure becomes smooth and the cue sheet accurate. If this is done at rehearsals well in advance of technical or dress rehearsals, the sound effects will be under control at the time when other elements of production should occupy the attention of the director. Only actual volume levels then remain to be set when the production goes on stage.

Instead of controlling sound effects in this way, the director may arrange to record all sound and music cues in sequence on tape. Normally this is a job he must supervise himself, since at this stage only he knows the cues, their length, and their ultimate use. Taping should always be done under rigidly controlled conditions, in a room free of extraneous sounds. The best available recording equipment should be used, and the turntables used should be equipped with record quality controls. Except for sounds to be produced live at the time of performance, all cues, recorded or manual, should be recorded consecutively so that during the performance the operator need only turn on the tape machine and set his level for each cue. It is always wise for the director to make a duplicate or two of the completed tape to ensure against loss, breakage, or deterioration.

Occasional sound cues do not fit into a regular sequence pattern. For instance, the music for a dance may be playing when at a certain point in the action the trampling of horses is heard drawing near. Since the action time could vary considerably, it would be difficult, if not foolish, to try to record this in sequence, guessing at the time the horses should be heard. Such problems are readily solved with the use of two tapes and two recorders, one containing the dance music cue, the other the horses. At the proper time the operator blends the two sounds through a mixer panel.

Speakers should be placed wherever they will do the job best —backstage, on one side, out on the apron, or even within the setting itself. In this connection, it is possible that in the years ahead binaural or stereophonic sound may offer great possibilities to theatrical producers. If a selector panel is provided as part of the sound equipment, the operator can select whichever of the speakers variously placed about the stage and apron he wishes for each cue. The speaker designation then becomes part of his cue sheet.

The best way to coordinate sound cues with action on stage is to place the operator within view of the action, perhaps in the orchestra pit or in a booth out in the house. This is especially important when a character is supposedly playing an instrument on stage—pipe, flute, piano, violin—and the sound is actually supplied by record. Absolute coordination is essential here, and several hours of rehearsals usually are required to perfect the illusion.

While a sound operator need not be a skilled musician, it helps if he is not completely tone deaf. He should at least be able to recognize when he has an incorrect cue playing, when his volume level is too low for light instrumentation to carry, or when the music is blasting. It also helps if he is alert to unusual opportunities to build music subtly under action or tense sequences, to punctuate lines and action with music as a continuation of the rhythm established by the scene, or to adjust volume levels to the changing volumes of the actors. While everything that can be written down will appear on his cue sheet, there is no real substitute for a high degree of artistry in the performance of this job.

SPECIAL EFFECTS

Most special effects can be classified under lighting, scenery, properties, or sound, depending upon the principal technical element involved. A few, however, involve several elements almost equally.

FLYING

While flying characters are actually specified in only a few plays such as *Peter Pan, Hansel and Gretel,* and *Mary Poppins,* several others can be considerably enhanced by the inclusion of this most spectacular phenomenon in children's theatre production. The apparatus required to fly actors is the same as that used for the many articles which appear to fly about, though it must be stronger.

Ingenious technicians have developed elaborate flying mechanisms which carry actors up and down, across stage, and out over the audience. The cost of such apparatus is prohibitive for most producing groups, but fortunately a much simpler principle works equally well.

The flying scheme diagramed here is based upon the pendulum, the simple swinging action of a clock mechanism. The body of the actor furnishes the weight necessary for the swinging to occur regularly. The actor who flies must wear a special harness of heavy canvas to which is attached a sturdy metal eye accessible through a split in the costume back. Shortly before his flight cue, he backs toward the wings, and a crew member snaps on the fly line, which is a piece of piano wire treated with gun bluing to cut light glare. This fly line extends out of sight into the loft above the stage where it is attached to a standard hemp fly rope. The rope passes over a pulley in the grid which is centered on the traversable area, thence to another pulley over the off-stage area and down to a hefty "fly man" or two who guide the flight by exerting lifts and releases on the rope.

It goes almost without saying that flying requires perfect cooperation and coordination between actor and fly man. The fly man senses through his hands the exact timing of pulls and releases and hence must know the exact course of each flight. An infinite number of small cues must pass between him and the actor. At the beginning of a flight the fly man stands on a chair, grasping the rope tightly. As the actor gives a slight take-off jump, the fly man follows through instantly by leaping to the floor, thus pulling the actor aloft. The actor's momentum carries him in the direction of the flight and must be timed to expire at the exact landing spot. When the fly man receives a clear cue

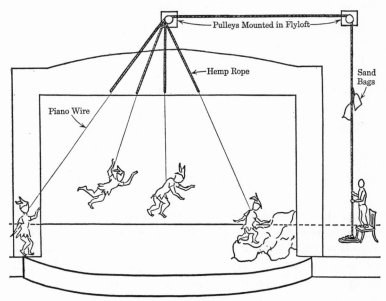

Fig. 12. A flying mechanism.

that the flier has reached that spot, he lets him down by gently releasing the rope. Obviously the fly man should have an unobstructed view of the stage.

When the designer is calculating sight lines on his setting he must plan to keep unused fly lines out of sight. If flying takes place inside a room, as it does in the Darling nursery in *Peter Pan*, provision must be made for passing a wire through the wall above the window through which Peter flies. Vantage points where actors can have wires hooked on must also be provided in the set, as well as landing places. If several characters fly at once it is important that there is no chance for tangled lines.

Theatres without a standard grid—which means one at a height three times the proscenium height—and some without any grid at all nevertheless often have sufficient space above the proscenium for successful flying. As long as pulleys can be mounted securely in the loft we need have few worries about the safety of actors who fly.

APPEARANCES AND DISAPPEARANCES

A quick magical appearance is usually managed by setting off a flash of light, momentarily blinding the audience, while the actor makes a quick entrance from a vantage point close by. Frequently it is necessary to build a false door for this purpose in order that the actor will be close enough to capitalize on the effect of the flash. Like the secret panels described earlier (p. 218), this is a door which cannot be distinguished from its surroundings. A magic appearance too close to a wing or a doorway is seldom effective. Children quickly solve the trick and are disgusted with its obviousness. It is usually well worth the extra trouble it causes to have the actor appear from inside a hollow tree, part of a rock formation, or a plain section of wall.

A disappearance can be handled in the same way, but there are also other possibilities: the actor can quickly drop out of sight behind a ground rise; he can be dropped down a trap in the stage floor or in a level formation or rock structure.

Every effort should be made to utilize the full potential of stage mechanics to augment appearances and disappearances. Thus flash pots can go off; thunder can crash; harp music can glide; area lights can flicker and go out, returning slowly to normal when the effect is accomplished; swirling clouds can cover the entire stage. The total effect is what the producer seeks.

SHRINKING AND GROWING

The most unusual impression in *Alice in Wonderland*—where Alice shrinks as she eats bits of the cake that lie on the table—has delighted children for generations, though in some versions of the play this effect happens off stage. Some producers create an illusion of size by extending some of the properties, such as the table itself, or even by enlarging a nearby door. Such effects are contrived through special construction and rigging of the units involved.

When the director cannot rely on altering the proportion between Alice and a nearby property, and there is no other way to give the effect of Alice's stretching upward like a telescope, he is obliged to try imaginative tricks. For example, a movie might be made of Alice alone against black drapery, wearing an amazed expression as the camera moves in closer and closer, making her image larger and larger. For the shrinking sequence the camera would move farther and farther away. At the critical cue during the play, immediately after she eats the cake, Alice would then move into position in front of the part of the setting which is to serve as a movie screen. There could be a flash of light and then a blackout, during which Alice hides quickly from view. The movie picks up the action from there, with Alice's voice continuing to speak the lines. A goodly amount of experimentation, principally with lights, will be needed to give a fairly realistic effect, with as little discrepancy as possible between the live actress and the movie image.

Another method of handling this particular sequence involves Alice's leaving the stage briefly and standing in front of a carefully placed spotlight so that her shadow moves higher and higher up a wall as the light is brought closer to her.

The foregoing discussion covers only a few of the multitude of special effects and staging problems found in children's plays, but enough to demonstrate that children's theatre challenges the ingenuity of designers and technicians to the utmost. In fact, some have become so engrossed with the unusual and spectacular they have neglected the ordinary aspects of substantial construction, adhering scene paint, and production schedules. Obviously, designers should never slight the basic demands of the production. They will find plenty of opportunity to experience the fun and satisfaction of manufacturing illusion and of seeing the results of their work on the delighted faces of the children.

9

Children's Theatre
Is a Business

ALTHOUGH children's theatre activity is sometimes subsidized, most producers must prove by efficient business practices that they are worthy of continued support. Pleas for subsidy have been made since the earliest days of the movement; but until children's theatre is recognized as deserving of full financial support, these organizations must remain solvent. They cannot take refuge in the values of the activity as an excuse for inefficient operation.

Many kinds of groups and institutions are presently engaged in children's theatre work as a means of accomplishing specific objectives. A municipal recreation department may regard children's theatre as an ideal means of integrating the artistic phases of its total program with the bonus factor of providing entertainment for its playground audiences. A local Junior League usually stresses service to the community in providing live theatre experiences for children. A college or university department of drama commonly stresses the opportunities of giving its students basic acting and staging experience and increasing its impact upon the community and the state. A high school, private studio, or professional school often expresses these same purposes. A community theatre which engages in children's theatre production as part of its regular season is probably most concerned with increasing the effectiveness of its program in the city and establishing an early habit of theatre attendance.

Organizations using child actors exclusively naturally stress the values of participation in drama. Some think of the child primarily as a social being taking part in a program that demands the utmost of cooperation and interaction with his fellows. Another may think of him as a human being who will benefit from a temporary escape from mundane or ugly surroundings into a world of beauty and idealism. Still another may feel that the drama's chief value to the child participant is that it exposes him to great literary works, to the folk tales and traditions which are his heritage. Again, practice in the social graces or the use of voice and body to express emotions and to communicate ideas may be the primary objective. A very few provide preprofessional training for talented children who intend to become the actors of tomorrow—though unfortunately some of these thrive on the gullibility of misguided parents who are pushing their suggestible offspring into the theatre to satisfy their own frustrated ambitions.

Each of these kinds of organizations is likely to operate on a different financial basis. Some community-sponsored recreation groups are forbidden to charge admission to productions and are therefore dependent upon a budgetary allotment which may or may not be sufficient to keep production standards high. Junior Leagues and community theatres sometimes have a "cushion" to fall back on in case of financial need but are otherwise expected to balance costs with income from admissions. College and university organizations may be subsidized to the extent of staff salaries but are usually expected to pay all costs of production from the box office. Fees required of participants in some programs are an added source of income, supplementing admissions. These include membership fees, laboratory fees, registrations, and instructional charges for related activities. Professional children's theatres are financed entirely from admissions or performance charges based on box office receipts.

Regardless of subsidies and the accounting demanded by the subsidizing agency, effective children's theatre organizations are obliged to direct a considerable part of their efforts toward efficient organization and sound financial operation. Their dreams and aspirations may reach the clouds, but their feet must be firmly planted on the ground. If those of us in children's theatre believe in our purposes and our goals, we owe our constituents—both those in the house and those behind the footlights—every possible assurance of continuity in the program.

This chapter is concerned with types of organization and management which have proved of value in bringing together the child audience and the play and in assuring a pleasurable experience in the theatre. If these two objectives are accomplished, our children's theatres may expect a long and prosperous life.

TWO KINDS OF CHILDREN'S THEATRES

Functionally, there are only two kinds of children's theatres: those which *sponsor* performances and those which *produce* plays. A given group may operate in either of these capacities at various times, but the organizational structure will be geared to the duties being performed.

Sponsoring Organizations

Sponsorship of both commercial and noncommercial productions for the child audience is undertaken by a wide variety of groups. An individual Parent-Teacher Association may simply appoint one of its members to negotiate for the visit of a producing company. The Parent-Teacher Council of a large school system may appoint a children's theatre committee empowered to make all arrangements. Chapters of the American Association of University Women or local Junior Leagues may regularly appoint committees to arrange for visiting performers. Associations of elementary principals or the administration of a school system itself may elect or appoint persons to bring producing groups to the city. Child study clubs, Rotary, Kiwanis, or Lions clubs sometimes designate certain members to be the local contact for a producing company. In each of these instances, the organization as a whole is the sponsor, but the actual work is done by the elected or appointed children's theatre chairman who functions with the aid of a working committee.

THE CHILDREN'S THEATRE COMMITTEE.   As soon as a chairman is designated, he should organize his committee to cover each separate phase of the sponsoring operation. Specific members must be made responsible for the following activities:

> Publicity
> Ticket sales
> School liaison
> House management
> Transportation of school children
> Community public relations
> Housing and meals (if required)

Sometimes not all of these activities require attention. For example, certain sponsoring groups, notably school systems and principals' associations, can ignore such matters as community public relations and school liaison; performances will probably be given on school time, and all contacts are made within the schools.

Certain members of the children's theatre committee must

be responsible for all arrangements at the auditorium. Dates and times must be made definite, with no chance for misinterpretation. If a local stage crew is to be used, its members must be informed about the specific staging requirements of the play and about the company's arrival time. Any necessary union help, electrical service men, and janitors must be on hand to assist in the setup. Arrangements must be made for sound amplification. The stage must be cleared of anything which is likely to interfere with the efficient setup and operation of the visiting production. Dressing room and make-up facilities must be cleared and made ready for occupancy.

If the sponsor contracts to provide overnight housing and meals for a visiting company, certain committee members should be assigned to make these arrangements. Some companies prefer hotel or motel accommodations while others are just as happy split into groups of two's and three's in private homes. Elaborate transportation arrangements are sometimes needed to get performers to and from the auditorium at specified hours. Meals provided by sponsors are usually a great help to the producing organization, especially if they are served at the place of performance. This is especially true between performances when the removal of costumes and make-up can create serious complications.

The chairman of the children's theatre committee should always be one of the sponsoring group's ablest executives, able to inspire confidence in his co-workers and willing to delegate responsibility. If he plans well, he should find it possible to devote his efforts to general supervision of the work of the committee, concentrating on the overall progress of the operation. He should not be burdened with the routine of ticket sales or ushering. He should receive reports from his committee members often enough so that he knows the total picture at any moment and can stimulate further effort where it is most needed. He should be "public relations minded," able to communicate effectively with local school authorities and to further their mutual interests. Especially at the time of performance he should be free of routine duties so that he can concentrate on public relations. When the production is over, the chairman should be expected to submit a complete attendance and financial report to the parent organization, together with his recommendations for the improvement of future operations.

If possible, the children's theatre chairman should be continued in office for more than one year, since it takes about that long to learn his job and establish the contacts which are needed to assure success. In organizations where annual rotation of the chairmanship is a standard policy, a vice-chairman should by all means work closely with the chairman to insure continuation of contacts and policies and to carry through with improvements in the operation. At best, however, the results are not as satisfactory as they would be if the chairmanship remained constant for at least two seasons.

THE CHILDREN'S THEATRE BOARD.   Many sponsoring groups have discovered the advantage of assembling an advisory board from the membership of other community organizations interested in the welfare of children. In these cases invitations from the principal sponsoring group are extended to the board of education, various parent-teacher associations, local museums, art galleries, libraries, churches, recreation departments, and other service clubs and community agencies that work with children.

A board composed of such a diversity of specialists needs to be carefully oriented to the philosophy of children's theatre production and what it can mean to children. The chief advantage of such a board is the broad point of view it brings to its work. The members are respected leaders who will bring prestige to the children's theatre operation. If they are convinced of the value of the program they will be an invaluable spearhead for its acceptance throughout the community.

The board considers available programs and probable costs of each and then makes recommendations to the principal sponsoring group. In some organizations this board remains purely advisory. In others it takes on executive functions and is then subdivided, duties being assigned as they are within the children's theatre committee.

THE INDEPENDENT CORPORATION.   After a sponsoring group has been engaged in operations for some time and its program has become quite extensive, it sometimes considers it advisable to establish its own independent theatre organization. The new group frequently uses its parent committee or children's theatre board as a nucleus for the new corporation's board of directors. One of the first articles of incorporation prescribes the composition of the board itself. The theatre is given a title; a constitution and bylaws are established; subscription and ticket memberships are established; and standard operating procedures are defined. The new corporation is then in a position to contract directly with professional agencies and local or regional producers for the programs that will comprise its season. As a legally independent body, this corporation can provide for its own future development without jeopardizing the program of the parent organization. It can engage in operations considerably more extensive than are feasible when the children's theatre is simply one of the parent body's many community service projects.

The financial responsibility assumed by such a group should force it to consider its prospects of success very carefully. Normally a group does not take such a step until it is well acquainted with the community, its needs, and its resources.

The people most deeply involved should have appraised the total picture firsthand and should certainly see to it that key people in the community are represented and actively supporting the aims of the corporation. They may even be fortunate enough to receive from the parent body and affiliated groups a substantial reserve fund to fall back on in case of need while the corporation is building its name and reputation.

If the expanding program of sponsorship which showed the need for a children's theatre board has not led the group into the field of actual production, it is quite likely that the establishment of an independent corporation will do so.

PRODUCING ORGANIZATIONS

All of the people who assist in the complex process of bringing a script to life in the presence of an audience, and whose work we have been discussing in the preceding chapters, are no different from their counterparts in the adult theatre. Many children's theatres, in fact, exist simply as extensions of established adult theatre organizations, using the same directors, designers, technicians, and actors. Two things, however, complicate the producer's organizational pattern in the children's theatre beyond what is normally required in the adult theatre: getting in touch with the child audience, and the occasional need for children in the cast.

ACCESS TO THE CHILD AUDIENCE. Obviously children can attend the theatre only when interested adults make it possible for them to do so. Although most children would probably respond enthusiastically to an invitation to see one of their favorite stories on the stage, it often takes some effort to convince adults who order the children's lives that such an experience would be worthwhile.

For this reason the children's theatre producer must often

solicit community support. He may organize an *advisory board* made up of educators, community leaders and service club representatives. Such a body can be most helpful in interpreting the program to the community and in clearing the way for integration with the school program. It goes without saying that unless the schools are willing to lend their cooperation the children's theatre will have a bumpy uphill climb.

A producer may discover that school cooperation is easier to get if the production is brought to the audience rather than requiring the audience to be brought to the production. Thus a very real transportation problem is minimized. The decision to tour to various schools within the community brings with it a galaxy of other problems, both artistic and administrative. And an extension of the tour to other cities will involve a whole series of sponsoring organizations whose problems the producer must help to solve.

SECURING CHILD ACTORS. A close affiliation with the elementary school system, the city recreation department, or various private studio, library, or museum programs for children may be brought about as the producer discovers a need for child performers in his casts. The simpler these arrangements can be the better. Frequently, however, a producer needs to expand his program in children's theatre to include classes in creative dramatics, puppetry, and related fields in order to satisfy the intense interest generated among the children who have appeared or hope to perform in the children's theatre. An entire series of plays done by the children may result from these mutual interests and cooperation.

COMPLEX ORGANIZATIONAL STRUCTURES. The most complex patterns of organization arise from the cooperative efforts of several community agencies and an independent children's theatre corporation. One result may be both the production and the sponsorship of an extended series of children's theatre performances, perhaps involving both resident and touring productions which encompass an entire school system as well as surrounding communities. Directors, technicians, and managers may be hired for each unit of the series. Contracts may be written with local colleges, private studios, high schools, and even with distant professional and nonprofessional troups. Elaborate schemes of promotion and ticket sales may be devised which require the combined efforts of many people. Such ambitious programs as these usually evolve after several years of continuous effort, and they have an enormous impact on the community.

Other elaborate organizational schemes may come about as a result of an alliance between a children's theatre producer and some special resource of the community—an arts foundation, a settlement house, a museum, or art gallery. One party to such an alliance may provide the facilities for production and the other the personnel—actors, directors, technicians. One party may act in a purely advisory capacity, or both may be actively engaged in carrying out designated portions of the operation.

In all programs which rely upon the cooperative functioning of several groups of people, it is important to keep the lines of communication as clear as possible and responsibility for each of the necessary phases of the operation clearly fixed. Too many cooks may indeed spoil the broth of children's drama. The director cannot be hamstrung by a number of committees who must rule on each decision he has to make. The aim of organization should be to clarify, not to confuse. The group's primary purpose is to bring the very best theatre experiences to the greatest number of children. All assignments should be made from this point of view, all alliances established to bring about this result.

BUSINESS MANAGEMENT

Common to all children's theatre organizations, both sponsoring and producing, are the problems usually classified under business management—in general terms, the problems involved in bringing the audience and the play together.

Frequently the director of a producing organization is his own business manager. Even when he has assistants to handle or to help with business matters, it is his responsibility to advise on the proper conduct of promotion and publicity to carry through the aims of the children's theatre and the scheme of the particular production. The meticulousness with which the business affairs are handled may easily mean the success or failure of an entire children's theatre operation. The director should therefore certainly enlist the aid of several competent people. It will pay him to devote some effort to training his business manager and helpers so that they can take primary responsibility for this important phase of the operation. He should be able to do this without jeopardizing the artistic success of the production—a responsibility the director cannot delegate. The problems of business management involve promotion, publicity, costs, ticket sales, transportation, and accounting.

PROMOTION

One of the first and most important tasks of any children's theatre producing or sponsoring organization is establishing prestige for children's theatre in the community. No time should be lost in initiating an active program for broadcasting information about the aims and objectives of the activity, for pointing out the needs of children and how children's theatre will help to satisfy them.

A PLANNED CAMPAIGN. It is impossible to overemphasize the importance of a planned campaign extending over several years and never really relaxed. Part of this campaign would be conferences with school administrators as well as scheduled appearances of effective speakers and demonstrations at PTA meetings, service clubs, and church organizations. Contacts with key newspaper editors or reporters, television personalities, and radio interviewers can bring about wide discussion of the purposes of the local children's theatre and its plans for the future. Attractively designed brochures help to call the attention of the community to the program. All material, speeches, and contacts should be kept on a high plane, worthy of the purposes of the activity. As the program grows, a certain amount of stress can be placed upon accomplishments, but most of the emphasis in a promotion campaign should be directed toward goals to be achieved.

SEASONAL PROMOTION. A fairly large part of the promotional effort of an organization is naturally concentrated at the beginning of each new season before the first play is given. Purely promotional items are likely to be mixed with those more accurately classed as publicity. Even so, the promotion campaign at this point is better focused upon the specifics of the season than upon generalities of children's theatre. The season itself should exemplify the basic principles being promoted in the total campaign.

The opening play, usually a dramatization of a well-loved familiar story, is calculated to attract the utmost attention. This is usually a play with a boy protagonist, since both girls and boys are attracted by such plays. It should be a play full of color and life, excitement, and idealism. It should attract adults as well as children, thereby assuring parental support for the rest of the season. The attraction of the first play should generate enough momentum throughout the community to carry through to succeeding plays, which may not be so popular but which merit an equal space in a balanced program.

Succeeding plays should of course contrast in type with the first, but the season to be sold on a single ticket should be carefully constructed to appeal to a specific age range. As indicated in Chapter 3, interests vary roughly according to age, and it is therefore unwise to plan a season which contains plays appealing to different ages. The wisest plan, at least at first, is to direct the series toward a middle elementary group, taking care that each play contains elements which have some appeal on either side of this group. As soon as it can be managed, two seasons for different ages should be planned, perhaps one for fourth graders and younger, and one for those in fifth grade and above. It is difficult to justify promoting the sale of single season tickets which include plays appealing to first through ninth graders.

If the season's offerings represent a wide variety of historical periods, of male and female protagonists, of poetic and realistic qualities, and of intellectual and sensual appeal, the promotion committee's job of furthering the educational functions of children's theatre is made much easier.

TEACHER'S AIDS. An excellent practice that is common in both the professional and the nonprofessional children's theatre is that of supplying teachers with instructional materials they can use to prepare youngsters for the theatre experience. Care should be taken, however, that the climax or outcome of the play is not revealed by such material, for to do so would be to rob the children of one of the greatest joys of seeing the play performed.

Instead of simply referring the teacher to a variety of readings on the subject of the play, the promotion committee should condense a reasonable amount of background information that may arouse interest in the subject of the play, its historical perspective, its author, or in the social or economic conditions which gave rise to the story. This information, perhaps with suggestions of stories related to the play, should be distributed in either mimeographed or printed form to the teachers whose groups will be attending a performance. Such information can be used in a number of ways, from providing motivation for individual projects to group activities of various kinds.

Regardless of what is actually done with these teaching aids, the promotion committee should consider its time and effort well spent in establishing good will and a feeling of cooperation for the mutual benefit of teachers and the children's theatre.

PUBLICITY

Any scheme which is designed to attract an audience to performances of a specific play is called publicity. The season, too, is usually publicized prior to the first play. Publicity is calculated to produce an immediate effect, whereas promotion is directed toward a long-range goal.

Publicity is usually aimed at two groups of people: the children and their parents. Since they exert pressures on one another, convincing one group or the other is really only half the job. The extent to which either group must be persuaded depends upon the conditions under which performances are given.

TO REACH CHILDREN.   If the children's theatre has the support of the school system, publicity may be limited simply to the distribution of attractively designed handbills to each child in the grades concerned. These bills will contain the title or titles, a brief description of the subject, admission price, and the dates, places, and times of the ticket sale and performances. They will not be distributed so long in advance that the children will forget the essential information or that their enthusiasm will cool by the time the actual sale comes along.

If for some reason the children's theatre is not permitted to publicize through the schools, the publicity committee is obliged to seek out other channels to reach the children. Artistically designed and colorful posters placed in strategic locations about town, in children's apparel sections of department stores, in shoe stores, in libraries and museums will help attract youngsters' attention to the program. Educational or even commercial television stations will frequently cooperate with a worthy project by contributing time for spot announcements during periods of heavy child viewing. Novel displays of costumes, properties, or scenic models placed in shop windows, lobbies, or galleries are certain to arouse interest in the program. The essential information—dates, times, places, and admission price—should be included in all forms of publicity.

Children are always thrilled when characters in costume make an invited appearance in the classroom to tell about the play. A short sequence from the actual play is sometimes done, or a terse synopsis of the plot may be sufficient to arouse their curiosity. If handbills can be distributed as part of this appearance, all the better.

Contests of several kinds frequently serve to stimulate interest in the play, such as a "Typical Tom Sawyer" or a "Real-life Cinderella" nominated from each school in the system and judged by a board from the children's theatre. Some groups regularly select a winning program cover design or even a scenic design from those submitted by school children. Champion ticket sellers from a Scout troop or Campfire Girls may be rewarded with a free season ticket.

It is well to remember that children are reached more effectively through visual material than through text. However, a minimum amount of factual information is always necessary.

Since children do not always get the facts straight, and since parents usually insist on some sort of verification, it is helpful to have a supply of "take home" handbills near each display or publicity center.

TO REACH PARENTS.   Newspaper stories and feature articles accompanied by pictures attract the attention of both children and their parents. As a general rule, news stories are devoted exclusively to the current production; but feature stories can sometimes be built around the promotional aspects of the children's theatre, its progress, its goals, and interesting sidelights— all of which will be of value in acquainting parents with the total program. Publicity committees should have supplies of news releases with photographs—preferably of local people or cast members in costume, against a fairly light background—ready to supply to newspapers at a moment's notice. The editorial staff of the paper almost always prefers to select specific items from such material. Lists of casts and crews should always accompany these releases, since newspapers are more interested in reporting the activities of specific people than of nebulous organizations.

Prominent local columnists can sometimes be persuaded to devote a single article or a series to the children's theatre. Local television personalities—the woman who has a sustaining homemaking series or the MC of a locally produced variety show, for example—are often pleased to devote a portion of one or more programs to the activities of the children's theatre. Sometimes a short sequence from the play can be presented, though care must be taken that TV rights retained by the publishers of the play are not violated. Characters in costume can be interviewed, or a special talent may be displayed. Since these are usually daytime programs, and hence not watched by the youngsters who attend the children's theatre, the material and its format must be geared to parents who will be watching. Again, the essential information about the performances should be included.

Something of the same sort of brief presentation might be planned for a PTA meeting, a luncheon meeting of the Kiwanis or Lions clubs, or for an afternoon session of the church women's society or the library board. Emphasis in all of these presentations should be upon the purposes and goals of the children's theatre as exemplified by the present production. In most cases they will be oriented to promotion as well as to publicity.

Brochures can be mailed to membership lists of several prominent service organizations, alumni of the local university or college, and members of influential boards. This is considered by many to be the most effective method of promoting and publicizing a children's theatre program. The brochure itself should be tastefully designed, attractive but not garish. It should exemplify the basic spirit of the children's theatre, yet be of such quality that the people for whom it is intended will be likely to read it.

Novel schemes of publicizing children's plays can be developed to take advantage of special features of community life or of the plays themselves. If a local celebration is taking place, the children's theatre might contribute or take part. A "Children's Theatre Week" has sometimes been proclaimed by the mayor and observed in several ways. The more novel the scheme is, however, the greater chance there is of offending the sensibilities of some people. Producing organizations must always remember that they represent a basically educational endeavor; even though they are obliged to consider its business aspects the children's theatre can exist only on the good will and faith of the community in its higher purposes. Even in this day of high pressure advertising, the children's theatre can easily negate all previous promotional campaigns with just one publicity scheme that reflects bad taste.

Costs of Sponsorship and Production

An appraisal of costs is the first duty of the business manager. There can be no set formula for budgeting either for production or sponsorship, since every organization has different items which appear regularly on its budget. Furthermore, simplicity or elaborateness of the production materially affects the proportionate amounts assigned to the different departments. The amount of usable equipment on hand from previous productions also affects the cost figures of a given production.

A sponsoring organization will be concerned with the following items commonly included in a children's theatre budget:

1. *Production fees.* The charges made by a visiting company for a definite number of performances are always specified in the contract drawn up by the producer or booking agency and signed by an agent of the sponsoring group. This fee is usually large and represents a major item of expense to the sponsor, though the actual sum will depend upon the size and elaborateness of the production and the distance the company must travel. This expense item is not necessarily itemized in the contract.

2. *Labor.* Another substantial sum in some sponsorship budgets is assigned to labor. Some stages on which children's theatre producing companies appear, even in some high schools, are unionized. Even if union stage hands are not required, sponsors are often obligated to provide help for setting up or striking the sets, for which they must often pay. Some theatres require that their own house manager be hired for a minimum number of hours. Janitors and electricians are also often included in the labor budget.

3. *Theatre rental.* Unless a suitable auditorium is donated,

anything from a nominal charge to a major appropriation may have to be assigned for theatre rental. Sponsors should make certain that services to be included in the rental fee are spelled out in the contract. Services of janitors, house manager, and even the union stage manager may constitute a part of the rental charges.

4. *Meals and housing.* If the contract provides that meals and housing for the visiting company are to be provided, these will constitute additional items of expense. A sponsor can often arrange to have both services donated by its members, thus saving the organization a considerable sum.

5. *Advertising and house expenses.* Costs of newspaper advertising, posters, programs, and tickets can sometimes be eliminated if it is possible to obtain donation of these services. Costs of transporting ticket sellers to the schools, of ushers' uniforms, of painted signs, and ticket booths must also be included.

A sponsoring group naturally tries to keep all of these items within reasonable limits. Care should be taken, however, that elimination of an item does not also eliminate an essential service or jeopardize the eventual success of the program. It is equally a mistake to assume obligations which cannot possibly be met with income, whether from the single play or the season as a whole. Sometimes a program must be initiated in a somewhat less elaborate way to assure financial solvency and build upon a solid foundation.

A producing organization will be concerned with the following items.

1. *Royalties.* It should be assumed that any play worth producing carries with it a royalty fee, the payment of which constitutes permission to perform the play in the presence of an audience—few published children's plays are in the public

domain. Special rates are often made when a considerable number of performances are to be given.

2. *Scripts.* If the play is available in book form, it is usually cheaper to buy copies from the publisher than to secure permission to have copies duplicated for each cast member and each key member of the crew.

3. *Scenery.* The costs of scenery vary according to the design, the number of usable stock items on hand, and the material which can be recovered from former construction. Units of scenery sometimes become capital investments after a play because they can be used in future productions. Platforms, a portal, draperies, and scrims would be such units.

4. *Costumes.* The cost of costuming a play will depend on the same variables as those just listed. If all items are well made and alteration possibilities for future productions are kept in mind during construction, a good stock of costumes is soon built up, and this may reduce costume expenses for many future plays. Even so, costuming children's plays is likely to be expensive, and the charges for dry cleaning after performances will seem exhorbitant unless this item has been anticipated.

5. *Make-up.* While make-up costs are usually a minor item in a budget, they may be substantial if the play requires a quantity of national or racial skin coloring or fantastic animals. Wigs are also expensive, either to purchase or to rent.

6. *Properties.* Compared to the items thus far mentioned, charges for properties are likely to appear modest indeed, unless a substantial amount of furniture has been bought, or some valuable borrowed property gets lost or broken.

7. *Special effects.* Costs of special effects mechanisms vary considerably from play to play. Usually they can be made inexpensively from materials on hand, unless a flying contrivance or other elaborate equipment is involved.

8. *Lights.* Basic lighting equipment is likely to be fur-

nished with the auditorium; if not, it should be part of the capital investment of the group. Only rarely will the purchase of equipment have to be charged to a single production budget, though some organizations may regularly have to figure on rental charges for lighting equipment. Color gelatins and special effects apparatus which must be built must be allowed for in the budget.

9. *Sound.* Costs of recordings, manual sound effects, tapes, and rental of any necessary equipment should be included in the budget. If the organization owns its sound reproducing equipment, this becomes a capital investment and is not carried in any one production budget.

10. *Transportation.* If the production is set up and performed in some location other than where it is built, transportation charges must be expected. In the case of a touring production, truck and bus or car rentals may easily run these charges into the highest single cost item in the entire budget.

11. *Meals and lodging.* Meals and lodging for the company figure in the production budget only in touring situations or under unusual resident conditions. When they are required they can amount to a large sum in a short time.

In addition to the foregoing items, producers may have to budget some of the same expenses incurred by sponsors, such as theatre rental, labor, advertising and house costs. Whether or not these become major items will depend upon the exact producing situation, whether resident or touring, whether productions are in the group's own theatre or a rented auditorium, whether they are part of an inclusive program of both adult and children's plays, and so forth.

Generally speaking, costs of producing children's theatre plays are likely to run rather high. While the size of the budget is not always a yardstick of success, there is usually a positive correlation between the cost and the quality of the production. Good costume materials are expensive, and there are often many people to be dressed in period fashions. Special staging devices and effects calculated to delight and hold the attention of the child audience may run costs up in spite of everything. The only solution is to set a minimum standard of quality for a production and then refuse to compromise. A way can usually be found to meet costs with income.

Bookings

Financial arrangements between sponsors and producing groups may vary a good deal. The usual contract made by professional children's theatres stipulates a guaranteed amount plus a percentage of the gross receipts. The producer thus has a very real interest in the success of the publicity campaign and in the reputation his group establishes in the community. Some of these companies obtain their engagements through booking agencies. These usually provide abundant publicity and study materials relevant to the production and make every effort to help the local sponsor get the required attendance.

Some noncommercial producers, especially colleges, universities, and private studios, book performances at a flexible rate which takes into consideration the size of the community, the seating capacity of the auditorium, the distance the group must travel in order to perform, and the accommodations such as meals and lodging which the sponsoring group can provide. Producers who confine their tours to a limited area often prefer to contract on a flat fee basis determined by average expenditures of previous tours. Occasionally these fees can be reduced by specified amounts if the sponsor is willing to provide meals or lodging for the visiting company. Some noncommercial producing groups, usually those within the vicinity of the sponsor, will accept a contract to produce a play specifically for a given occasion. The sponsor may agree to a "cost plus" or a "shared cost" arrangement, or it may set aside a given amount for the producer to use in staging the play.

Arrangements between producers and sponsors should not be considered complete until a contract is signed by both parties, obligating the producer to present the play at the dates and times specified and the sponsor to make certain arrangements and to pay the fee, usually before the company leaves the premises.

Admissions

Balancing production or sponsorship costs with income is an important part of the business manager's responsibilities. While a certain amount of income may be in the form of subsidy, most children's theatres are obliged to consider ticket sales their major source of operating revenue.

Setting the price or prices of tickets is a comparatively standard procedure. Obviously adults, with the exception of teachers accompanying groups of students, should be charged more than children, and children should not be admitted for less than the cost of admission to local movies. Ticket prices should be neither so high that the performance is priced out of the market nor so low that the experience tends to become undervalued in the community. A season ticket for all plays should cost less per show than the same number of single admissions.

With these principles in mind, the business manager calculates the number of seats available for the entire run of the production and divides this figure roughly in half, for only under the most unusual circumstances can he count on full houses at every performance. Dividing probable costs by anticipated admissions will give an average admission price, at least within a limited range. If the figure seems too high for parents in the particular community concerned he may reduce it, though he must then realize that he will have to compensate by either increasing attendance or reducing costs. If there is reasonable assurance of a good ticket sale through the public schools a reduced admission price may not be disastrous.

Scheduling performances in the largest available auditorium is unfortunately not uncommon in children's theatre. For the sake of both performers and children in the audience, a theatre seating no more than a thousand is vastly preferable. Even this is too large for intimate contact between actors and audience, for optimum sight lines and acoustics. An auditorium capacity of six to eight hundred is considerably better. Better a slightly higher admission price than risking an unsatisfying theatre experience for the children.

Free admission for needy children is a consistently recurring problem and is especially difficult in the case of total school or grade attendance at the play. Where it is possible to arrange free admission, the business manager should inform all teachers affected that a special fund has been arranged to make sure that no child will be denied admission. He can usually arrange such a fund through service groups or foundations. Such groups are sometimes willing to subsidize complete performances for settlement house children, or even a special performance in the children's ward of the local hospital. Any teacher in the system should be able to make application for a ticket for a needy child; often she helps the child to earn the ticket by doing small chores after school, at recess, or during the noon hour, thus giving him the feeling that he has paid his way just like all the others.

TICKET SALES

Permission to sell tickets in the schools is always the goal of the children's theatre business manager. Ideally, entire grades attend a performance; study of the play or related material is incorporated in the curriculum; and the school collects the admission fees. This practice is standard in many cities and is growing with the increased integration of children's theatre with the total school program.

Some school systems, however, have definite policies which prevent teachers from collecting money for any cause, regardless of its worth. In this situation the business manager can usually get permission to sell tickets in the school halls on specified dates. An attractive but simple booth for this purpose could become something of a trademark of the children's theatre; its appearance often generates considerable excitement.

If even this access to the schools is denied, other community resources must be tapped. A centrally located drugstore, bank, department store, or toy shop may welcome an attractive ticket booth. The children's room of the library may be the announced place of the ticket sale. None of these will be as effective in reaching the children as the schools; however, if publicity is well handled there need be no fear of empty houses.

Receiving and handling the children once they arrive at the theatre is the responsibility of the house manager, but the box office ticket sale remains the business manager's job. Regardless of the way in which the children arrive, the ticket sellers must be ready for them. If the youngsters come by busloads and all at once, the situation will be eased if the tickets have been purchased ahead of time and are in the hands of the teachers. The group can then proceed directly into the auditorium. If tickets have not been obtained in advance the box office can set aside the number of tickets previously requested by the school, putting them in an envelope clearly marked as to recipient and amount due. As each group arrives it is a relatively simple matter for the representative of that school to call for the tickets, pay for them, and escort the group directly into the auditorium. Some such system can also be used with individual rooms or grades, but this involves considerably more work.

The arrival of small, disorganized, heterogeneous groups of children, who may or may not be accompanied by parents, can be extremely difficult to handle. Those who come early are no real problem for ticket sellers, but just before curtain time the lobby may suddenly fill up with impatient youngsters who are afraid of missing part of the play. It is never a good idea to allow long lines to form. If several ticket stations can be spaced around the lobby and a few members of the business manager's staff are on hand to distribute the children to the different stations, the situation can be handled with reasonable efficiency. Experience in each community soon shows how many stations are needed to cope with the problem. When only one box office is used, long lines are inevitable, a delay in curtain time will result, and the patience of children who arrived early will be sorely taxed. A serious problem of discipline may be caused by inefficient ticket sale procedures.

TRANSPORTATION

A special committee is sometimes appointed to arrange the transportation of school children to the place of performance; sometimes this responsibility rests with the business manager or with the schools attending the play. This problem is unique to children's theatre. Adults can get themselves to a performance by one means or another, but children must be brought. School busses are by far the most common means of transporting children to the theatre, especially when entire grades or whole schools attend a performance in a body. Since the busses must be returned for their normal duties by school closing time, the hours of performance must conform to their schedules. Even so, they are the most obvious answer for the school which must transport its children across town or to a neighboring community to attend a play.

In large cities, busses or streetcars may have to be chartered to transport children to a play. The additional cost of this transportation is sometimes included in the price of the theatre ticket, and sometimes special tickets are sold just for that purpose. In some cases the children's theatre can persuade a civic service organization to underwrite the cost of chartered busses or streetcars; others have solved the problem by appointing the president of the transit company to the children's theatre board.

The job of the transportation committee is really not complete until the children are safely back home, or at least back to their points of departure. It takes considerable effort to get many children to the right place at the right time, and in the process some adjustments in the performance schedule may have to be made. For this reason it is advisable to complete all transportation arrangements as early as possible and to keep those concerned informed of any needed changes in schedule.

Saturday and evening performances seldom present a transportation problem, since parents are usually free to bring their children by cars or on public conveyances.

ACCOUNTS AND THE FINANCIAL REPORT

Meaningful and realistic budgets for children's theatre productions can be set up only after accurate records of income and expenditures have been kept for at least one season. An elaborate system of accounting is seldom necessary, though every business manager should form the habit of promptly recording every payment he makes, classifying it as scenery, properties, royalty, and the like. A simple system of columns for each major category of expense, together with a running balance column, should provide an accurate financial picture at a glance. As soon as the production is over and all bills have been paid, a summary account can be compiled without much trouble. However, the business manager should never make the mistake of postponing his accounting until the whole operation is finished. He should be expected to act as "watchdog" over the budget, to caution about excessive expenditures in any category, and to keep the technicians informed as to the status of their allotments. He can do this only if he has an up-to-the-minute record of both cash and credit expenditures. He needs to work ahead, anticipating needs, in order to forestall a financial crisis. The final accounting for the production should not come as a shock, either to him or to those who spent the money.

HOUSE MANAGEMENT

The house manager is responsible for the well-being of the children once they reach the auditorium. He works closely with the business manager in planning traffic lines in the lobby, making sure that groups and individuals who have their tickets proceed directly into the house. The ticket takers, ushers, and audience supervisors are under his jurisdiction. It makes no difference in his duties whether a sponsoring or a producing group is presenting the play.

SEATING

Seating arrangements in the auditorium are the house manager's biggest problem. Whether or not seats are to be reserved is likely to depend upon whether large groups arrive together or attendance is in small groups and individuals. One good plan is to designate sections of the house for large groups during school matinees and to sell individual reserved seats for evenings and Saturday performances.

Specific seating arrangements for school matinees must always be planned ahead of time. A system of rotating the most desirable sections of the house among groups or schools which attend regularly may prove to be the fairest way to handle the problem. If there is considerable discrepancy between the ages of children attending in large groups, the smaller youngsters should be seated nearer the front so that the larger children will not block their view.

The ushers should be informed of all arrangements and know where each group is to be seated. As the groups arrive the ushers should direct them down as many aisles as possible and make certain that no vacant seats are left to throw off the section arrangement. This can be managed if the ushers stand ahead of the row being filled until each seat is occupied, then move back to the next, and so on until the section is filled.

When seats are reserved there should be someone to act as traffic director in the lobby, or the ticket takers themselves can tell each child which aisle is closest to his seat. An usher at that aisle then escorts him to his seat. If attendance at reserved seat performances is large, a large corps of ushers will be needed to keep traffic moving and to avoid long delays in seating the children.

USHERS

Some groups arrange with the school safety patrol, Boy or Girl Scouts, or some other organized body of children to usher at performances of the children's theatre throughout a season. Other groups prefer to draw their ushers from sons and daughters of sponsors. Either way, the corps should be trained in courteous and efficient performance of its duties. Unless they understand thoroughly the arrangement of the seats in the house and the system of designating the seat on the ticket stub, confusion is bound to occur. They should also understand the importance of greeting each customer, of walking before him down the aisle, of standing in front of the row and of asking pardon if those already seated must be disturbed. This is all part of providing a complete theatre-going experience for the children.

Scout uniforms or uniforms of the school patrol are perfectly acceptable as ushers' uniforms, though some theatres prefer to have a distinguishing uniform for their ushers. Arm bands, cummerbunds, or diagonal bands of bright material across the chest set ushers apart and make them easily recognizable to the children in the audience. A simple designation is usually preferable to an elaborate costume.

Controlling the Audience

When ushers and adult supervisors cooperate in a children's theatre audience, a pleasurable theatre experience is likely to be in store for all. All of the factors likely to cause distractions can usually be prevented. Aisle racing should never be permitted. Any tendency on the part of children to go in and out of the house for drinks of water or to look for friends or for better seats should be promptly and emphatically discouraged.

Whether his seat was reserved or not, once a child has been seated, he should be encouraged to regard it as his for the duration of the performance. Producing or sponsoring organizations which seek additional revenue by selling candy or popcorn in the lobby should remember that this merely encourages the movie-going habit of leaving the seat at any time, littering the floor, crunching noisily during the performance. These results are inevitable, and they cause a great deal of disturbance.

A wise practice is to ask each child who attends to *check* whatever candy, gum, or toys he has with him before he enters the house, assuring him that he will get them back right after the performance.

Adult supervisors should be spaced around the house, ready to handle any emergency that may arise or quell disturbances. Unsupervised children, especially at Saturday performances, often display a sense of freedom and holiday exuberance which is distracting to the other children. Usually the quiet presence of the adult supervisors in the audience is enough to discourage such disturbances and remind the children of their manners; if not, the supervisors should inform them that if they refuse to consider the other children they will be asked to leave. Unfortunately, a few rowdy youngsters in an audience are enough to spoil the performance for everyone, and producers owe it to their customers to maintain the very best conditions possible for the enjoyment of the play.

Adults who assume these obligations should be warned about quelling normal audience involvement in the play by supressing vocal reactions. They must learn to distinguish normal responses from trouble making.

PROGRAMS

Most children's theatres have discovered the advantages of distributing printed programs only at evening or reserved seat performances. As discussed in Chapter 6, the information necessary for an understanding of the play is best given from the stage as a curtain speech—children are seldom interested in the names of the performers anyway. The only real use for a program, as far as they are concerned, is to take it home after the show as a momento. Unfortunately, they also find programs useful as airplanes during the performance unless parents or supervisors are there to quell the urge.

The house manager and his many assistants have a very important opportunity to complement the work of the director and actors. Not only can their efficient operation keep a performance on schedule by anticipating seating problems and keeping the director or stage manager informed as to the progress of the seating, but their effective control of the audience can assure a performance free of distraction. At intermissions their efforts to keep the children in their seats rather than allowing free travel in and out of the auditorium will mean few delayed curtains. The calmly efficient operation of the house is one of the most important aspects of the entire children's theatre enterprise.

EVALUATION

No discussion of organization and management problems would be complete without some mention of the process of evaluating the production after it has closed its run.

Sometimes a committee is specially charged with this responsibility; but even if the evaluation is carried through by the director and the children's theatre committee as a whole, the basis of future operations may well be established at this time. The attendance record is not the only criterion for the success of children's theatre; nor can a balanced budget always be taken as the final word on the production.

An effort must be made to judge the play and its staging from the point of view of the very highest standards of which the group is capable. Teachers and the children themselves should be encouraged to contribute their frank opinions to the evaluation committee. Evaluators should attend as many performances as possible. They should sit with the children and observe their reactions. Accepted standards of criticism, both literary and theatrical, should be applied, and recommendations for improvement should be as specific as possible. A satisfactory community response to the children's theatre means that as many children as possible were in attendance at the performance of an excellent play beautifully performed and staged. No group should be satisfied with less.

10 ∾

Children's Theatre
on Tour

ANY CHILDREN'S THEATRE organization which elects to tour brings untold pleasure to countless children who otherwise might never be exposed to the delightful experience of sharing in a live theatrical performance. The touring company also provides invaluable experiences for its members as they meet the challenges and enjoy the rewards of bringing a play into various communities.

As a result of requests from communities within the geographic areas they serve and also because of the educational benefits available to students participating in such programs, college and university theatres in increasing numbers are establishing children's theatre touring programs. Many high school drama groups are trouping children's plays to elementary schools within their communities. A number of community producing organizations also are presenting touring productions.

The scope of any touring program must be realistically determined according to the basic purposes and operational program of each individual organization. Obviously the educational or community theatre cannot undertake as extensive a program as can the professional group whose members devote their time exclusively to working in productions. Except in cases where the curriculum provides for academic credit for an entire term of touring theatre, the usual pattern for educational and other nonprofessional groups is a series of week-end appearances. Bookings are made according to geographic area to cut travel time to a minimum.

All the members of the production staff will find that their plans will be affected to some extent when a play is to go on the road. Business management also becomes somewhat more complex in the touring situation, although the principles of sound organization and financial planning apply equally whether the show is to play in one theatre or a dozen. Because of these similarities the discussion of the business aspects of touring was included in Chapter 9.

THE DIRECTOR'S ROLE

From the director's point of view, touring poses problems similar to those encountered in any extended series of performances. However, going on the road is certain to be an exciting experience for young actors, and the director is sometimes hard put to control their exuberant spirits and conserve precious energy to withstand the rigors of continuous travel and the pressures of constant adaptation to new environments.

Realistically speaking, it is unwise to undertake touring outside the home community with a cast of children or even high school students. If the production requires a mixed cast of children and adults, the children must be carefully selected; their parents must be thoroughly acquainted with all plans and arrangements; special provisions must be made to safeguard their health while they are away from home.

When a play is to tour the director carefully selects all the members of his company. Customarily only a skeleton backstage crew goes with the show. This group may include only the stage manager and the lighting and sound technicians, although sometimes a property crew head and a wardrobe and make-up crew head may be added to the company. Members of the cast normally double as crew members, each having a specific backstage assignment in addition to his role. Obviously then, stamina and a willingness to work are almost as vital as acting ability in touring children's theatre.

In addition, the director should bear in mind that even minor disharmony can lead to difficulty when a group lives and works together under circumstances that require them to make continuous adjustments to other groups and to a variety of living and working conditions. Negligible personality conflicts become magnified through continuous association. Once the director has assembled the company it is up to him to establish a working environment which will encourage company unity.

On the road the children's theatre touring group has an obligation to maintain a high moral tone and to strive diligently to leave a favorable impression in each community visited. Veterans of children's theatre tours often jokingly comment that they are expected to be "pure as the driven snow"—a remark that is not as facetious as it may seem. Communities do not ask too much when they expect exemplary behavior from individuals who come in to entertain their children.

Touring productions are booked into all types of communities; they are presented in auditoriums ranging from the most modern and complete to those offering only minimum facilities for staging plays; advance arrangements will vary from sponsor to sponsor, as will the warmth and quality of the reception extended the players. The company should not allow its performance to be adversely affected by substandard stages or inept sponsor arrangements. Frequently the most appreciative audiences gather in the most unlikely spots, and cool reception from adults in no way foreshadows indifference in the audience.

The director's presence is essential when the nonprofessional group goes on tour. He is able to keep the company functioning as a unified group; he serves as a liaison between the company, the sponsors, and the staff of each school or theatre visited; he carries out arrangements for meals and housing; he is able to note signs of fatigue or illness and takes steps to forestall major health problems; he can keep his finger on the pulse of the show, assuring that performances remain consistent throughout the run. In every respect he remains the stabilizing factor in the company.

SCENERY FOR TOURING PRODUCTIONS

The design and planning of scenery is usually materially affected when the production is to go on tour. The necessity for transporting scenery by truck and setting it up in a wide variety of auditoriums sometimes causes a technical staff to reduce the scenery to the point where it loses its effectiveness. However, if he has the children's interests at heart, the designer will make every effort to design as ideally for tour audiences as he would for the resident audience. Nevertheless, he will need to take a number of precautions.

All flats or wall sections will probably need to be supported by jacks rather than by stage braces. They can be loose-pin hinged to the flats and weighted with sandbags or stage weights to hold the unit steady. These can be easily removed for transport. Stage braces require the use of screws or pegs, and on many stages their use is forbidden both by the school administration and by the hardwood flooring of the stage.

All scenic units intended for touring should be carefully

designed to break down into segments or parts no larger than the dimensions of the bed of the truck which will transport them. No section should be too large to go through an ordinary doorway, or too bulky to be carried upstairs and around corners. As many units as possible should stack flat on the truck.

Since a variety of stage widths and heights are usually encountered on tour, the designer must know in advance what the dimensions will be in each case. Settings should always be designed to permit a certain amount of both expansion and compression in overall width. When extreme differences of stage height are to be encountered, scenic units should be of variable height, or the highest unit should be limited to the measurement of the lowest stage.

Standard parallels, or collapsible platform units, are often too bulky for stacking on a truck, and a supply of much simpler platform assemblies is advised for tour. These consist of flat sheets of $\frac{3}{4}''$ plywood, to which are bolted eight floor flanges. Pipe sections of any desired length and preferably $1\frac{1}{4}''$ in diameter are screwed into the flanges when setting up and removed when striking. These platforms are obviously not as sturdy as standard parallels, but they are substantial enough for most purposes, especially if patches of rubber are wired to the pipe ends to prevent slipping on the stage floor. The advantages of flat storage in the truck and reduced construction should make this a practical and popular solution to the problems of levels on tour.

Wagons for shifting sets are sometimes essential even on tour. While their size and weight are both formidable, the problem of off-stage storage is frequently even more serious. When no off-stage space exists, the designer can sometimes plan his setting to accommodate an unused wagon within the playing area, perhaps behind a unit presently in use, perhaps as part of that setting, the inside of the house, or the view

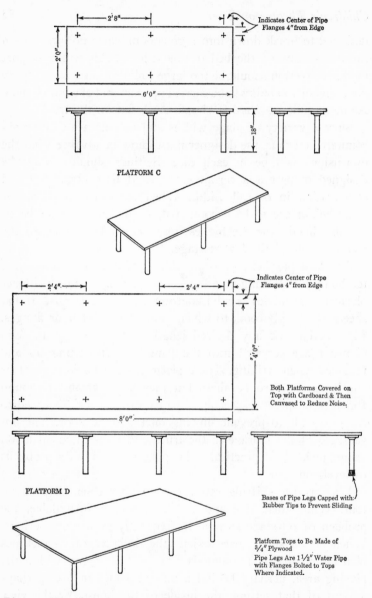

2' 8"

Indicates Center of Pipe
Flanges 4" from Edge

2' 0"

6' 0"

18"

PLATFORM C

2' 4"   2' 4"

Indicates Center of Pipe
Flanges 4" from Edge

3' 4"

Both Platforms Covered on
Top with Cardboard & Then
Canvased to Reduce Noise.

8' 0"

PLATFORM D

Bases of Pipe Legs Capped with
Rubber Tips to Prevent Sliding

Platform Tops to Be Made of
3/4" Plywood
Pipe Legs Are 1 1/2" Water Pipe
with Flanges Bolted to Tops
Where Indicated.

*Fig. 13. Working drawings showing the construction of easily dis-
assembled platforms for touring. Designs by Merlin E. Bement.*

to be seen through the doorway. Other scenic units may have to be similarly planned in order to make use of whatever dead storage space is available.

A false proscenium or portal—a free-standing unit that breaks down into transportable sections—is highly recommended for touring children's theatre groups which encounter many different proscenium widths. Its advantages are that it can be expanded and contracted somewhat and will contain the playing space within narrow limits on each stage regardless of existing dimensions. The proportions of the setting and properties, the effectiveness of the lighting, and the blocking of the actors will thus remain relatively constant.

This false proscenium should be set up before any other portion of the setting, and as far downstage as possible, just clear of the act curtain. It may be decorated in keeping with the design of the play itself, or it may be kept completely neutral, covered only with straight black drapes hung across the top and down the sides. Erecting a portal like the one shown at the bottom of Plate 21 takes about fifteen minutes. Crew members bolt together the three center span sections, bolt on the two side jacks, and tie on the covering drapes. A concerted effort pulls the entire structure erect, and the three-fold jacks are then opened up and weighted. A structure as solid as this can be used to support lighting instruments, cables, or even a special traveler for an inner curtain or scrim.

Once the portal is built, it can be used over and over, becoming something different for each play. Its versatility makes it a most reliable piece of standard touring equipment. Variations of the same basic idea can be used to enclose the acting area in drapes or to provide a mounting position for a sky drop in theatres which lack flexible lines for the suspension of scenery.

LIGHTING ON TOUR

Touring groups learn quickly that they cannot rely on finding any lighting facilities in many of the auditoriums in which they play. Such groups are advised, therefore, to carry with them everything they will need to light the production, from control boards to mounting devices.

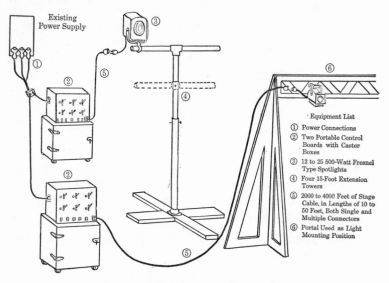

· Equipment List

① Power Connections
② Two Portable Control Boards with Caster Boxes
③ 12 to 25 500-Watt Fresnel Type Spotlights
④ Four 15-Foot Extension Towers
⑤ 2000 to 4000 Feet of Stage Cable, in Lengths of 10 to 50 Feet, Both Single and Multiple Connectors
⑥ Portal Used as Light Mounting Position

Fig. 14. A lighting setup for touring.

One useful assemblage of touring equipment is illustrated in the accompanying diagram. The heart of this system is two portable control boards which are connected to an existing power supply with alligator clips. Towers and a portal serve as mounting positions. Spotlights of the 500-watt Fresnel lens variety are mounted and connected with flexible cable to a control board. The spotlights, gelatin frames, tools, and supplies are carried in a caster box, and the boards also are enclosed in caster boxes for transportation. Setting up lighting arrangements for the average children's play with this equipment takes from two to four hours—not an unwarranted amount of time when one considers that an independent and flexible system makes possible a fair amount of lighting artistry.

ORGANIZING EQUIPMENT FOR TOURING

It has been noted that the designer must know the dimensions of every stage on which the production will appear. A simple questionnaire filled out by someone who is well acquainted with each theatre is a valuable source of information for all members of the production staff. This questionnaire should include spaces to record pertinent data about the stage and its equipment, the power source, the auditorium, dressing room facilities, access doors, and any other information the producer wishes to have at hand. This information later can be supplemented by the observations of the company director.

Even with such information in hand, however, it is well to be prepared for the unforeseen and to carry mirrors, an ironing board and iron, a ladder, extra drapes to mask off unusually high proscenium arches, a sky drop, stage weights, and any other equipment essential to efficient mounting procedure.

Careful organization and a continuous check on all the equipment and supplies that will go with the production will eliminate many problems. The stage manager keeps a master check list, plans a system for loading and unloading the truck, and supervises the setup in each auditorium. Each crew head must also have a complete list of the items for which he is responsible; he should work out a system for packing his supplies and follow it consistently. Sturdy, easily portable containers should be assembled to carry costumes, make-up, properties, lighting and sound equipment, tools, and supplies for emergency repairs.

Essentially, the keys to successful touring lie in the same artistry and organization a company brings to any quality production. The additional planning and preparation necessary to touring are a small price to pay for the rich rewards a producing organization will reap as it extends its operation to include an ever widening children's theatre audience.

11 ∾

Children's Theatre
Is a Profession

THE BIRTH OF A CHILDREN'S THEATRE

THE FOLLOWING ACCOUNT is undoubtedly fictitious, and yet it is typical of the way many children's theatres are started. A group of young matrons, all intelligent women with growing families, gathered for the first meeting of the neighborhood mothers' club. The routine of winter had begun—the children were in school; the bridge club had reconvened; household activities were relieved only by the usual community activities and occasional social events. Seeking release from this confining routine the mothers cast about for a project, one that would be different, something of a challenge, and an outlet for their creative energies. The logical course was to do something that also would benefit the children. But what could it be? Was there anything the community did not already provide? What project would fulfill their purpose?

Why not put on a play? This certainly should be challenging and fun for the adults, and a play for children should not be too difficult to produce. Children are easy to amuse, and everyone knows that they like dramatic entertainment. Certainly they should be able to find a play more appropriate for children than the westerns and crime shows that keep them transfixed before television sets for hours on end.

One mother had taken some drama courses in college and had been in several plays. She certainly should be able to direct the production. The auditorium at the neighborhood elementary school should be available for one Saturday afternoon. Perhaps the PTA would help by decorating the stage. Money? Oh, it shouldn't be too expensive. In fact, it should cost next to nothing. Everyone had a couple of evening dresses tucked away. These would do nicely to costume a fairy tale.

Someone volunteered to go to the library to see if the children's collection included a book of plays. Others formed a telephone committee to enlist the support of other housewives in the neighborhood. A few meetings, a week or so of rehearsal, a scramble through attics and storage closets, trips to local merchants to gather remnants and colored paper and other odds and ends not to be found in a dozen or so cooperative households, and the project was launched.

On the big day spots of rouge were applied to cheeks already flushed with fatigue and excitement. Makeshift costumes were donned. The mother assigned to take tickets rushed backstage to announce that the auditorium was almost filled and there still was a line in the lobby. The din was frightening. But as the house lights clicked out one by one something magic seemed to happen. Whistles and cheers were followed by an electric silence. The red, white, and blue border lights were flicked on, and the curtain opened on a stage decorated with crepe paper and cardboard cutouts arranged to represent a palace garden. The earnest actresses smiled bravely and set out to entertain their audience.

In retrospect, however, the whole thing seemed to have been rather unsatisfying. The stage decorations had looked terribly artificial, and, worse than that, homemade. In spite of heroic efforts to make them look like the raiment of fairies and princesses, the rejuvenated evening gowns seemed pathetically inadequate. The little play found in a collection of nonroyalty entertainments based on favorite fairy tales lacked excitement and meaning. Oh, yes, the children seemed to like it. They clapped sometimes, and they laughed a great deal. But did they laugh because the court chamberlain was an amusing character or because he was so obviously somebody's mother dressed and made up to look like a man and talking in a strained, gruff voice?

At their next meeting the mothers' club took stock and decided that perhaps this project had not been too rewarding after all. But then, they were only amateurs, and they did the best they could. Some suggested that they try something else next year—that all this had not been worth the effort. However, not everyone agreed. Didn't the unexpectedly large audience indicate something? Although there had been no intensive publicity campaign, a number of children had come from neighborhoods far away from the school. Might this not mean that there is more interest in children's theatre than the group ever suspected? If so many children came to see such a poorly publicized production, what might happen if there were some real promotion? If the audience seemed to enjoy this inadequate presentation, what might their reaction be to a good play well produced? Would a really well-organized children's theatre directed by someone with some background and talent have a chance of success? And wouldn't the community be a better place for its children if it offered them something truly fine in the way of dramatic entertainment?

Thus another children's theatre was launched. The same

energetic enthusiasm that carried them through their first production was put to work enlisting the support of other organizations. A steering committee was formed. A neighboring college children's theatre director was invited to conduct a workshop and to advise them on organization and production matters. Enough money was raised through the generosity of numerous community organizations interested in serving youth to subsidize a children's theatre for one year. It took effort, but a little skillful persuasion convinced the sponsoring organizations that the subsidy should be large enough to enlist the services of a trained director for the production program.

AN EVALUATION AND A CHALLENGE

Although individual circumstances differ, this fictitious account of the birth of a children's theatre reflects quite accurately events which have occurred countless times in cities and towns across the nation. However, the outcome is not always as fortunate, nor does it ever come about as quickly and easily as our story suggests. After one unsatisfying attempt many a producing organization is never heard from again. Sometimes members of the group fail to recognize the weaknesses of their amateurish efforts and continue to support a program which perpetuates a standard of mediocrity that does little to advance the cause of children's theatre.

For many years those of us concerned with children's theatre have looked with satisfaction upon the establishment of each new program. The movement is growing, we say; each day a new group springs into being. Soon the country will be alive with children's plays, and every youngster in the United States may eventually have a chance to see fine plays.

There is nothing wrong with these dreams, except that they are dreams. There is more involved in developing good children's theatre than working toward an increasing number of producing groups, groups whose enthusiasm all too often is born solely of good intentions. There is more to measuring success than gathering columns of impressive statistics, which are frequently misinterpreted. Even the very people who accept responsibility for nurturing the growth of children's theatre often abuse it by tolerant indulgence.

At its present stage of development the children's theatre movement may well pause to examine its motives, take stock of its assets, admit its liabilities, and point out specific directions toward achieving its goals.

An objective examination of children's theatre today would reveal that much substandard production is tolerated. Many plays repeatedly produced for child audiences lack literary merit and fail to present the greatest truths of our time. Many directors do not interpret their goals effectively to the community—some of them, in fact, are not too certain of those goals. Many children's theatre workers undervalue their services to a degree that causes administrators to respond by undervaluing the programs they represent. Some workers habitually substitute enthusiasm and sentimentality for factual knowledge and respect for their profession. For a profession it most certainly is.

Are we then to assume that there is no place in children's theatre for the housewife, the community youth organization, the classroom teacher, or any of the countless dedicated amateurs who each year devote untold numbers of hours to promoting and producing theatre for children? Should nonprofessional producing groups dim their lights, lock their doors, and surrender the field to companies producing plays as a means of livelihood? The answer here is a resounding *No!*

Children's theatre never could have reached its present level of achievement without the vision and persistent efforts of dedicated amateurs. Strong in numbers, venturesome in spirit, and firm in their conviction that children's theatre is worthy of time and effort, they have taken the lead away from the professional theatre, and there is little doubt that they will continue to dominate the field, challenged to achieve the level of excellence associated with professional work. Dedicated amateurs who set high standards and objectively evaluate each of their productions on the basis of those standards, constantly seeking better ways to bring theatre to children, can eventually eliminate forever the amateurish "kiddie show."

As more and more producing organizations turn to trained children's theatre directors for leadership, these specialists assume a large measure of responsibility for building children's theatre as a profession. Those who make children's theatre a career must accept the obligations of professional status. They must evaluate themselves and the programs they direct according to a few simple precepts, realizing that children's theatre will truly be a profession when the following standards are achieved:

1. It is recognized as on equal status with adult theatre programs. No theatre program is complete without the production of children's plays—but these should never be considered the season's "filler."
2. Those in charge of children's theatre programs respect their work. No one can do even a passable job while maintaining an attitude of condescension.
3. Directors are thoroughly trained in this specialized branch of theatrical production. An increasing number of colleges and universities must offer practical and theoretical training in child drama to outstanding candidates for the new professional children's theatre; and those chosen to implement such training programs must themselves be specially trained.
4. Children's theatre workers place a high value on their serv-

ices. Children's theatre is not second-rate theatre, and highly trained directors must be recognized as equal to their counterparts in adult theatre and worth equal salaries in every type of organization.

We cannot afford any longer to leave this important area of educational endeavor to dabblers. The years ahead are much too critical in the development of mankind and of civilization.

CHILDREN'S THEATRE IN THE SPACE AGE

No one was really surprised when the announcement of the first artificial earth satellite produced a spurt of interest in scientific study. Many people in high places proclaimed that scientific and mathematical pursuits could not possibly assume their rightful importance in elementary and secondary school curricula so long as so much time was being "wasted" on artistic and "personality development" subjects. Even our colleges, they said, were offering too many electives. The arts—music, drawing and painting, the drama—suddenly were forced on the defensive, and many programs in these fields were actually curtailed as administrators yielded to public pressure. "Stop wasting the taxpayers' money," they cried. "Our children don't need all those extra subjects to get along in today's world. What they need is a good old solid course in the three R's!"

But in the days that followed, people who understood the full and lasting value of the arts and artistic experience solidified their ground. This experience was good for them. A challenge was to be met, and the arguments had to be strong.

The first justification for continued emphasis on the arts in all levels of education is that all advances in the history of civilization have been made by creative thinkers, people who have been able to go beyond proved facts to dream of new combinations and relationships, people whose modes of thinking have not been bound by methods of the past but have drawn upon and adapted those methods to advance new theories and possibilities. The headlong progress of the twentieth century should never curtail subjects that encourage creative thinking. Rather, it should demand their expansion to reach an even larger part of our population.

Second, what will earth-man carry with him when he goes out into space? Complex scientific apparatus, to be sure, and much knowledge to enable him to guide his ship and bring it back. But in addition he will take with him thousands of years of cultural heritage. The understanding of mankind's struggles from the murky depths, of his conquest of animals and nature which threaten to engulf him in forces much larger and more powerful than he, of the story tellers who explained people to themselves and bound their wounds with the fabric of magic words—these he will carry in the compressed air compartment as it whizzes through blackness. He will know of the philosophers who thought long and deeply about the purpose of life itself, of the old astrologers who gazed at the stars in wonderment and saw in them a key to man's inevitable fate, never suspecting that one day man himself would be journeying among them.

He will take with him the poets, those who look deep into man's soul and record his desires, his griefs, and his ambitions. A line or two of Shakespeare, Sophocles, Shaw, or Arthur Miller is bound to come into the conversation somewhere between Earth and Venus. And surely the musicians who have kept man's head high throughout every known struggle will be riding in the cabin—Beethoven, Schubert, Gershwin, and the rest.

Third, in spite of all, mankind will continue to be the most fascinating study of man. This creature who evolved in miraculous fashion from the lowest life, who is endowed with a spark of divinity, who possesses an instrument capable of mastering the universe itself—this creature still remains unfathomable. Who can really say he *understands* his neighbor or even himself? Who can trace the myriad influences, ideas, and people possessed of that creative power that culminated in the design of the first wheel, the first boat, the first automobile, airplane, or rocketship? In what way were those influences any different from the ones that produced the dramas of Aeschylus and the paintings of Matisse? Now is not the time to diminish our study of mankind or to lessen our efforts to enlarge the scope of the creative life—rather, it is the time to double our efforts. Our world is expanding, and it will need the assistance of everyone endowed with creative gifts to help us evaluate our gains and put our ambitions in perspective. We must make sure that we are inheriting something other than interplanetary war.

Children's theatre is certainly not the only answer. However, as we reach out to stir the souls of young people by bringing them universal truth, feeding their imaginations, widening their horizons, exposing them to the beauty inherent in the fusion of all the arts that emerges in fine theatrical production, we can rightfully feel that we have made no small contribution to their growth as creative and humane members of society.

In the space age, man's destiny will be met by people with imagination. The development of this essential quality must not be left in untrained hands.

Here lie our inspiration and our challenge.

Appendixes

Sample Prompt Book Pages

THE FOLLOWING EXCERPT from Act I of Mary Jane Larson Watkins' *The Rose and the Ring* is included here to show the extent and kind of action needed in directing a children's play and to show a practical system for blocking notation in a prompt script.

The scene is one of exposition—the kind usually requiring the addition of visual appeal by the director in order to center audience attention on important background information. It contains essential conversation, exits, and two major entrances introducing key characters. Movement is planned to fit into the floor plan sketched at the top of each facing page. The main entrance is stage left. The covered throne is stage right, a window seat upstage center, and a tall cupboard up left. The cupboard contains evidence of Betsinda's royal birth.

On the facing pages the characters' names are abbreviated: GL for Glumboso, GR for Gruffanuff, Q for the Queen, and the like. VA is used for Valoroso, since the letter V might easily be confused with an arrow pointing downward, used to indicate a sitting movement. If the director elects to use the blocking movements described in the script, they should be underlined; if not, they should be crossed out. *All* movement to be included in the produced play should be recorded on the facing page.

Stage areas and characters' movements are designated in abbreviated form: DS means downstage (toward the audience); C, center; DLC, down left center; UR, up right; X, a cross; $_\wedge$, rise; ←○ indicates that the actor is facing stage right (this symbol indicates not a turning movement but rather the position of the actor in relation to the audience). Each director usually develops a system of blocking notation best suited to his purpose, which should always be explained to the cast and followed consistently. Clarity as well as brevity are important.

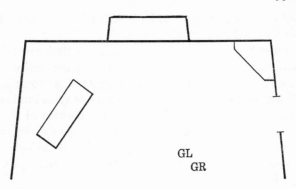

GL
GR

(1) X away from GR. RC to.

(2) Step toward GL from DLC.

(3) Quick movement ULC. GL slips behind GR, then to R of her on entrance.

(4) Q leads, X to throne, ⌣ on US end, has embroidery, sews.
A X to window seat, one knee on L end, looks out.
VA X C, pause, X DL.
GR & GL hold ULC, bowing.

(5) X C, pause, X RC almost to Q.

(6) Starts L, stops C.

(7) Both snap to attention, GL starts backing to door, GR counter.

(8) VA advances on GL who stops.

(9) VA X DRC.

(10) GL X toward VA. VA X DR.

(11) GL X toward door — backwards.

(12) As GL X's her. GL turns L & quick exit.
GR X to L of A.
VA X L, faces L to DL.

(13) A ⌣ on window seat, ε.

(14) GR exit L.
VA counter C.

(15) VA ⌣ on DS end of throne.

GLUMBOSO: Don't raise your voice! (1)

GRUFFANUFF: You robber of the royal treasury! You'll pay for your insults! (2)

(Voices are heard offstage. GRUFFANUFF *and* GLUMBOSO *scurry out of the way as* VALOROSO, *the* QUEEN, *and* ANGELICA *enter.* GRUFFANUFF *and* GLUMBOSO *bow low as they murmur,* "Good morning, your Majesties." *They are ignored.* VALOROSO *is preoccupied and paces.* ANGELICA *indifferently crosses to the window seat. The* QUEEN *goes to the throne.)* (3) (4)

QUEEN: Valoroso, do sit down.

VALOROSO: Don't nag, Mrs. V.—Where is Giglio? (5)

QUEEN: In his room, I suppose . . . that's where you sent him.

VALOROSO: So I did. *(Spying* GRUFFANUFF *and* GLUMBOSO*)* What are you doing here? Glumboso! Who is taking care of my royal business while you stand there? Go and check the morning dispatches. (6) (7) (8) (9)

GLUMBOSO: Yes, your Majesty . . . by all means, your Majesty. But begging your pardon, Royal Highness . . . (10)

QUEEN: You heard the King. Now go!

*(*GLUMBOSO *bows and scrapes his way to the door.)* (11)

GRUFFANUFF: *(Whispering)* And good day to you, you old time waster. (12)

GLUMBOSO: *(angrily sweeping out)* Humph!

QUEEN: Angelica, dear, isn't it time for your lessons?

ANGELICA: I can't study unless Betsinda is here. If I have to suffer, she must suffer, too. What else is a maid for? (13)

QUEEN: There's no need for a maid to be well educated, my pet . . . but if you want her with you, all right. Summon Betsinda, Gruffanuff.

*(*GRUFFANUFF *bows her way out.)* (14)

And, Valoroso, do stop wandering about, and sit down.

(With a sigh of resignation VALOROSO *joins her on the throne.)* (15)

Angelica, my sweet, what are you going to do today?

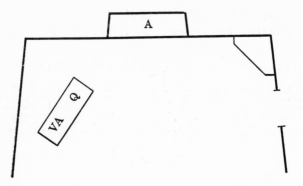

NOTE: Each new page, the blocking movements
begin again with No. 1.

(1) Λ, X to Q.

(2) X DC + DLC.

(3) Face throne.

(4) X to A.

(5) Turn DLC.

(6) To Q.

(7) X DS to DRC but L of throne.

(8) Turn to Q.

(9) VA Λ; Q X quickly to him.

(10) Move toward DC; then X to VA.

(11) Q eases VA onto DS end of throne.
A X DR of throne.

(12) GR + B enter L, B DS of GR. GR pushes B DL + X's C.

(13) ✓ US end of throne.

(14) X front of throne to above Q.

(15) GR slight move LC.

(16) GR move toward DLC.

(17) B slips around above + just R of GR.

ANGELICA: I think I'll order some new clothes. And I may have Betsinda do my hair a new way. And I haven't counted my jewels for weeks. *(4)*

QUEEN: Aren't you going to play with Giglio? Poor boy, you haven't paid much attention to him lately.

ANGELICA: Bother Giglio! He's not the only prince in the world. I'm tired of him. Gruffanuff showed me a picture of Prince Bulbo of Crim Tartary, and I think he looks much nicer.

VALOROSO: Oh you do, do you!

ANGELICA: Yes, and I'd like to meet him. (*struck by a sudden idea*) Papa, couldn't I go to Crim Tartary? Travel would be good for me. *(11)*

VALOROSO: You may not. We'll have nothing to do with Crim Tartary.

(GRUFFANUFF enters with BETSINDA. GRUFFANUFF, who carries a large book, pushes BETSINDA aside.)

GRUFFANUFF: Here is Betsinda. Shall we begin our lessons?

QUEEN: Yes, Angelica. Let us hear what you've learned this week.

GRUFFANUFF: Ready, your Highness?

ANGELICA: I suppose.

GRUFFANUFF: What country lies to the east of Paflagonia?

ANGELICA: That's easy. Crim Tartary. That's where Prince Bulbo lives.

VALOROSO: Oh, so that's where you got your notions!

QUEEN: But see how bright she is, Valoroso.

VALOROSO: Um hum.

GRUFFANUFF: And who is the king of Crim Tartary?

ANGELICA: Well . . . Bulbo will be some day . . . but . . .

(ANGELICA gropes for her answer. BETSINDA signals and mouths the answer.)

King Padella, who drove his brother from the throne in the great Crim Tartar revolution.

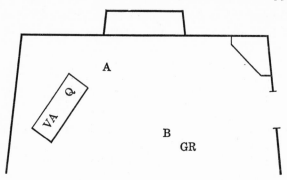

(1) X DL.

(2) X C (toward B); B X C a step (toward A);
   VA & Q focus on each other.
   GR looks off DL.

(3) A face front; hold C; B X to her L & above her.

(4) A X RC toward VA.

(5) X DLC.

(6) X DLC, R of GR.

(7) Turn R; X UC to window sect; ∨ L end.

(8) (C facing throne); free movement within C area.

GRUFFANUFF: Very good, my dear. Now tell us about the revolution.

ANGELICA: Well, before the revolution it was . . .

(She is at a loss. BETSINDA *prompts.* VALOROSO *and the* QUEEN *pay no attention, and* GRUFFANUFF *turns away so as not to see. Throughout the rest of the lesson* BETSINDA *supplies the answers.)*

It was King Savio who ruled . . . but Padella grew very strong and powerful and gathered an army. . . . He forced King Savio off the throne . . . and . . . Padella got to be king.

VALOROSO: *(virtuously)* He stole the throne, that's what he did.

GRUFFANUFF: And what happened next, my dear?

ANGELICA: Well . . . everyone got killed or ran away. . . . There was a princess named Rosalba. She was a tiny girl then . . . and . . . Oh, let Betsinda finish. Go on, Betsinda. Tell them what I know.

BETSINDA: They forgot the Princess when they ran away. She wandered into the forest, and Padella's men went after her . . . but all they found was some rags and a shoe. So everyone thinks she was eaten by wild beasts. And that means Prince Bulbo will be the next king.

Sample Light Plot

THE FOLLOWING light plot was designed for a touring production of Rosemary Musil's *Robin Hood*. The play requires two settings—one in the forest near a bridge, the other at Nottingham Fair—plus an interlude played in front of the main curtain. Technically speaking, the most severe limitation on the lighting scheme for this or any production is the control equipment. The challenge to the lighting artist is to make the best possible use of whatever facilities he has at his disposal. Because of the limitation on control equipment in the touring situation, this plot is not elaborate. However, it represents a reasonable compromise between what was desirable and what was possible. The plot consists of five parts: the Master Layout, a Connection Schedule, an Instrument Schedule, the Control Board Layout, and the Cue Sheet.

THE MASTER LAYOUT

On the Master Layout, the lighting scheme is superimposed on scale drawings of the floor plan of the setting. The acting area is divided into a suitable number of light areas, and the location of each instrument for lighting these areas is shown in its mounting position. Each group will probably want to develop and use consistently its own system of notation for these mounting positions,

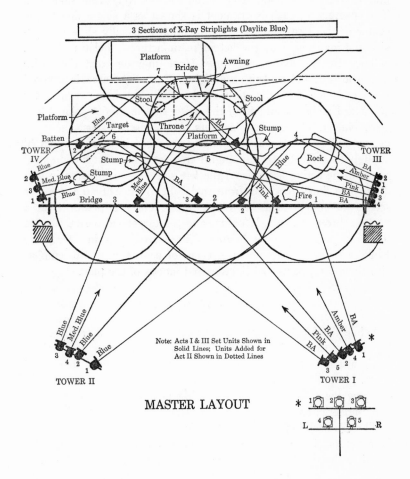

MASTER LAYOUT

such as BE for beam, BR for bridge, I for first pipe, II for second pipe, T for tower. Standard symbols for each kind of instrument should also appear on the layout, and these instruments should be numbered in each mounting position consecutively from stage left. The coverage of each instrument is shown as a single line to the center of the area, and the color medium is usually shown alongside the instrument as the actual manufacturer's gelatin number.

The Master Layout for *Robin Hood* indicates that the entire acting area is lighted with spotlights. Each light area is covered from one side (the direction of the sunlight) in a warm color ("bastard amber") and from the other side in a cool color ("no-color blue"). These particular tints were chosen because the color of sets and costumes was dominantly green. A suggestion of actual sunlight is given by two spotlights in a golden amber color aimed to flood the acting areas from the left side. Two spotlights in medium blue flood generally from the right to intensify the moodier scenes and complement the golden amber. The rear platform (area 7), the throne (in Act II only), and the target (also Act II) are the only areas specially lighted. Three spotlights in "DuBarry Pink" are mounted to enhance scenes of pageantry and to emphasize the more joyous and lighthearted moods of the play.

CONNECTION SCHEDULE

While the Master Layout shows the integration of settings and lights, the Connection Schedule shows the electrical connections from instrument to instrument and from instruments to control units. No particular scale is used, but the page is laid out roughly to show the relationships of mounting positions. The instruments are numbered as they are in the Master Layout.

The Connection Schedule for *Robin Hood* shows that some of the lamps in the X-ray striplights are removed to make the total wattage equal to the size of the available dimmers. It shows that the spotlights are 500-watts each and of the Fresnel type. The color of each is also indicated. Principally, it shows which instruments are connected together and to what control board (I, II, or III) and

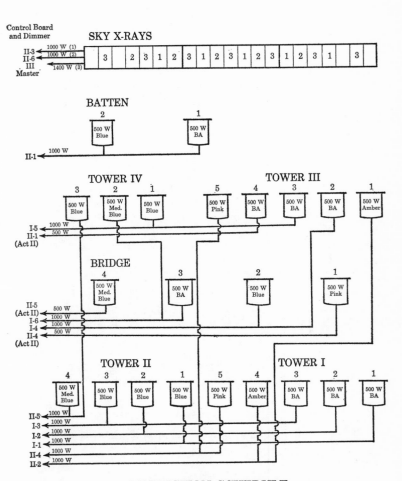

CONNECTION SCHEDULE

311

INSTRUMENT SCHEDULE

Location	Instrument	Wattage	Color[a]	Coverage	Control Unit	Act Used
Tower I	1	500	BA	Area 1	I-1	I, II, III
	2	500	BA	Area 2	I-2	I, II, III
	3	500	BA	Area 3	I-3	I, II, III
	4	500	Amber	General Sun	II-2	I, II, III
	5	500	Pink	General Pink	II-4	I,
Tower II	1	500	Blue	Area 1	I-1	I, II, III
	2	500	Blue	Area 2	I-2	I, II, III
	3	500	Blue	Area 3	I-3	I, II, III
	4	500	Med. Blue	General Blue	II-5	I,
Bridge	1	500	Pink	Throne	II-4	II, III
	2	500	Blue	Area 4	I-4	I, II, III
	3	500	BA	Area 6	I-6	I, II, III
	4	500	Med. Blue	Throne	II-5	II,

Tower III	1	500	Amber	General Sun	II-2	I, II, III
	2	500	BA	Area 4	I-4	I, II, III
	3	500	BA	Area 5	I-5	I, II, III
	4	500	BA	Target	II-1	II,
	5	500	Pink	General Pink	II-4	I, III
Tower IV	1	500	Blue	Area 5	I-5	I, II, III
	2	500	Blue	Area 6	I-6	I, II, III
	3	500	Med. Blue	General Blue	II-5	I, III
Batten	1	500	BA	Area 7	II-1	I, III
	2	500	Blue	Area 7	II-1	I, III
Sky X-rays	Ck. 1	1000	Daylite Blue	Sky	II-3	I, II, III
	Ck. 2	1000	Daylite Blue	Sky	II-6	I, II, III
	Ck. 3	1400	Daylite Blue	Sky	III-Master	I, II, III

ᵃ Color is usually indicated by the manufacturer's gelatin number.

dimmer unit they are plugged. The total load on the circuit is shown at the point of entry into the dimmer.

If plugging boxes, floor pockets, or wall outlets serve as intermediary connections between instruments and control units, these should also be indicated by number on the Connection Schedule. Since this was a touring production utilizing portable control boards with direct cable connections, such intermediaries do not appear.

INSTRUMENT SCHEDULE

The Instrument Schedule gives all the pertinent information on each lighting instrument used in the production. It is in table form, with column headings for location, instrument number, wattage and type, color, coverage, control unit, and the act in which it is used.

Since all the spotlights used in this production of *Robin Hood* were of the Fresnel type, it was not necessary to include a separate column for this information. Note that "coverage" may be shown either as an area number or special name by which the area is always designated. Thus, for example, we have "throne" area, "general pinks," "general sun," and "target."

CONTROL BOARD LAYOUT

The Control Board Layout shows only the face of the board and the scheme by which instruments are grouped for easy manipulation by the operator. If possible the board should be laid out to approximate the areas of the stage. Specials should be placed more or less together on the board, and background instruments which are not often changed during the action may be in the least accessible positions. The pertinent designations of control units (bank numbers or letters, dimmer numbers, auxiliary units) should be clearly shown. The total capacity of each unit is given along with the load actually connected to it.

For *Robin Hood,* three small portable dimmer boards were used. Two of them contained six 1000-watt dimmers each, and the

BOARD I
Contains
Six 1000-W
Dimmers

1	2	3
Capacity: 1000 W	Capacity: 1000 W	Capacity: 1000 W
AREA 1	AREA 2	AREA 3
Load: 1000 W	Load: 1000 W	Load: 1000 W
4	**5**	**6**
Capacity: 1000 W	Capacity: 1000 W	Capacity: 1000 W
AREA 4	AREA 5	AREA 6
Load: 1000 W	Load: 1000 W	Load: 1000 W

BOARD II
Contains
Six 1000-W
Dimmers

1	2	3
Capacity: 1000 W	Capacity: 1000 W	Capacity: 1000 W
AREA 7	GENERAL SUN	SKY CYC #1
(Acts I & III)		
Load: 1000 W	Load: 1000 W	Load: 1000 W
TARGET		
(Act II)		
Load: 500 W		
4	**5**	**6**
Capacity: 1000 W	Capacity: 1000 W	Capacity: 1000 W
GENERAL PINKS	GENERAL MED. BLUE	SKY CYC #2
(Acts I & III)	(Acts I & III)	
Load: 1000 W	Load: 1000 W	Load: 1000 W
THRONE PINK	THRONE MED. BLUE	
(Act II)	(Act II)	
Load: 500 W	Load: 500 W	

BOARD III
Contains One 2000-W Dimmer
and Four 650-W Dimmers

MASTER	1	2
Capacity: 2000 W	(Not Used)	(Not Used)
SKY CYC #3	**3**	**4**
Load: 1400 W	(Not Used)	(Not Used)

CONTROL BOARD LAYOUT

third contained a master dimmer of 2000-watt capacity that could be used independently of the other four dimmers on the board. Only the master dimmer was used on Board III. For convenience in operation, Board I controlled the six constant light areas. All re-plugging to accommodate special Act II instruments was done on Board II.

CUE SHEET

The Cue Sheet is the final form of the entire light plot. This is what the operator needs to follow during the play. It is both the beginning and the end, for the lights are laid out, connected, colored, and controlled to accomplish the effects decided upon by the director, the designer, the costumer, and the lighting artist at the start of the planning period.

CUE SHEET

Cue	Cue Number	Instrument(s)	Control Unit	Reading	Special
Before curtain, Act I	1	Sky	II-3	10	
			II-6	10	
			III-Mas.	Full	
		Fire	I-hot	On	
Curtain	2	House		Out	
		Gen. Blues	II-5	8	
		Gen. Pinks	II-4	6½	
Right after #2	3	Areas 1–6	All I	8	
		Area 7	II-1	8	
		Gen. Sun	II-2	6½	
Right after #3	4	Fire	I-hot	Out	
John's entrance	5	Area 7	II-1	8½	
		Areas 1–6	All I	8½	
Song	6	Areas 1–6	All I	9	
		Area 7	II-1	9	
		Gen. Sun	II-2	8	
Curtain closes, Act I	7	Gen. Sun	II-2	Out	(Interlude
		Gen. Pinks	II-4	Out	before
		Gen. Blues	II-5	Out	curtain)
		Area 3	I-3	10	

CUE SHEET (*Continued*)

CUE	CUE NUMBER	INSTRUMENT(S)	CONTROL UNIT	READING	SPECIAL
Friar's exit	8	Areas 1–3	I-1, 2, 3	Out	
Before curtain, Act II	9	Sky	II-3	10	
			II-6	10	
			III-Mas.	Full	
		Target	II-1	6	Replug
		Throne Pink	II-4	6½	Replug
		Throne Blue	II-5	7½	Replug
Curtain, right after #8	10	Areas 1–6	All I	9½	
		Gen. Sun	II-2	8	
		Target	II-1	8	
On approach to throne	11	Throne Pink	II-4	7½	
		Throne Blue	II-5	8½	
Wrestling	12	Area 2	I-2	10	
Shooting match	13	Areas 1, 3–6	All I	10	
		Target	II-1	10	
Curtain closes, Act II	14	Gen. Sun	II-2	Out	
		Areas 1–3	I-1, 2, 3	Out	
		House		Up to ¾	

Cue	No.		Dimmer	Reading	
Before curtain, Act III	15	Sky			
		Area 7	II-3	10	Replug
		Gen. Pinks	II-6	10	Replug
		Gen. Blues	III-Mas.	Full	Replug
Curtain	16	House		Out	
		Areas 1-6	II-1	8	
		Area 7	II-4	8	
		Gen. Sun	II-5	5	
Sheriff's entrance	17	Areas 1-6	All I	9½	
		Area 7	II-1	9½	
		Gen. Sun	II-2	8	
King's recognition	18	Gen. Sun	II-2	9	
		Gen. Pinks	II-4	7½	
		Gen. Blues	II-5	9	
Final curtain	19	Areas 1-3	I-1, 2, 3	Out	
		Gen. Sun	II-2	Out	
		Gen. Pinks	II-4	Out	
		Gen. Blues	II-5	Out	
		House		Full	

$\mathcal{A}$ $\mathcal{C}$abulation of
120 $\mathcal{C}$hildren's $\mathcal{T}$heatre $\mathcal{P}$lays

THE PLAYS listed here are not by any means to be regarded as the only ones "recommended" for children's theatre production. The fact is that any "Recommended List" is out of date by the time it is printed. Fortunately for the children's theatre movement, new scripts are appearing regularly and a number of authors circulate their most recent efforts in manuscript form for the consideration of prospective producers. A few of the plays we have included can be recommended only with the utmost reservation. Actually, there is no substitute for choosing a play on the basis of a personal evaluation, arrived at with script-in-hand.

The plays are arranged alphabetically by title in order to group most of the versions of the same story. The publisher is listed under the author's name in the second column. These abbreviations are used:

Baker. Walter H. Baker Co., 100 Summer St., Boston 10, Massachusetts.
CTP. Children's Theatre Press, Cloverlot, Anchorage, Kentucky.
Coach House. Coach House Press, 53 W. Jackson Blvd., Chicago 4, Illinois.

Dramatic. Dramatic Publishing Co., 179 N. Michigan Avenue, Chicago 1, Illinois.

French. Samuel French, Inc., 25 W. 45th St., New York 36, New York.

Longmans. Longmans, Green & Co., 55 Fifth Ave., New York 3, New York.

Macmillan. The Macmillan Co., 60 Fifth Ave., New York 11, New York.

Row, Peterson. Row, Peterson & Co., 1911 Ridge Ave., Evanston, Illinois.

The plays originally published by the Century Co., Dodd, Mead & Co., Charles Scribner's Sons, and Henry Holt are presently handled by Samuel French.

The anthologies in which several of the plays appear are cited in shortened form. The volumes referred to are:

Another Treasury of Plays for Children, ed. by Montrose J. Moses, Little, Brown, 1926.

First Performance, ed. by Virginia Lee Comer and Nora Tully MacAlvay, Harcourt, Brace, 1952.

Miniature Plays, by Madge Miller, Children's Theatre Press, 1954.

Ring Up the Curtain! ed. by Montrose J. Moses, Little, Brown, 1932.

A Treasury of Plays for Children, ed. by Montrose J. Moses, Little, Brown, 1921.

There is usually some difficulty in indicating the number of characters in a children's play, though in some they are obvious enough. In others one must account for strange characters such as detached voices with puppet bodies, animals supposed to be more-or-less real animals, animals who are frankly men or women under enchantment, man-made articles brought to life, little people who may be played as small men, small women, or children of either sex, or even animated trees. We have tried to remain consistent in listing roles according to the gender intended by the author, on the assumption that producers will be more successful when casting this way. Roles in which the sex of the actor is immaterial are listed separately.

The "Settings" column gives the number of interiors and exteriors required for the action, with a brief description of each. Except in a few plays constructed on the "unit set" or "simultaneous set" plans, no allowance is made for suggested methods of economical staging usually found in the texts. Each producing group will want to make its own decision on how it will meet the set requirements of the play.

Under "Special Requirements" are listed problems of costuming, make-up, sound, lighting, dancing, singing, fencing, special construction of setting units, unusual properties, need for certain rigging or shifting facilities, and tricks of staging. This list of items is a purely arbitrary one. Seasoned producers may find prosaic items listed, while some beginners may discover omissions that prove to be serious problems. The length of some of these lists should not frighten producers away from these plays—usually some of the effects can be omitted or modified. Almost all children's plays demand plenty of imagination and ingenuity for effective staging, and these qualities will usually bring about a solution to whatever problems are involved. Often suggestions given in the texts serve as a starting point.

ADDITIONAL SOURCES OF PLAYS

Other sources of plays, in addition to the 120 listed in the tabulation, are the following firms and organizations which publish children's theatre plays or duplicate them for distribution to producers:

The Ash Arbor Press, 651½ N. Huntley Drive, Los Angeles 46, California.

The Association of the Junior Leagues of America, Waldorf-Astoria Hotel, New York 22, New York.

The Harlequin Press, Box 4161, Santa Barbara, California.

Plays, Inc., 8 Arlington St., Boston 16, Massachusetts.

Seattle Junior Programs, Inc., 1386 Dexter Horton Building, Seattle 4, Washington.

Musical plays and operettas are available from the following:

Carl Fisher, Inc., 56-62 Cooper Square, New York 3, New York.
Willis Music Co., 124 E. Fourth St., Cincinnati 1, Ohio.

There are many books containing plays for children to perform and plays for the child audience. Some are royalty free, but most of the good ones require the payment of royalty. While the plays in the volumes listed below are not of uniformly high quality, all contain plays of various lengths worthy of consideration.

Coit, Dorothy, *Kai Khosru and Other Plays for Children,* Theatre Arts, 1934.

Drama League of America, *Dickon Goes to the Fair and Other Plays,* George H. Doran, 1927.

Field, Rachel, *Patchwork Plays,* Doubleday, Doran, 1930.

Folmsbee, Beulah, *Guki the Moon Boy and Other Plays,* Harcourt, Brace, 1928.

Fyleman, Rose, *Eight Little Plays for Children,* Doubleday, Doran, 1925.

Goulding, Dorothy Jane, *The Master Cat and Other Plays,* Coach House Press, 1957.

Jagendorf, Moritz, *One-Act Plays for Young Folks,* French, 1924.

Mackay, Constance D'Arcy, *The Silver Thread and Other Folk Plays,* Holt, 1910.

Major, Clare Tree, *Playing Theatre: Six Plays for Children,* Oxford, 1930.

McCaslin, Nellie, *Legends in Action,* Row, Peterson, 1945.

McCaslin, Nellie, *More Legends in Action,* Row, Peterson, 1950.

McCaslin, Nellie, *Tall Tales for Tall Men,* Macrae-Smith, 1956.

Walker, Pamela Prince, *Seven Steps to Creative Children's Dramatics,* Hill & Wang, 1957.

Walker, Stuart, *More Portmanteau Plays,* Stewart and Kidd, 1919.

Walker, Stuart, *Portmanteau Plays,* Stewart and Kidd, 1917.

TABULATION OF PLAYS FOR CHILDREN

Title	Author	Characters	Settings	Special Requirements
1. *Abe Lincoln— New Salem Days*	Chorpenning, Charlotte B. (Coach House, 1954)	9m, 7w, 3 children	1 *interior* General store	Sounds of horses off stage. Sun shines through the window. A practical store counter, with much action on and over it. Rustic and fine 1830 costumes. A loft that characters climb into. Horses' heads are seen outside the window, fed candy. A hand coffee grinder. Several barrels. Fireplace with fire. Some singing and dancing. Seasonal changes seen through the window (winter to spring). A set of surveying instruments. A churn. Many small hand props, sold at the store.
2. *The Adventures of Tom Sawyer*	Chorpenning, Charlotte B. (Coach House, 1956)	9m, 5w, 6 children, extras	3 *exteriors* 1 *interior* Backyard Graveyard Island with house ruins	1850 costumes. Board fence that gets whitewashed. Dim moonlight, graveyard scene. Box of money buried under rock. Staircase of ruined house must be climbed (III).

			Bedroom	Injun Joe falls through broken board of stairs. Storm, thunder, lightning. Characters climb through window. Portable organ for funeral scene.
3. *Aladdin*	DuBois, Theodora (Little, Brown, 1932) in Moses, *Ring Up the Curtain*	7m, 3w, 1 child, extras	*2 exteriors* *3 interiors* Street in Cathay Palace court Cavern House Sultan's palace	Grand and ragged Chinese costumes. Some action through audience. Princess arrives in a golden palanquin. Aladdin descends by ladder into the magic cavern. Dog idols guard the niche with the lamp. Trap door above closes. Great treasure is revealed. Clash of cymbals, lights go on and off as Genie appears. Clouds of smoke. Dishes of food and fine garments appear magically. Singing and dancing. Gorgeous palace disclosed as arras curtains open. Aladdin tosses candies to audience. Fast change of background as palace is returned to Cathay from Africa.

TABULATION OF PLAYS FOR CHILDREN (*Continued*)

TITLE	AUTHOR	CHARACTERS	SETTINGS	SPECIAL REQUIREMENTS
4. *Aladdin and the Wonderful Lamp*	Norris, James (CTP, 1940)	8m, 4w, extras	1 *exterior* 2 *interiors* A glen Magic cave Princess' palace	Large rock with trap door in top (entrance to cave). Arabian costumes. Genie of the Ring appears magically with rolls of thunder and change of lights. A blast of blue smoke (magic spell). Magic cave glitters with colored lights, trees with gold and silver fruit, urns of coins; a niche with the burning lamp. Aladdin enters from up high. Slaves of the Ring dance fantastically, chant in chorus, weird lights. Sunlight comes through opening into cave, cut down as cover is replaced. Lamp and sleeves of slaves' costumes are phosphorescent. Genie of the Lamp appears in puff of smoke and crash of cymbals. Slaves of the Lamp carry in rich repast on gold and silver plates. Costumes phosphorescent on back side. Gossamer castle appears in background by magic.

				Aladdin appears suddenly in rich garments.
				Palace disappears from view.
				Aladdin comes through locked window of the palace.
				Palace flies back home—seen as stars passing window at high speed.
5. *Alice in Wonderland*	Chorpenning, Charlotte B. (Coach House, 1956)	13m, 4w, 1 child, extras	Draped stage suggested	Fantastic costumes and masks.
				Shaft of light for Rabbit hole.
				Caterpillar pushes his mushroom on stage.
				Duchess' house comes rolling on.
				Hare and Hatter bring on table and 5 chairs, teapot big enough for the Dormouse.
				Pieces of garden are sneaked on.
				Rock formation for Mock Turtle scene.
				Much singing and dancing.
				A large picture of Walrus and Carpenter as per Tenniel.
				Flamingo croquet mallets.
				Treadmill action at end of II.
				Jury boxes with chairs (III).
				Dais with 2 thrones.
				Scroll 5 to 6 feet long.

Title	Author	Characters	Settings	Special Requirements
6. *Alice in Wonderland*	Gerstenberg, Alice (Longmans, 1941)	16 m, 5 w	4 *interiors* 3 *exteriors* Alice's home Room in looking-glass house Hall with doors Court of Hearts Seashore March Hare's garden Garden of flowers	Fireplace with huge mirror where Red and White Queens appear. Alice goes through the mirror. A shawl flies into the room. Lightning shafts essential in blackout. Rabbit disappears into a trap door. Humpty-Dumpty appears and disappears on a wall. Much use of specific and effect lights. Alice extends like a telescope. She almost drowns in a lake of tears. Mock Turtle and Gryphon fly with Alice into the air. Small silhouettes of Mock Turtle, Gryphon, and Alice "in an orange colored moon far away in the sky." Many fantastic costumes. Huge tea table in March Hare's garden is on a platform. The whole platform moves off on cue. Dish breaks over Frog footman's head. Head of Cheshire Cat appears in a tree and then vanishes.

			7 *interiors* 11 *exteriors*	
7. *Alice in Wonderland*	LeGallienne, Eva, and Friebus, Florida (French, 1932)	50 speaking parts, extras	Alice's home Little door Duchess' kitchen Railway carriage Sheep shop Court of 3 Queens Banquet Pool of Tears Caucus Race Mushroom and door to Duchess'	Baby turns into a pig and crawls away. Alice should disappear down a trap door at end of II. Garden of enormous flowers. Gold crown and sceptre appear on the mushroom. Large mirror to go through. Table top grows higher, then shrinks. Little door does the same. Table vanishes (on a wagon). Cake and bottle appear on table. Ripple effects used for Pool of Tears, also scrim. A system of travelers to change backdrops desirable. Animals, birds, etc., call for fantastic costumes after Tenniel. Blackout between scenes. Alice is pin-spotted for her soliloquies. Baby changes to a real pig who runs off stage on cue. Processional of moving scenery through the garden.

TITLE	AUTHOR	CHARACTERS	SETTINGS	SPECIAL REQUIREMENTS
7. *Alice in Wonderland*			Cheshire Cat tree	Oysters are marionettes.
			Mad tea party	White Queen's shawl flies about.
			Garden	White Queen herself flies in and out.
			Mock Turtle's rock	White Knight rides a 2-man horse.
			Land in chessboard squares	Lots of songs and music.
			Land of Tweedles	Mutton leg (marionette) rises, bows, speaks lines.
			Humpty's wall	Pudding is drawn up into flies for its exit.
			White Knight's woods	Dishes fly off the banquet table.
8. *Arthur and the Magic Sword*	Engar, Keith M. (CTP, 1952)	17m, 4w, 4 children	3 *interiors* 2 *exteriors* Great hall of castle Lot's castle	A unit set suggested. Split acting areas, curtains between planes, shifting behind, action in front. Dais and throne. Flash as Merlin appears before curtain.

			Urien's castle Courtyard Churchyard	Fanciful 7th-century costumes. Much specific lighting. Flash when King waves magic sword. Sword fight. Kay and Arthur shoot arrows at off-stage target. Sword imbedded in anvil and stone. Flash as stone is revealed. Weird lights as Morgan incants. Parachute sails down with scroll. Harp music as sword is drawn.
9. *Beauty and the Beast*	Beers, Jesse, Jr. (French, 1954)	5m, 4w, 1 dwarf	*Simultaneously set:* Beauty's cottage Sybil's cottage Beast's castle	Partial sets, all with fireplaces, are set at once, with action flowing freely among them. Spinning wheel. Play depends on lights to shift attention to desired setting or area. Beast's mask and hands. Secret panel in Sybil's cottage. Fire and candle go out on Beast's entrance. Flash when Beast puts log on fire. Many thunder cues. A Pavanne is danced. Beast's transformation.

TABULATION OF PLAYS FOR CHILDREN (*Continued*)

Title	Author	Characters	Settings	Special Requirements
10. *Beauty and the Beast*	Gray, Nicolas Stuart (French, 1951)	3m, 3w, 1 small dragon	3 *exteriors* 2 *interiors* Wizard's garden Gate at Beast's castle Doorway to Beast's castle Beauty's home Beast's salon	Dragon costume, Victorian costumes, fantastic costumes and mask. Lie-detector pulley arrangement on Wizard's house ("storm cone"). Cocky-olly's egg flashes light on magic spells. Lights dim and flicker, thunder rolls. 6 branches of candelabra light one by one by themselves. Pitcher pours glass of wine without help. Rose wilts. Dragon and Wizard enter castle through window. Gate swings open by itself. Beast's transformation. Magic voices beckon Beauty into the castle. Many rose bushes and white roses. Victorian furnishings in house. Large portrait of Beauty's mother. Small tree in I-i is large in I-ii.

11. *Beauty and the Beast*	MacAlvay, Nora (Coach House, 1955)	6m, 7w, extras	1 *interior* Room in the secret palace	Flicker and flash of colored lights precede magician's entrance. Dancing by Antoinette. Flicker and flash introduce Godmother who appears from nowhere. Large mirror frame in which scenes appear and fade. Ape costumes for Renard and Antoinette. Flash as spell is cast. Beast's head and paws. Godmother in pool of light. Doors hiding portrait open themselves. Rose picked from bushes. Magic tricks may be included as entertainment sequence, II-ii. Portrait of Prince in coronation robes appears in what was empty space. Fountain hides Prince's transformation.
12. *The Blue Bird*	Maeterlinck, Maurice (Dodd, Mead, 1907)	10m, 12w, 24 children, extras	5 *interiors* 4 *exteriors* Woodcutter's cottage Palace of the Fairy	Many fantastic costumes: Light, Time, Night, Dog, Cat, Bread, Sugar, Fire, Water, Milk, animals, trees. Woodcutter's cottage must hide souls of elements for quick entrance. Bird in a cage.

Title	Author	Characters	Settings	Special Requirements
12. *The Blue Bird*			Palace of Night	Lamp lights itself in fantastic color.
			Palace of Happiness	Neighbor Berlingote transforms herself into beautiful fairy.
			Azure Palace	Complete change in aspect of set as Tyltyl turns diamond. Everything in hut comes to life.
			Land of Memory	Fog in Land of Memory.
			Forest	Ghosts escape and are driven back (Palace of Night).
			Graveyard	Hundreds of flying bluebirds in Palace of Night.
			Before the house	Souls of trees come out.
				Graveyard transforms into a garden.
				Gyrations of inventions by unborn children.
				Many light cues.
13. *Buffalo Bill*	Harris, Aurand (CTP, 1954)	13m, 1w, 3 children, extras	5 *exteriors* Roadside trading wagon Indian village	A scene of covered wagons crossing prairie is projected on act curtain at opening.
				Settlers push all kinds of equipment across the stage.
				Side and end of covered wagon for roadside trading post.

			Cutaway teepee with action both inside and out.
		Shipping Co. office	Action of riding horses in dance mime.
		A cliff	Portion of Shipping Co. office.
		Speaker's platform	Bill shoots knob off gatepost, a bird off Becky's hat.
			Campfire center stage (II-iii).
			A rock Bill climbs on (II-iv).
			Scenes progress alternately in front of and behind act curtain.
			Indian ceremonial dance.
			A speaker's stand draped in bunting.
			Stylized U.S. map projected on back drapes with Pony Express route clearly marked (III-iii).
			Storm, lightning.
			Much gun shooting.
14. *Caddie Woodlawn*	Brink, Carol Ryrie (Macmillan, 1945)	7m, 4w, 8 children	*2 interiors*
		Kitchen of pioneer farmhouse	A pump for water in kitchen.
			Sky lighting changes to sunset and dark.
			Northern lights.
		Barn	Dim lighting in barn scene.
			Dawn comes up (III-ii).
			American pioneer and Indian costumes.
			Rustic props.

335

TABULATION OF PLAYS FOR CHILDREN (*Continued*)

TITLE	AUTHOR	CHARACTERS	SETTINGS	SPECIAL REQUIREMENTS
15. *A Christmas Carol*	King, Martha Bennett (CTP, 1941)	14m, 6w, 8 children	4 *interiors* 1 *exterior* Scrooge's office Cratchit kitchen Schoolroom Fezziwig's office Graveyard	Fire in fireplace. Singing and dancing. Light cues: area lights and special lights to follow action. Ghosts and Scrooge must overlook action in all scenes. Many tolling bell cues. Cupboard large enough to hold Martha, Cratchit kitchen. Large turkey for roasting.
16. *The Christmas Nightingale*	Groff, Phyllis Newman (CTP, 1935)	8m, 3w, 6 children, extras	2 *interiors* 1 *exterior* Cottage kitchen Room in the castle Before the castle gates	Peasant and Gothic furnishings and costumes. Boy soprano for leading character. Fire in fireplace. Szopka, Polish puppet show, in various stages of preparation and finally performed. Christmas tree dragged in and set up. Lamp posts before the gate. Doors of stable must open to reveal nativity scene.

Native Polish dances to violin accompaniment (II).
Tartar girl whirls and dances (II).
Candles and candelabra used to light the castle scene (III).
Atmospheric lighting needed.
Nightingale sings several Polish Christmas carols.
Chimes from cathedral.

17. *Cinderella* Chorpenning, Charlotte B. (CTP, 1940) 4m, 7w, extras 1 *interior* 1 *exterior* Kitchen Palace garden

A fireplace, glowing coals.
Dream scene, played behind gauze section of wall.
Many pumpkins.
Many special light cues.
Mother tears Cinderella's dress.
Another gauze panel which opens. Dress appears there (I); Godmother (I); slipper (III).
Small pumpkin coach, drawn by mice, goes across and out. In III it returns, pumpkin rolls off the carriage into blank space of lined-up pumpkins.
Large coach appears behind gauze, drives off to the ball.
Costumes of 17th century.

TITLE	AUTHOR	CHARACTERS	SETTINGS	SPECIAL REQUIREMENTS
17. *Cinderella*				Prince and Roland disguised as beggar and Herald.
				Prince's dance. Also comic version by sisters and fops.
				After flight from ball, Cinderella seen in rags running across gateway.
				Godmother appears in circle of light.
				"Glass" slippers.
18. *Cinderella of Loreland*	Homer, Frances (Dramatic, 1934)	6m, 9w, 1 cat, extras	*2 interiors* Kitchen Palace reception room	A cat (little boy or girl).
				Light cues: gradual dimming.
				Godmother appears during blackout.
				Costume change for Cinderella: rags to ball gown, done in the midst of a fairy dance.
				Cake with candles on it which are blown out by the Prince.
19. *Circus Day*	Harris, Aurand (French, 1949)	6m, 4w, 2 children, extras	*1 exterior* *1 interior* Outside the big top Inside the dressing room	An elephant tub.
				A covered cage on wheels.
				A section of the center ring.
				A baby that cries on cue.
				Parade chariot is pulled across.
				Fritz has a nose that lights.
				A hurdling wall carried across.

				A magician's box in which characters get lost.
				An animal box large enough for a boy to hide in.
				Calliope music off stage.
				A barrel big enough for a man.
				2-man horse costume.
				Platform carried in.
20. *The Clown Who Ran Away*	Seiler, Conrad (Longmans, 1948)	8m, 7w, 7 children	Before the curtain, and bare draped stage (Dodo erects street scene)	Dodo takes from suitcase: lamp post in sections, tree of pieces of cardboard, 2 windows of cardboard, colored rods for doorway and front window of shop.
				Lamp lights up.
				6 dolls (girls).
				Cardboard automobile with 3 girls drives past.
				A 2-girl horse named Gladys.
				A music box that plays.
				Specific lighting called for.
21. *Crazy Cricket Farm*	Masters, Robert, and Masters, Lillian (CTP, 1941)	2m, 4w, 6 children	1 *interior* 1 *exterior* Farmhouse kitchen Echo well in meadow	Rustic and fashionable modern costumes.
				Barn burns off stage.
				A chair collapses.
				Reuben's invention.
				Fence in the meadow is climbed.
				A movable stile.

Title	Author	Characters	Settings	Special Requirements
22. *Davy Crockett and His Coonskin Cap*	Evernden, Margery (Coach House, 1956)	5m, 1w, 1 bear, 3 children, extras	2 *exteriors* Clearing with cabin Forest	A bear, alligator, puppet coon, squirrel, rabbit. Cradle swinging in a tree. Outdoor oven. Fiddler plays a square dance. Gun shoots, twigs snap off trees. Animal masks on Indian dancers. Johnny hides in a hollow log. Thunder and lightning as Davy splits Injun rock.
23. *The Elves and the Shoemaker*	Tully, Nora, and Chorpenning, Charlotte B. (CTP, 1946)	1m, 9w, 3 elves	1 *interior* Shoemaker's shop	Moonlight streams in (I-i). Off-stage sounds: elf hammers; elf music. Sunlight streams in (I-ii). Many pieces of varicolored leather. Widget (elf) plays pipe music. Trick chalk stick is snapped out of Rhoda's hand. Many pairs of shoes are made by elves. Sunrise outside window (III).

24. *The Emperor's New Clothes*	Chorpenning, Charlotte B. (French, 1938)	7m, 4w, 1 child, extras	1 *exterior* 1 *interior* Street of Weavers Room in palace	Several houses of weavers required for I and III. Secret door for Empress (II). Secret panels with cupboard behind. Large ruby removable from center of panel. Large treasure of jewels and cloth. Oriental costumes, all classes.
25. *Five Little Peppers*	Musil, Rosemary Gabbert (CTP, 1940)	2m, 4w, 9 children	2 *interiors* Kitchen-living-dining room Mansion library	Live dog (Prince). Much food prepared and eaten, cake baked. Simple and elegant early 1900 costumes, props. Bugle sounds, coach heard approaching. Piano practicing heard off stage.
26. *Flibbertygibbet (His Last Chance)*	Chorpenning, Charlotte B., and MacAlvay, Nora Tully (CTP, 1952)	4m, 3w, 1 child	1 *exterior* 1 *interior* Outside Grandpop's cottage Second floor of barn (or on drying green)	Special lighting and sound (wind, music, echo) as Flib. appears. A well with low stone curb. A stile. Much dancing. Magic light comes from well. Kaleidoscopic whirl of lights as Flib.'s reed kilts, wig and cap fly through the air, his jacket and trousers appear in black light upon a tree. (In ordinary light the garments blend with bark.)

341

TABULATION OF PLAYS FOR CHILDREN (*Continued*)

Title	Author	Characters	Settings	Special Requirements
26. *Flibberty-gibbet (His Last Chance)*				Light of Flib.'s magic shows through door of barn.
				Grain sacks both painted and real in barn set (II).
				Trap entrance from below required in barn set.
				Much magic light in varying colors.
				Flib. shows in black light (II).
				Paper money floats in through barn doors, moving up and down to rhythm of music.
				Light flashes.
				Characters dance Highland Fling.
				Scottish costumes.
				Nannie also seen in black light.
27. *The Forest Ring*	deMille, William C., and Bernard, Charles (Little, Brown, 1921) in Moses, *A Treasury*	1m, 6w, 2 children, 1 bear, 1 deer, 1 fox, 1 owl	2 *exteriors* Forest with cave Farmyard	A hollow tree from which dreams (on parchment scrolls) are dispensed.
				Moonlight through foliage. The fairy ring is in an arc of light.
				A magic wand that glows when the Queen uses it.
				Animals (deer, fox, owl) appear as humans with animal skins over them.
				Ursa appears both as a bear and as a human. She goes behind rock for transformation.

	Author (Publisher)	Cast	Sets	Notes
28. *The Ghost of Mr. Penny*	Musil, Rosemary Gabbert (CTP, 1939)	4m, 4 children	*2 interiors* Old coach house Living room of deserted home	Jane Adams enters asleep on a bed. Jane's clothes fly off end of the bed and disappear under the bed clothes. The bed disappears. (End of I.) A "sweep well" and bucket. Ursa's head appears at 2nd story window of farmhouse. Hank's gun flies out of his hand and disappears. A leaf pitcher and flower glasses for "cup of dew" toast. Door of coach house is pushed down but must stand by itself again. Manger is part of coach house set but divided from it.
29. *Greensleeves' Magic*	Jonson, Marian (Coach House, 1951)	6m, 5w, extras	*1 exterior* Garden of castle (Changes to fantastic garden III-i)	Special green lights for Greensleeves' areas. Duchess goes up in smoke (III). Black light gives magic atmosphere to the "secret place" (III). Special ultraviolet treatment of costumes, make-up and set. Singing and dancing.

Title	Author	Characters	Settings	Special Requirements
30. *Hans Brinker and the Silver Skates*	Chorpenning, Charlotte B. (CTP, 1938)	5m, 2w, 12 children	1 *exterior* 2 *interiors* On the canal Room at Red Lion Inn Brinker cottage	Cutout "snow banks" suggested for canal scene. Dutch costumes, upper and lower class. Dutch props and furnishings. Skating on ice simulated. Carved wooden chains made by Hans. Christmas carols sung off stage. Lights are blown out (dimmed). Hans climbs in cottage window. Stocking and pouch filled with gold. Orchestra off stage plays for race. Flags and speaker stand added to canal set for III.
31. *Hans Brinker or The Silver Skates*	Taggart, Tom (French, 1937)	4m, 3w, 7 children	1 *interior* Cottage kitchen	Dutch costumes, wooden shoes. Fire in fireplace.
32. *Hansel and*	Chorpenning, Charlotte B.	2m, 5w, 11 children,	3 *exteriors* Before the	First act shows "a transition from the everyday doing and thinking of the house to the

Gretel	extras	house at edge of forest	mysterious and glowing quality of the forest."
(Coach House, 1956)			The opening is a panorama, each with its own lighting effects, of the forces of good and evil that surround the house: dwarfs with pickaxes appear here and there in spot areas; witch rides in on a broom which turns red on action cue; angel appears out of nowhere and fades out after plucking a coat from nowhere.
		Deep in the forest	Witch's broom turns red when it is angry, green when sly.
			Special spot area for Ole, the sandman, as he gives dreams.
		Before the witch's house	Witch's broom stands up after it has been laid down.
			Oven large enough to be entered erect.
			Candy house, pieces detachable.
			Cage for Hansel.
			Oven door opens when Witch points, closes when she sighs.
			Oven glows beautifully, not terrifyingly.
			Much business with broom which bucks, starts to fly away alone, won't stand when leaned, then stands by itself.

TITLE	AUTHOR	CHARACTERS	SETTINGS	SPECIAL REQUIREMENTS
33. *Hansel and Gretel: A Legend Brought To Life*	Masters, Lillian, and Masters, Robert (French, 1949)	2m, 2w, 9 children	1 *interior* 2 *exteriors* Inside hut "Great rock" in forest Witch's house in forest	Flash, Witch flies in on a broom. The Witch's ride: she flies about on her broom amidst flashing lights. Many dances by children (I, III). Large white cat, changes to boy. Gingerbread children in fence come to life. Baskets of treasure.
34. *Hansel and Gretel*	Miller, Madge (CTP, 1951)	1m, 3w, 3 children, extras	3 *exteriors* Forest clearing with hut In the forest Witch's hut in clearing	Black cat (actor) changes into a girl. Trick oven with open back. Jack-in-the-box (actor).
35. *Heidi*	Miller, Lucille (CTP, 1936)	3m, 6w, 4 children	1 *exterior* 2 *interiors* The Alm Grandmother's hut Clara's	Mountains in the background. A live goat. Live kittens. Wheel chair for Clara. Swiss peasant and late 19th-century upper-class costumes.

346

			living room	Characters go in and out of hut (The Alm, I, IV).
36. *Helga and the White Peacock*	Meigs, Cornelia (Macmillan, 1922)	2w, 3 children, West Wind, Grey Goose, Peacock	1 *interior*	Cobwebs all over Trolls' house. A loom on which colorful weaving is in progress. Dim lighting for dingy interior. Spider Woman and other Trolls in special costumes.
			1 *exterior* House of Trolls	Grey Goose with torn feathered cloak. A Peacock gets new feathers. Some singing. Dawn breaks (II).
			Forest	Young Troll blows bubbles.
37. *Hiawatha*	Norris, James (CTP, 1953)	14m, 2w, 1 girl, 1 rabbit puppet, 1 raccoon puppet	1 *interior* 2 *exteriors* Inside longhouse	Skin hangings in longhouse. Fire in center of floor. Indian costumes, make-up. A cloth mask with long nose. Ceremonial dances. Rock and stump conceal Rabbit and Raccoon puppets.
			In the forest	Fire started on stage with flints. Striped goal-post for gauntlet. Wind and thunder. Spherical hut added to forest set for III-i. Bear spirit, costume problem.
			Outside longhouse	Hiawatha sails away in magic canoe.

TITLE	AUTHOR	CHARACTERS	SETTINGS	SPECIAL REQUIREMENTS
38. *Huckleberry Finn*	Whiting, Frank M, and Rickert, Corinne H. (CTP, 1948)	9m, 5w, 4 children	5 *exteriors* 1 *interior* Cabin clearing, woods Raft in cove Raft afloat Raft in bushes Backyard of farm Sitting room	Suggested false proscenium throughout. 2 rocks and tree stump. Huck saws hole in wall of cabin. Raft with box cabin. Raft on rockers to suggest movement. Moving cloud projection on cyclorama for raft in motion. Specific light for Huck's narratives. Jim carries in dead pig. Off-stage shooting. Dead rattlesnake. Suggested music cues, some dancing. Snake slips off house eaves and down Sally's neck. Night lighting (III-iii). Much shooting of guns in escape sequence. Off-stage dogs barking. 1850 rustic costumes.
39. *The Indian Captive*	Chorpenning, Charlotte B. (CTP, 1937)	3m, 3w, 5 children	2 *exteriors* Forest clearing and cabin	Brewing tub. Children go in and out of cabin. Pioneer and Indian costumes and make-up. Indian songs.

Title	Author (Publisher)	Cast	Settings	Production notes
			Lookout rock near Indian village	Large rock with thongs for torture scene. Outdoor fire, tripod, and kettle. Crescent moon in sky.
40. *Jack and the Beanstalk*	Chorpenning, Charlotte B. (CTP, 1935)	7m, 5w, 1 child	2 *exteriors* 1 *interior* Garden outside house On beanstalk Kitchen of Giant	A movable cow stretches over the fence, moves all visible parts. Harp (II, III), actor with ornamental head. Beanstalk which grows on cue must support several actors at once on concealed rope ladder. Garden table with magic lights in blue, green, and red (I). Special lighting, not realistic, for Giant's sky kitchen. Fireplace with side oven, big enough for boy. Kettle big enough for boy. Also other over-sized props: carrot, knife. Golden hen on nest of golden eggs. Man in the Moon, sits on a crescent. Beanstalk with Giant crashes to ground when cut (III).
41. *Jack and the Beanstalk*	Nixon, Nora Fortson (French, 1936)	2m, 3w, 1 boy, 1 cow (2w), hen (child)	2 *exteriors* 2 *interiors*, Country road with cottage	A 2-man cow, flicks tail at flies. Light cues for different times of day. Beanstalk grows in sight of audience. Jack climbs it. Jack appears in upper land from below (upstage of boulders).

TABULATION OF PLAYS FOR CHILDREN (*Continued*)

TITLE	AUTHOR	CHARACTERS	SETTINGS	SPECIAL REQUIREMENTS
41. *Jack and the Beanstalk*			Top of beanstalk Giant's kitchen Jack's cottage (remodeled for III-ii)	A ballet to open II. Oversized furniture and props for Giant's kitchen. Steam pours from kettle. A hen (actor) that walks and speaks; lays golden eggs all over. Fire leaps up on cue. Grindstone to sharpen ax. Beanstalk falls when cut.
42. *King Midas and the Golden Touch*	Chorpenning, Charlotte B. (CTP, 1950)	2m, 2w, 4 children	1 *exterior* King's garden	Phrygian costumes, several centuries B.C. A pool or fountain with blue, then gold, lights. Egyptian water clock. Life-sized statue of Goddess, comes to life occasionally. Dancing, much playing of games. Specific light on statue. Extra pedestal for Tyra. Props turn to gold on Midas' touch, end of I, II. All props gold at opening of II.

| 43. *The King of the Golden River* | Margery Evernden (Coach House, 1955) | 4m, 2w, 2 children | 1 *interior* 1 *exterior* Farmhouse kitchen Mountain top | Some gold chairs and benches replaced with marble for III. Midas drinks wine, eats apple, spits out pieces of gold. Tyra, the Princess, turns into golden statue on cue. "A dark Germanic atmosphere" in the wealthy farmhouse. A tile stove. A gale rages outside. Fantastic costume and make-up on South-west Wind, Esq. A magic walking stick, intercepts flying rolling pin. Gale blows window open, roof off house. Lighting changes, goes dim on cue. Fantastic lights on S. W. Wind. King of Golden River comes out of oven. Wears fancy gold costume. Characters go out through window. Thunder and lightning on cue. Rocks and shrubs on mountain. As King touches spots of ground, blades of grass and trees appear. A dog appears and vanishes on rock. |

TABULATION OF PLAYS FOR CHILDREN (*Continued*)

Title	Author	Characters	Settings	Special Requirements
43. *The King of the Golden River*				Rock rolls, pinning Hans' foot. A flower, then many, appear from nowhere. Dog appears again, almost dead. A tall white lily grows from rock. Rocks of Hans and Schwartz appear in their likenesses.
44. *The Land of Oz*	Goodspeed, Elizabeth Fuller (French, 1928)	6m, 5w, 1 girl, Woggle Bug, Gump, 2 monkeys, extras	4 *interiors* 1 *exterior* Kitchen of the witch Throne room of Emerald Palace Tin Woodman's royal bed chamber Glinda's throne room	Tip makes a Pumpkin man on the stage. Replaced in cupboard by character. Comes out alive. Steaming kettle of witch's brew. Dancing of Gillikins, Army, and principals. Saw Horse comes to life. Winged monkeys. Canopied bed for Tin Woodman. Dance of sunflowers. Costume problem for Woggle Bug, Pumpkin Head, Scarecrow, Winged Monkeys, Tin Woodman, Saw Horse, and others. Mouse runs across stage on cue. Characters build the "Gump" out of 2 sofas, palm leaves, etc. Gump comes to life, talks and flaps wings.

			On the road to the Emerald City	Several special light cues, spot areas, flickers. Cloud effect. Wind sound. Red flare during charm. Transformation of Tip to Ozma.
45. *The Land of the Dragon*	Miller, Madge (CTP, 1946)	5m, 5w, 1 dragon	1 *basic set* Oriental stage	A series of cut out shrubs, trees, boxes, flowers, and painted "scenes" on scrolls to suggest 9 locales. Oriental costumes, make-up, props. Dragon costume (Small One). 2 fake dragon costumes, 1 of them for two people.
46. *Lee Bobo, Detective for Chinatown*	Lee, Rose Hum, and Chorpenning, Charlotte B. (CTP, 1948)	6m, 3w, 6 children	1 *interior* 1 *exterior* Curio shop Chinatown street	Sliding wall panels in Curio shop. Jade Goddess (Goon Yum). Chinese-American costumes, make-up. Unusual Oriental props in Curio shop, unspecified.
47. *Lincoln's Secret Messenger*	Chorpenning, Charlotte B. (Coach House, 1955)	8m, 2w, extras	1 *exterior* 1 *interior* Street in Washington	A practical window in a house along the street. 2 street lights, practical. Moonlight (I).

Title	Author	Characters	Settings	Special Requirements
47. *Lincoln's Secret Messenger*			Reception room at White House	Fire in fireplace (II). 1860 furnishings in realistic White House room (II). Historically accurate costumes.
48. *The Little Princess*	Burnett, Frances Hodgson (French, 1911)	5m, 5w, 11 children	3 *interiors* Drawing room of boarding school Garret Study of neighbor's house	A monkey enters the garret. Complete change of props and furniture through window in a very short time. Rats enter and exit on cue.
49. *Little Red Riding Hood, or Grandmother Slyboots*	Chorpenning, Charlotte B. (CTP, 1946)	1 m, 2w, 2 children 2 wolves	2 *exteriors* 1 *interior* Forest clearing with house deep in forest Wolves' cave Grandmother's cottage	Storybook costumes. 2 wolves' costumes. Much singing and dancing. House with front and rear access for chases (I). Cave structure to sustain racing into, over and around. Grandmother's house: mantel to support R.R.H., reached by ladder. People come down chimney. Grandmother escapes through window.

50. *Little Women*	Spencer, Sara (CTP, 1940)	2m, 10w,	1 *interior* Sitting room of Concord home	1863 costumes. Realistic detail in set strongly suggested. Hallway and curtains for stage of Jo's play. Also rough scenery of cardboard. Jo's long hair is cut off to sell.
51. *The Magic Horn*	Nicholson, Anne, and Chorpenning, Charlotte B. (Coach House, 1951)	5m, 4w, extras	2 *exteriors* Inner court of French castle / Magic garden	Pieces of armor line walls of castle court (I). A glowing jewel on Falerina's (sorceress') headpiece. A Book of Fate, larger than a man, on an easel (II). A misty effect in garden. Falerina plays the flute. Sword rises by itself and hangs in mid air in a wall recess (II). A ring of fire rises around it. White wine turns red as it is poured into a glass. Robe glows brilliantly as it is being enchanted. Fruits and sweets also glow. Flames guarding sword change color. Steps and niche turn red as Prince tries to get sword. Lights dim. A time candle is burning (III).

355

TABULATION OF PLAYS FOR CHILDREN (*Continued*)

TITLE	AUTHOR	CHARACTERS	SETTINGS	SPECIAL REQUIREMENTS
51. *The Magic Horn*				A crystal ball. A wax tablet and stylus. A mime is played. Falerina whirls and melts into a heap of misty folds. The mist music is especially important. Gregorian chant is sung by Roland and Charlemagne.
52. *Make-Believe*	Milne, A. A. (French, 1918)	32m, 16w, 15 children, 1 bird, extras	3 *exteriors* 3 *interiors* Forest glade Tropical island Outside the Hubbard's house Schoolroom Drawing room Court of Father Christmas	Modern storybook costumes. Forest glade has woodcutter's cottage. Practical door. Many songs. Fast shift to desert island for almost continuous action. Daylight comes on cue. Dance of Pirates and Dusky Maidens. Cave on desert island, glows red. Trees needed.

53. *Many Moons*	Chorpenning, Charlotte B. (Dramatic, 1946)	5m, 3w, 2 children	3 *interiors* Room in the palace Throne room Princess' bedroom	Stairway to Princess Lenore's bedroom. 5 bell cords. Table and royal chair. Jester in motley. Throne and dais. "Moonlight Sonata" plays every time Jester waves hands over lute. Moonlight through window on cue, flickers. (Or built moon rises in the window.)
54. *Marco Polo*	Siks, Geraldine Brain (CTP, 1941)	11m, 4w, extras	2 *exteriors* 1 *interior* Quay at Venice Tartar Mountain camp Khan's throne room	Section of deck and ship at wharf (I). Dawn rises. Marco hides in big basket of figs. Flag hoisted up mast. Night lighting (II). Campfire on stage. Smoke from fire glows red and green on cue. Statuette (Tartar image) contains urn of magic powder. Thunder and lightning. Hut in which Princess is locked (II). Oriental gong (III). Chests of treasure. Silver prophecy ball. Dance of Dragon Slave. Incense burner gives off red and green smoke on cue.

357

TITLE	AUTHOR	CHARACTERS	SETTINGS	SPECIAL REQUIREMENTS
55. *Master Skylark* or *Will Shakespeare's Ward*	Burrill, Edgar White (Century, 1916)	12m, 4w, extras	2 *exteriors* 4 *interiors* Country lane with thatched cottage Garden at Stratford Tavern room Carew's house Throne room of Queen Elizabeth Dungeon corridor	Inn yard stage visible through tavern window. A few light cues. An upper story window overlooks the garden. Much singing, some dancing. Elizabethan costumes, both rustic and upper class.
56. *Mr. Dooley, Jr.*	Franken, Rose, and Lewin, Jane (French, 1931)	4m, 4w, 2 children	2 *interiors* Pet shop Anders' living room	Pets in cages (1). Dog (live) quite prominent in action. Children paint the wall of the living room, spill paint on set, floor, selves. Piano lesson on stage.

57. *Mr. Popper's Penguins*	Mitchell, Albert O. (CTP, 1952)	8m, 2w, 4 children, 12 penguins	2 *interiors* Living room Draped stage (Transition scene before curtain)	Dog makes noises on cue. Bicycle on stage. Children's slide and revolving teeter-totter. 12 penguins' costumes. Refrigerator in alcove (only the door is seen). Mama plays the piano. Contemporary costumes.
58. *Mr. Popper's Penguins*	Musil, Rosemary Gabbert (Ms. from author, 293 W. Fremont St., Elmhurst, Ill.)	11m, 7w, 2 children, 12 penguins, extras	2 *interiors* Living room Backstage of theatre	Cuckoo clock (doorbell). Ladder slide for penguins. Icebox wheeled in, set against wall, false back for penguins' entrances. Trays of fish are "eaten," removed through rear wall. 12 penguins' costumes. Mama plays the piano.
59. *Mystery at the Old Fort*	Musil, Rosemary Gabbert (CTP, 1944)	6m, 2w, 2 children	2 *interiors* Living room, re-modeled fort	Live dog. Combination living-dining room-kitchen for main set. Passage set may be in front of curtain or screens. Fireplace with side oven.

Title	Author	Characters	Settings	Special Requirements
59. *Mystery at the Old Fort*			Subterranean passage	Victorian furnishings. Wardrobe large enough to hide in. Moonlight through window. Moody lighting several scenes. Costumes modern. One Indian. Large kettle over fire. Cereal cooked. Workbench in passageway scene, littered with test tubes, vials, tools, and machinery. Lizzie drops and breaks plate. Draped alcove to hide in.
60. *Niccolo and Nicollette* or *The Puppet Prince*	Cullen, Alan (CTP, 1957)	7m, 3w, extras	3 *interiors* 2 *exteriors* Toyshop Castle corridor Magnus' workshop Crossroads Outside the castle	A fantastic toyshop with large assorted dolls, puppets, toy theatre, soldiers; also a life-sized mechanical soldier in a box. He comes to life (Niccolo). A leprechaun. A flash as magic causes door to lock. Moonlight in crossroads scene. A log across US at crossroads. Tiny gleams of light appear all over the stage (I-ii). A human-sized golden cockerel.

"The Dance of Dawn" ballet is performed by an assortment of birds.

Blackouts and other light cues.

Leprechaun "nails" tail feathers back on High Cockalorum.

Seamus' shoes remain "rooted to the ground" as he is kicked out of them.

Castle gateway has practical door.

Silver feather is pulled from High Cockalorum.

Mountebank's stall is set up.

Castle door opens magically.

Alchemist's workshop is littered with paraphernalia.

Nikki wears mask when he is a puppet.

Leprechaun comes down chimney.

A flash in the mortar as Magnus mixes magic potion.

Music plays on signal from Magnus.

"A huge magnificent porcelain stove ornamented richly with bright colored figures and scenes."

A modeled Bethlehem scene.

A voice from the stove.

Fire in stove goes off and on.

August climbs into stove to hide.

61. *The Nuremberg Stove*	Silks, Geraldine Brain (CTP, 1956)	4m, 1w, 4 children	3 *interiors* Living room Curiosity shop Throne room of Berg castle

Title	Author	Characters	Settings	Special Requirements
61. The Nuremberg Stove				Curiosity shop has 2 knights in armor, spinet piano, Saxe poodle, and tall Dutch clock. Shadowy lighting in shop. Window of shop is too high for August to unbolt. Chiming of many clocks. All above objects come to life, candles light, piano plays, clock swings pendulum. 4 teapots come out of the cupboard and dance. Apostle-Krug jug comes out of cupboard. A china princess enters and dances with August. Hirschvogel speaks, lighted with a golden beam of light.
62. Ozma of Oz	Buchanan, Mary Isabel (French, 1935)	7m, 3w, 1 girl, hen, Saw Horse, Nome King, extras	3 interiors 1 exterior Cave Palace reception room	A hen character (Billina). Tiktok, a round copper man. Many light cues. Cabinets full of heads for Langwidere. Palace reception room is a divided scene. Tower room (L).

			Nome King's throne room	Other fantastic characters: Scarecrow, Tin Woodman, Lion, Tiger, Saw Horse. Ozma rides chariot drawn by Lion and Tiger.
			underground	Iron Giant (of which we see only the foot) hammers the ground.
			Road to Nome King's	Nome sprites flit back and forth.
63. *Oliver Twist*	Browne, Muriel (CTP, 1938)	7m, 5w, 2 youths	*2 interiors* Thieves' den	Rough, dirty, broken furnishings and props in thieves' den. Fire in fireplace, sausages cooking. Pile of dirty old rags in corner. Stolen jewelry and articles in red leather box.
			Sitting room	Costumes of 1800's upper and lower classes: Dickensian. Portrait of Oliver's mother. Storm outside, IV.
64. *The Panda and the Spy*	Heinlein, Mary Virginia (CTP, 1954)	4m, 8w, 2 children	*1 interior* Suburban living room	An old house, remodeled; has a staircase. Fireplace with safe in old Dutch oven. Trap door used by Panda. Realistic household props. A panda (actor). Vase is shot off window seat. Moonlight outside; some moody lighting. Contemporary costumes.

Title	Author	Characters	Settings	Special Requirements
65. *Papa Pompino and the Prize Fighter*	King, Martha Bennett (Harcourt, Brace, 1952) in *First Performance*	3m, 1w, 8 children	1 *exterior* Wall of a deserted estate	The wall is practical. Characters run and jump on it. An apple tree behind wall, with a seat in it for Papa. Bush, tree, L and R. A ladder against the wall. A flagpole with pennant flying. A clown costume for Papa—the rest are contemporary. Wall has one removable stone, behind which a paper is concealed.
66. *The Patchwork Girl of Oz*	Marshall, Mrs. James Waller (French, 1930)	16m, 14w, cat, owl, donkey, Woozy, Yoop	2 *interiors* 7 *exteriors* Pipt's workshop Emerald City throne room Roadside house and fence Place of	Dr. Pipt, the magician, is crooked. A glass cat is alive, dances. Huge patchwork doll comes alive. 2 characters turned to marble. Some lighting effects called for. Costume problems: Owl, Saw Horse, Donkey, Woozy, Scarecrow, Patchwork Girl, Jack Pumpkinhead, Yoop with Claws, Tin Woodman. Woozy's eyes flash fire, burn fence.

				Scene	Notes
				Bending Trees	Clutching hands of leaves lower onto the travelers.
				Near the Emerald City	Lantern slides projected as Shaggy Man sings.
				Outside Jack Pumpkinhead's house	A pumpkin house with small pumpkins attached.
				Rocky country	A scarecrow dummy to be tossed about.
				Outside Tin Woodman's house	Magic appearance of Ozma and Wizard, in flashing lights.
67. *Peter Pan*	Barrie, James M. (Scribner's, 1928)	12m, 3w, 10 children, dog, ostrich, crocodile, mermaids, pirates, Indians	1 *interior* 4 *exteriors* 1 *combined*	Nursery Forest in Never Land Mermaid Lagoon	Dog (Nana), an actor. Tinker Bell is a ball of light. Flying of Peter, Wendy, John, and Michael. Trees with doors in them lead to Peter's house below. Ostrich, wolves, crocodile costumes. Indian costumes and makeup. Mermaids. Indians build a fire on stage.

TABULATION OF PLAYS FOR CHILDREN—(Continued)

Title	Author	Characters	Settings	Special Requirements
67. *Peter Pan*			Pirate ship Treetops Underground house and ground above it	A smoking chimney hid by a giant mushroom. Lost Boys build house over Wendy. Smoke then comes from chimney (John's hat). Large rock in lagoon must hold characters. Boat moves on lagoon. Kite carries Wendy off rock. Peter escapes in bird's nest which floats on rising tide. Michael's bed is a wall basket. Table collapses like accordion. Little house flies in and lands on tree tops.
68. *Peter, Peter, Pumpkin Eater*	King, Martha Bennett (CTP, 1945)	2m, 6w	1 *exterior* Farmyard (Large pumpkin house added for III)	Pumpkin vine with large blossom grows across stage on cue. Vine cut by Pruella. Practical pumpkin house: characters go in, sit, and hang curtains in it. Practical balcony on farmhouse. Owl hoots off stage as dialogue with meaning.

69. *The Pied Piper of Hamelin*	Miller, Madge (CTP, 1951)	3m, 3w, 3 youths, extras	1 *exterior* Public square	Stone benches R and L, shrubs. Platform with a bust of a disagreeable-looking man on a column. Pied Piper wears parti-colored costume. Pipe music played by Dirk and Piper. Much dancing, both groups and solos. Tumbling. Sound of mountain's opening. Bust of the Baron opens its mouth, laughs, and spits out gold coins.
70. *Pinocchio*	Miller, Madge (CTP, 1954) in *Miniature Plays*	2m, 1w, 2 children, cricket, cat, fox	2 *interiors* 4 *exteriors* Gepetto's house Inside Dog-fish Forest Before the Fairy's cottage Field Boobyland Transitions before curtain	Fire, fireplace, kettle painted on wall. Cricket is a "large black movable prop" who appears on wall. Gepetto works on puppet prop. Harp glides accompany waves of wand. Pinocchio's nose grows longer. Music of traveling puppet show. Storybook costumes throughout. White cricket (ghost) also a prop. Pinocchio is hung from tree. Blue Fairy twice appears in disguise. Land of Boobies has backdrop of distorted amusement park items. A practical distortion mirror. Donkey ears on Pinocchio and Candlewick.

TITLE	AUTHOR	CHARACTERS	SETTINGS	SPECIAL REQUIREMENTS
70. *Pinocchio*				Sound of rushing water as Pinocchio dives into the sea. Cutaway dogfish. Inside seen through scrim. Fish's eye moves. Pinocchio with Gepetto on his back swims out of the fish's mouth. Transformation from puppet to boy occurs under fairy's cape.
71. *Pinocchio*	Stone, Dorothy Dayton (Dramatic, 1946)	4m, 2w, 2 children	2 *interiors* 3 *exteriors* Gepetto's cottage Puppet theatre Outside puppet theatre Land of Hookey On the road	Costume problem for Pinocchio and Blue Fairy. Blue Fairy extends Pinocchio's nose to full length. Nose grows longer with lies he tells. Urn of fire for Fire Eater. Pinocchio and Candlewick each get a set of donkey ears, tail. Transformation of Pinocchio to a real boy.

| 72. *Pinocchio and the Indians* | Harris, Aurand (French, 1950) | 7m, 6w, extras | 3 *exteriors* Behind tent of animal show On the ocean Indian village | Sets move rapidly from one to next. Interludes with Pinocchio's excursions through audience. Linnebach projection suggested for tent show scene. Drum, bugle, and band playing during tent show scene. 2 bears, 1 tiger, Whitecaps require special costuming. Others in fantasy and story-book fashion. Large book walks on, hiding cricket. Trick hat from which a bird flies. Rocking "waves" (flats) moved on for ocean scene. A large fish chases Pinocchio in the ocean. He eats a small candy fish while "swimming." Indians chant and dance. Bear's head on wooden tray for feast. Long scrolls. Cricket enters through door in tree. Pinocchio enters full of arrows. Fire lighted on stage, red glow all over. Thunder and lightning. Splashes and sprays of water during ocean crossing scenes. Pinocchio's hat is full of water for final sequence. |

TABULATION OF PLAYS FOR CHILDREN—*(Continued)*

Title	Author	Characters	Settings	Special Requirements
73. *The Plain Princess*	Harris, Aurand (CTP, 1955)	4m, 7w, extras	*2 interiors* Royal playroom Cottage	Dame Goodwit sings prologue. A puppet show booth, performs Punch and Judy show to hurdy-gurdy. Table with balloons and confetti for party. Magician does several tricks: causes sun "to go out"; music box lid opens; doll near wall bows and says lines; stage changes colors; coaster wagon rolls off stage; Princess is transformed with a mask which has flashing lights for eyes. Knit scarf unravels. Princess makes batch of muffins; a big mess. Rainbow shines outside window. Bird in cage sings on cue. Princess' features (nose, mouth, eyes) change from ugly to pretty on cue. Small cake on table magically replaced by large one with candles which light by themselves one by one. A Roman candle spouts at top.

74. *The Prince and the Pauper*	Chorpenning, Charlotte B. (CTP, 1951)	13m, 16w	*4 exteriors* *2 interiors* Outside palace wall Palace garden London street Canty's hovel Woods camp Cathedral	Settings must flow from one to the next as action continues. Secret jewel closet in palace garden. Elaborate late-medieval costumes. Pageantry of a coronation. Great Seal of England, used to crack nuts.
75. *Prince Fairyfoot*	Brain, Geraldine (CTP, 1947)	10m, 3w, extras	*2 exteriors* Town square Forest clearing with hut	Fanciful costumes. Big feet on most characters. A foot-measuring block. Robin hops along the wall chirping (II). He flies in, chirps, and flies off several times.
76. *The Princess and Mr. Parker*	Seiler, Gwendolen (French, 1934)	12m, 10w, 2 children	*2 interiors* Palace sitting room Banquet hall	Mr. Parker carries a duck. Blinding flash and bang takes all characters back to 1583 from modern times. Madrigal singers. Red glow of fire off stage.

TABULATION OF PLAYS FOR CHILDREN—(*Continued*)

TITLE	AUTHOR	CHARACTERS	SETTINGS	SPECIAL REQUIREMENTS
77. *The Princess and the Swineherd*	Miller, Madge (CTP, 1956)	3m, 5w	1 *interior* 1 *exterior* Royal drawing room Royal pigpen	Nimble, the Jester, dances. Swineherd enters through windows. Bells from magic kettle play the Princess' tune. Candlelight scene (I-ii). Green-lighted weird dream dance. Pig masks for Ladies in Waiting, Princess, and Nimble. Fantastic ring for Nimble. Fence and fence post for hanging the crown at the pigpen. A lute resembling a woman's face ("Dame Gossip"); the lute speaks gossip when the strings are plucked. (An unintelligible chattering.) Nimble disguises himself as a doctor, changes disguise with the Prince. Storybook costumes.
78. *The Princess and the Swineherd*	Seiler, Gwendolen (French, 1930)	17m, 5w, extras	2 *interiors* 1 *exterior* King Bingo's throne room	Shabbily furnished throne room. Characters dance the minuet. Other singing and dancing, too. Pigs carried on in a market basket.

			4 *interiors* 1 *exterior*	
			Princess' nursery	Sky changes to sunset. Swineherd climbs in and out of nursery window.
			Royal Piggeries	
79. *Racketty-Packetty House*	Burnett, Frances Hodgson (Little, Brown, 1926) in Moses, *Another Treasury*	12m, 14w, extras	Nursery	Large shabby doll house. Mixture of fantastic costumes. (Green Workers, Fairy Queen) and contemporary and Victorian realistic.
			Sitting room, RP house	Light inside old doll house, lights on cue.
			Drawing room, RP house	Large castle-type doll house. 6 dolls of Tidy Castle taken out and named. Upturned furniture, pictures all swinging on walls in opening of I. Peter with head through table top. Kilmanskeeg found upside down in grandfather clock.
			Bare room in Tidy Castle	Life-size legs seen passing window of RP house.
			Outside	
			Toy Church	Ceiling of RP house removed, a large hand places box in center of room. Box contains Lady Patsy. Ceiling replaced. Dancing. Fairy Queen appears out of big vase in RP house, also from table drawer. Tidy Castle with lighted windows seen through window of RP house. Sequence of action seen at one window of Tidy Castle.

Title	Author	Characters	Settings	Special Requirements
79. *Racketty-Packetty House*				Scene change to room in Tidy Castle done in brief blackout. Lady Doris has enlarged nose which she loses later.
80. *Radio Rescue*	Chorpenning, Charlotte B. (Coach House, 1954)	4m, 2w, 6 children	2 *interiors* 1 *exterior* Attic of Orphan Home Abandoned mill Railroad embankment	Unit set for I and II suggested. Radio receiver and transmitter hidden in trunks. Voices over radio. Much dim, shadowy lighting. Escape through window. A storm outside (II). Some specific music cues. Must suggest operating parts of mill. Trap door to fish through (II). Fire built on millstone. Broken railroad trestle. Fire built on the tracks. Wreckage pins Mike to track.
81. *Rama and the Tigers*	Chorpenning, Charlotte B.	6m, 6w, 4 tigers, 5 monkeys	2 *exteriors* Clearing with hut	Costumes for Tigers and Monkeys. Indian make-up.

Title	Author (Publisher, date)	Cast	Setting	Staging notes
(Little Black Sambo and the Tigers, 1938)	(Coach House, 1954)		Deep in the jungle	A vine up which monkeys and Rama climb. Tigers change to butter after chase around tree (II-iii). Lightning flashes, lights dim and flicker to hide change.
82. *Rapunzel and the Witch*	Melanos, Jack A. (CTP, 1957)	2m, 3w, voices	2 *exteriors* Outside the house and witch's garden Outside the prison tower	A high wall separates Margot's yard from Witch's garden. Wall has a door in it. Lights flash on and off with Witch's entrance. Garden contains a Wizard's stone, big enough to hide behind. Its eyes light up. The tree (enchanted King) speaks. A plant (enchanted Queen) speaks. Wizard stone speaks when it lights up. Other lights dim. Flower speaks. Special lights on tree and plant. Rapunzel lets down her long hair so witch can climb up tower. Tower can be seen into clearly.
83. *Rip Van Winkle*	Chorpenning, Charlotte B. (Coach House, 1954)	13m, 9w, 11 children	1 *interior* 1 *exterior* Parlor of wealthy burgher	1771 period costumes. Model of "Half Moon" on stand in parlor. Rip climbs out window. "Portrait" of Henrick Hudson on wall smiles, eyes follow Rip around, salutes.

Title	Author	Characters	Settings	Special Requirements
83. *Rip Van Winkle*			In the mountains	Dancing. Large rock formation for mountain scene. Storm (II) suddenly clears, then moonlight. All play ninepins. Lightning, spotted areas and fadeouts (II). Old make-up for Rip and others after 20 years.
84. *Rip Van Winkle*	Ruthenberg, Grace Dorcas (CTP, 1935)	9m, 7w, 7 children, 6 dwarfs, extras	*2 exteriors* Inn yard Mountain glade	1771 period costumes. Dog (live) goes with Rip. Storm. Weird lighting suggested for mountain glade scene. Game of ninepins is played as thunder roars. Lights flash and fade (II). Dancing and singing. Old make-up on Rip after 20 years' sleep. Slight changes in inn yard set for III.
85. *Robin Hood*	Davis, Owen (French, 1923)	14m, 5w	*2 exteriors* *1 interior* Sherwood forest glade	A large tree necessary for action. Light changes required. Escape down ladder at window (we see only top of ladder). A little hut of boughs.

86. *Robin
Hood*

Norris,
James
(CTP, 1952)

11m, 2w

Greenwood tree in forest	Deer carcass. Sheriff climbs up into the Greenwood tree.
Great hall, Nottingham	
1 *interior*	Singing and dancing (the Hey figure).
2 *exteriors* Living room	Living room in style of Medieval England. Medieval costumes. Sir Guy in a horse's hide.
Sherwood forest	Bagpipe music in background. Robin comes through window, hides in closet. Specific lighting for flash-back sequence. Arrow in Sir Guy's seat.
Nottingham Fair	Trees moved from place to place. Large tree trunk, 3-dimensional, with knot hole to look through. Large camouflaged rock with door leading to cave. Dawn comes up. Awning-covered booths at Fair. Prize fight ring roped off. 2 targets. Taken off stage for actual shooting. Arrows shot into mattress. Little John's bow breaks in half.
(Interlude before the curtain)	

TITLE	AUTHOR	CHARACTERS	SETTINGS	SPECIAL REQUIREMENTS
87. *Robinson Crusoe*	Chorpenning, Charlotte B. (CTP, 1952)	10m, 2w, puppet parrot	1 *interior* 1 *exterior* Living room Island	17th-century English manor living room, realistic props. Large rock formation with cave for island scene. Rustic props: goatskin umbrella, chair, table, eating utensils, tools. Parrot is a puppet that must move and talk. Costumes elegant in I, rustic and scanty in II and III.
88. *Robinson Crusoe*	Miller, Madge (CTP, 1954) in *Miniature Plays*	5m, puppet parrot	1 *exterior* (Stockade added for Part II)	Tree can be climbed for lookout. Surf, thunder, lightning. Native costumes, make-up. Robin wears breeches and jacket, in I. Puppet parrot operated by rod through vegetation, atop wall. Witch Doctor wears grotesque mask. Sound of ship crashing on rocks. Robin hauls in several props from the ship: telescope, powder horn. Robin fires fowling piece; blossom falls off bush. Ladder leads over wall of stockade. Rough chair, primitive tools. Robin and Friday in goatskin clothes for II.

	Author (Publisher, date)	Cast	Settings	Production notes
89. *Rumpel-stiltskin*	Chorpenning, Charlotte B. (CTP, 1944)	6m, 7w, extras	2 *exteriors* 1 *interior* Edge of the World King's garden Queen's spinning room	Desirable that Edge of the World, behind scrim, literally overlook the garden. Specific lighting, Edge of the World and garden separately. Secret door from Edge of the World to garden. 3 off-stage rooms filled with straw which turns to gold; revealed through 3 different-sized doors. Spinning wheel which starts and stops on cue. Lights flash when it operates. Fairy tale costumes. Cauldron with varicolored lights. Regal cradle. Rumpel "flies to pieces" at end of play. Dueling by King's Son and courtiers. Dancing. Shadow of tree climbs a wall. Wind and thunder sound cues.
90. *The Sandalwood Box*	Siks, Geraldine Brain (CTP, 1954)	7m, 2w, 3 children, extras	3 *exteriors* 1 *interior* Spanish street Alcalde's patio	2 huts with shuttered windows. Sanchez plays guitar, sings. Several large water jugs. Dolores dances fandango. Chests of jewels on levels. Candle on level, flickers on cue.

TABULATION OF PLAYS FOR CHILDREN (*Continued*)

TITLE	AUTHOR	CHARACTERS	SETTINGS	SPECIAL REQUIREMENTS
90. *The Sandalwood Box*			Stone wall which opens on treasure cave	"Magic light of taper" floods area outside wall (III). Thunder, flashes of colored lights as wall reveals cave. Much treasure handled.
91. *The Scotch Twins*	Perkins, Eleanor (French, 1930)	4m, 2w, 4 children, extras	1 *interior* 3 *exteriors* Kitchen of peasant hut In forest by waterfall Another part of forest Before the castle door	A Dutch door to outside. Big fireplace with fire in it. Fire poked up, brightens. Exact business with fly rod: child is caught by the fly. Bagpipes played. Characters dance Highland fling. A cliff with broad ledge is required for action, entrance to cave off ledge, cliff split. Storm blows up (II). Off-stage waterfall is heard. Trees to hide behind (III). Terrace, stone steps, lawn, and castle door (IV).
92. *The Secret of Han Ho*	Evernden, Margery (Coach	10m, 1w, 1 child, extras	2 *exteriors* Street in Peking	Set has red gate to house L; temple grounds R (I). Shadow play stage erected and struck.

380

	House, 1956)		Street in So-ping	Shadow play presented. Kite dealer carries fantastic shaped kites to sell. A frightful mask worn briefly by Ho. Shadow figures torn by stepmother. Wu beats cymbals with his feet. Flower vendor's cart brought in. Wu plays the lute. Sheepskin shadow figure slashed to pieces.
93. *The Secret of Pat Pending*	McCreary, Bill, and McCreary, Marcie (French, 1948)	6m, 2w, 4 children	1 *interior* 1 *exterior* Basement workroom Wishington, D.C.	Furnace pipes and laundry tubs. Window in basement through which characters talk to those outside. Steps down from kitchen, and some from outside. Laundry chute. Washing machine and electric outlet. "Machine" goes into orgy of sounds and motion. Wishington set is fantastic, but basement should appear real. A red "Irish mail" (scooter) is ridden in. Ladder on which Pat was sitting vanishes overhead. Encyclopedia sails into Tink's hands. Tink's eyes light up when he gets an idea.

Title	Author	Characters	Settings	Special Requirements
93. *The Secret of Pat Pending*				Many light cues to concentrate attention. Lock of Mother's hair springs up. Machine smokes.
94. *The Secret of the Worn-out Shoes*	Clifford, Margaret Ellen (Harcourt, Brace, 1952) in *First Performance*	11m, 11w, 9 girls, 2 trees, extras	1 *exterior* 2 *interiors* Village square Dressing room Enchanted castle ballroom (changes to palace garden on cue)	A weathered medieval fountain in center of square; it has curb. Large water jars filled at the well. Much dancing, both peasant and stately court dances. Also Michael dances in the interpretative style. Gypsy dance. Ballets. Herald blows fanfares on trumpet. Storybook costumes, probably medieval. Lights dim and emphasize Lady of the Stars. Her costume gleams and glitters like a starry night. Two laurel trees in pots. They are as tall as Princess Lena by 11. Nine dressing tables and mirrors, 11. Blossoms appear magically on the laurel trees. Spirits of the trees come to life. They disappear after giving their gifts to Michael.

95. *The Seven League Boots*	Harris, Aurand (Row, Peterson, 1948)	5m, 5w	*2 exteriors* *1 interior* Forest clearing Forest clearing with large rock and cave added Ogre's bed and dining room

Clock strikes twelve. Trap door opens as Celestina turns ring.

Cold light in enchanted castle. Flash of lights as Michael breaks the golden goblet. Stage brightens, turns warm as scene becomes the regular castle garden.

Hanging vines are played like a harp.

Balloon "plum" floats down.

Other real plums fall on cue.

Large cobweb blocks the path.

Light changes required.

Large beds, fireplace, kettle in Ogre's house.

Children escape through window.

Very long legs taking very long steps projected on cyc. (Hop 'o My Thumb in boots.)

Ogrettes smear themselves with the fresh paint of window boxes.

Flashes of blue light silhouette 2 fairies in window.

Trick yellow flower attached to bottom of chest of gold. Stem breaks.

3 yellow flowers appear in flower box (Ogrettes transformed) Ogrettes melt away on stage.

TABULATION OF PLAYS FOR CHILDREN (*Continued*)

TITLE	AUTHOR	CHARACTERS	SETTINGS	SPECIAL REQUIREMENTS
95. *The Seven League Boots*				Chest fills with gold, overflows. Ogre transformed into flower. All 4 flowers sway rhythmically to music of finale.
96. *Seven Little Rebels*	Musil, Rosemary Gabbert (CTP, 1938)	3m, 5w, 8 children	*2 interiors* Kitchen of settlement house Dispensary	Stove, sink, cabinets required in kitchen. Boys play with a live dog. Large white live duck brought in. Contemporary costumes. Doll buggies played with. Letta sits in pan of jello. 2 counters in dispensary. Large box of adult-sized dress-up clothes. Letta drapes snake around her neck.
97. *The Silver Thread*	Mackay, Constance D'Arcy (Holt, 1910)	9m, 4w, 6 goblins, extras	*4 interiors* Cornish kitchen-living room Goblin's forge room Princess' bedroom	A spinning wheel. Off-stage explosions. A storm (I). Grotesque imitations of miners' tools for Goblins. Costumes fantastic for Goblins; others Cornish peasant and royal. Secret sliding panel in Princess' bedroom wall.

		Goblin's council chamber	Silver thread just appears and leads from ring to hidden door (III). Concealed stone door opens in the council room wall. Some special lighting cues.
98. *Simple Simon* or *Simon Big-Ears*	Harris, Aurand (CTP, 1953) 6m, 2w, 3 children, nightshirt, underwear, dress, extras	1 *exterior* Castle courtyard	Castle wall surrounds the acting area, containing towers and a dungeon window. Sun rises. Tower has a practical window. Simon has big ears. A pie wagon is drawn on stage. When Queen's nose turns red, all caps, aprons, signs, and banners turn red. When her nose turns green, all things turn green by command. Procession with May pole and Mardi Gras heads. A huge razor and bowl of shaving lather. Pieman gets his face shoved into open face cream pie. Large laundry basket extends off. Special lighting on it as Nightshirt, Dress, and Long Underwear come to life and dance. They return to basket. A clothesline across US with sheets, underwear, etc.

TABULATION OF PLAYS FOR CHILDREN (*Continued*)

TITLE	AUTHOR	CHARACTERS	SETTINGS	SPECIAL REQUIREMENTS
98. *Simple Simon* or *Simon Big-Ears*				Large penny. A tree appears, grows on stage, and sings. It gets chopped down. Another larger one with lights that blink grows in its place.
99. *Sing Ho for a Prince*	Grenzeback, Joe, and Bergh, Haakon (Coach House, 1951)	13m, 5w, 6 fairies, extras	*Simultaneously:* Forest DS Throne room US *Simultaneously:* Outside garden DS Palace garden US	Thunder and lightning flashes. Spotted areas for Treakle, change color on cue. Fizz (Magician) performs "standard magic tricks" throughout the play. Puffs of smoke rise from Fizz' pointed cap. Fairies with wings. Seat of throne opens and is loaded with props. Hogal (uninvited fairy) gets her trick wings crossed. Much dancing, many songs (a musical *Sleeping Beauty*). Horseshoe descends from flies. Lights on cradle change color with each wish of the fairies. Princess Rosamund lies on a bier in the garden. Briar hedge springs into place on cue, hiding garden.

100. *The Sleeping Beauty*	Chorpenning, Charlotte B. (CTP, 1947)	3m, 8w, 1 child	2 *interiors* 1 *exterior* Throne room Spinning room in tower Forest	Smoke rises about Hogal. Hogal pops balloons to emphasize lines. Magic hedge opens partially on cue. Firecracker that pops. Prince Plump rides in a wagon. Flash pot explodes, smoke rises. Throne room has small door to the tower. We see steps going up. Tablecloth with Fairies' names embroidered. Frytania is seen outside window waving her wand (I). Special lighting on Fairies' gift ceremony. Bells sound as each gift is given. All characters age 16 years. Cobweb covers tower door, pulls aside on spell, then closes. Panel in wall opens for Frytania. Door C opens by itself (II). Box with spindle opens by itself. Fairies appear in Tower room through secret panel. Special light as Beauty sleeps. Fairy forest rises, separating Una and Elano (Prince) from all others. Lights flicker as forest disappears. Singing by Frytania and Beauty, dancing by all at the end.

Title	Author	Characters	Settings	Special Requirements
101. *The Sleeping Beauty of Loreland*	Homer, Frances (Dramatic, 1935)	6m, 12w, 1 child, extras	1 *interior* 1 *exterior* Main hall of palace Before gate of palace	A cradle. All characters age 15 years. A peasant dance. Fairy tale costumes.
102. *The Snow Queen and the Goblin*	King, Martha Bennett (Coach House, 1956)	2m, 2w, 1 goblin, 2 children, extras	2 *interiors* Snow Queen's palace Grandmother's attic	Throne room should be "a scene of dazzling beauty." A throne on a dais. A frosty telescope. Northern lights move in slow arcs. Eerie wind music. Earth Children, blue with cold, wear masks. Snowbird in a cage. Dance and chant integrated. A rose tree in wooden tub. Attic set is detailed: a stove, cupboard to hide in. Snowbird flies in at window which opens by itself. Fantastic costume and make-up on Goblin.

An ice rose tree.
Gerda is encased in a block of ice. Ice dissolves into smoke on cue.
An explosion as Goblin throws magic mirror into black void.
Songs sung by children.
Indefinite period and fantastic costumes.

103. *Snow White and Rose Red*	Miller, Madge (CTP, 1954) in *Miniature Plays*	3m, 3w	1 *interior* 1 *exterior* Cottage Forest (Transitions before the curtain)

Rose trees outside cottage are seen through open doorway.
Hearth with a blazing fire.
French peasant costumes.
Sounds of wind on hearth.
Mother sings a song to the girls.
Complete bear outfit (enchanted Prince). He gets out and into it.
Scrim effect through fireplace shows background scenes.
Dolphe, the evil dwarf, wears a rock- and moss-patterned outfit.
Swinging panel in wall through which Philippe goes to be in scrim scenes.
Bluebird's song heard.
Forest has rocks and stump. Stump has cleft in which dwarf's beard is caught.
Large fish's head appears above rocks at edge of pool.

Title	Author	Characters	Settings	Special Requirements
103. *Snow White and Rose Red*				Small golden axe. Girls dance and sing. Bits of dwarf's beard are cut off.
104. *Snow White and the Seven Dwarfs*	Jonson, Marian (Coach House, 1957)	3m, 7w, 7 dwarfs	2 *interiors* Throne room with garden beyond Dwarf's cottage	Several dances. Housekeeper carries a large gold clipboard. Music of small orchestra comes from off stage. Music specified and supplied in text. Songs sung by various members of the cast. Prince dressed as a jester with domino mask of black and white. He carries a lute. Prince does magic tricks. Large magic mirror brought in, dropped, finally set against wall. It speaks in a deep voice. Fanfares. Dark Queen wears a constantly smiling mask. Lights change to cold and sombre on Queen's entrance. Prince builds a fire in fireplace of Dwarf's cottage.

105. *Snow White and the Seven Dwarfs*

White, Jessie Braham (French, 1912)

5m, 11w, 7 dwarfs, 3 cats, extras

3 *interiors* 1 *exterior*
Throne room
Dwarf's house
Cave of
Witch Hex

7 chairs, all different sizes, in cottage. 7 plates and cups.
Mining tools for Dwarfs.
Dwarf eats an icicle.
Cottage is an inset so that a sequence before the mirror can be played during the dwarfs' scene (II-i). Lights control attention in proper area.
Cottage has a Dutch door.
Snow White's song is answered by an Owl and a Dove. Then they appear on the door.
Queen puts on a disguise.
Snow White, apparently dead, lies on a golden couch in the garden.
While in a temper the Queen changes mask to one of evil ugliness. She tears mirror from wall and smashes it on the floor.
Lights flash and go out.
Prince does a quick change from jester to golden suit.
3 cats (little boys) go with Witch Hex.
Magic spell: smoke rises from center of circle traced on floor, then thunder, then, Witch Hex appears in the smoke.
A hand mirror that glows and beams like an opal.
Voice of the magic mirror.

TITLE	AUTHOR	CHARACTERS	SETTINGS	SPECIAL REQUIREMENTS
105. *Snow White and the Seven Dwarfs*			Deep in the forest	Witch Hex is bald.
				Blackouts on charm, earthquake sound as Hex disappears.
				Light fades in the forest.
				Bird sings in trees, is seen to fly past in 2 scenes.
				Pump draws water in Dwarf's house.
				7 very small dwarfs appear through floor.
				The mine is under the house.
				Quee gets washed in barrel of water.
				Hex's cavern covered with moss.
				Shadow of Hex crosses the moon.
				Cauldron and fire in cave.
				Pigtails all over Hex's head as she sticks it in the cauldron.
				Vision of old peddler woman appears in cauldron steam (scrim effect).
				Queen transforms to old peddler. Transforms back into Queen outside Dwarfs' window.

				Crystal coffin with Snow White in it is carried by Dwarfs. Queen sprouts a foot-long red nose. Much singing and dancing. 3 cats carried in basket for final scene.
106. *The Three Bears*	Chorpenning, Charlotte B. (CTP, 1949)	4m, 2w, 2 children	1 *interior* 1 *exterior* Bears' house Evergreen grove	Court-style medieval costumes. Bear costumes and make-up. Singing and dancing. A Christmas tree, trimmed. 3 different-sized beds, tables, chairs, bowls, spoons, cups, clocks. The beds store under each other. Characters hide and chase behind trees. Smallest chair collapses under Goldilocks. Big Bear fixes it. Characters dive out window.
107. *The Tinder Box*	McKelvey, Richard (Dramatic, 1946)	3m, 5w, 4 children, 1 dog, extras	2 *exteriors* 3 *interiors* Roadside in forest Village square Cave	A hollow high stump with ladder leading down inside. Some light cues. A large dog (actor). Three chests full of coins. House fronts in village square scene open up revealing the Princess' room.

TABULATION OF PLAYS FOR CHILDREN (*Continued*)

TITLE	AUTHOR	CHARACTERS	SETTINGS	SPECIAL REQUIREMENTS
107. The Tinder Box			Princess' room in castle Petrov's room in the inn	The Witch has the castle wall open up like a book; also the inn wall. Platform and 2 thrones are added to Princess' room.
108. Titian	Tully, Nora (Harcourt, Brace, 1952) in *First Performance*	6m, 3w, 3 children	2 *interiors* Kitchen Abandoned house	Sets and costumes Italian, 1487. Angelus rings. Titian paints a red devil on the back of a doublet. Titian squeezes flower petals and makes a stain on table leaf. A large painting on the wall of the abandoned house is covered with canvas to disguise it. Jars of water color paint. A brazier for heating water. Paint spills, stains the floor. Off-stage music is played. The girls dance. Salvatore smears paint on Lisa's dress. He smears dirty water on the wall painting. Catarina hides under a cask. Madonna miniature painted on sole of a shoe.

109. *Toad of Toad Hall*	Milne, A. A. (French, 1932)	4m, 5w, 16 animals, 2-man horse, extras	*4 exteriors 6 interiors* Willow wood River bank Middle of Wild Wood Canal bank Badger's home Court room Dungeon Rat's house Secret passage Banquet hall	Animal costumes: Mole, Rat, Toad, Badger, several ferrets, several weasels, several stoats, 2 field mice, Turkey, Duck, 4 rabbits, Fox, several squirrels, a 2-man horse, and another horse. Mole enters through earth UC. Tree with door. Badger appears from under pile of leaves. A large fitted traveling cart with horse. Weird incantation of Wild Wooders calls for special lighting. A bat flies across stage. Entrance to Badger's house is uncovered in the snow of the Wild Wood. 3 doors in Badger's house. A hollow tree for Toad to hide in. A barge gets towed on and off. Toad rides on back of horse. Singing and dancing. Toad gets in through window of Rat's house.
110. *Tom Sawyer*	Spencer, Sara (CTP, 1940)	10m, 3w, 12 children	*5 interiors 3 exteriors* Bedroom Schoolroom	Double bed, wash stand (I). Benches and desk in schoolroom. Eerie lighting in graveyard (II-i). Tombstones.

Title	Author	Characters	Settings	Special Requirements
110. *Tom Sawyer*			Church Courthouse Cave Street Graveyard Island	Board fence, part of which gets whitewashed (II-ii). Tree stump, boulders, bushes, camp fire for island (II-iii). Sound of cannon booming. Boys smoke corn cob pipes. Money box hidden in tree stump. Pulpit, pews in church (III-ii). Benches, statue of Justice in courthouse scene (III-iii). High boulder in cave (IV-i).
111. *Tom Sawyer's Treasure Hunt*	Chorpenning, Charlotte B. (French, 1937)	6m, 3w, 6 children	1 *exterior* Outside McDougal's cave	Scene shows mouth of cave and the secret trap door into it. Lighting atmospheric for murder scene, midnight, and waiting sequences. Costumes of 1850's, rustic. A tree with a dead limb. Treasure is dug up from around the rocks. "Corpse" brought on in wheelbarrow. A fire burns on stage. Skeleton of a cat is brought on.

| 112. *The Toymaker of Nuremberg* | Strong, Austin (Little, Brown, 1921) in Moses, *A Treasury* | 11m, 2w, 3 children, extras | 2 *exteriors* 1 *interior* Street outside garden wall Inside walled garden Toymaker's shop | A sentry box outside garden wall. A boy plays the flute. A very high wall is required in the street scene. Light changes suggested to conform to times of day. Many toys are hanging on the walls of the toyshop. |
| 113. *Treasure Island* | Drew, Dorothy (CTP, 1939) | 13m, 1w, 1 boy | 1 *interior* 2 *exteriors* Benbow Inn Aboard ship Before the stockade on island | 18th-century middle class, pirate, and special costumes. Old and weathered chest hidden under the stairs. Door to inn is broken open. Chest contents strewn all over. Room furnishings all messed up. Sound of horse trampling Blind Pew. Rope ladder into flies aboard ship. Several levels of deck needed. Long John Silver has wooden leg, carries a parrot on his shoulder. Parrot talks. Apple barrel big enough for Jim. Companionway appears to lead down. Flag is run up a pole in stockade. |

Title	Author	Characters	Settings	Special Requirements
113. *Treasure Island*				Campfire burns near stockade. Some shooting of guns.
114. *Treasure Island*	Goodman, Jules Eckert (French, 1915)	22m, 1w, 1 boy, 1 parrot	2 *interiors* 6 *exteriors* Admiral Benbow Inn Ben Gunn's cave Quay at Bristol Aboard ship off Treasure Island Front of Gunn's cave Stockade Aboard drifting ship Wooded hillside	Moody lighting in several scenes. Door splinters to pieces as pirates break into inn. Chest thrown down stairs and smashed open. Pirates tear up everything to find chart. Gangplank to ship from wharf. Cage with parrot, barrels, rope coils, boxes on wharf. Men appear on deck of docked ship and talk. Cannon on ship deck (II). Some men in the rigging (III-i). Sunrise suggested (III-i). Trees to hide behind, a hill to slide down. Ship in motion, tiller spins; ship lurches to side as it is beached (III-iii). Skeleton stands in specific position. Hillside with plateau where treasure is buried (IV-ii).

115. *The Utah Trail*	Mitchell, Albert O. (Harcourt, Brace, 1952) in *First Performance*	6m, 4w, 5 children, 1 dog	1 *interior* 1 *exterior* Log cabin Open place in forest	A built-in seat with its top in 2 sections, hinged, leads to cellar. Dutch door into the cabin. A live dog. A flour bin with flour. Mother lights fire in fireplace. Light changes: it begins to grow dark outside (I). Smoke comes in between logs as Indians set cabin afire. Much gun firing. Cabin door battered down with a battering ram. There are chinks in the walls. Sound of approaching militia. Pioneer and Indian costumes and make-up.
116. *Winnie-the-Pooh*	Sergel, Kristin (Dramatic, 1957)	1 boy, 1 man's voice, 11 animals, Extra animals	Stage represents 3 parts of the forest Area in front of curtain	Many animal costumes. A "buzzing sound." A rocking chair, nursery size. A hassock for Christopher. A wash cloth with foamy soap to scrub Roo's mouth. A cupboard; aerial root for entrance to Rabbit's hole. Pooh should get fatter after his meal.

Title	Author	Characters	Settings	Special Requirements
116. *Winnie-the-Pooh*				Wagon comes on in III, with cake and candles; candy to distribute to the audience.
117. *The Witch's Lullaby*	King, Martha Bennett (Coach House, 1955)	4m, 6w, 5 children	1 *interior* 2 *exteriors* Kitchen of cottage Rocky ledge by cave Village street	Cooking stove, cupboard, fireplace with fire in kitchen. Bagpipes prominent over mantel. Actual skirling off stage. G'tha and Gorina (witches) disappear "in a flash" and then return immediately. Gertrude (witch) loses facial hair, claws and hump on stage. G'tha and Gorina also lose facial hair. A mouse runs across the stage. A bag of gold hurtles through the air. Gertrude catches it. Broom collapses into a heap.
118. *The Wizard of Oz*	Chapman, Elizabeth Fuller (French, 1928)	4m, 4w, 1 girl, 1 dog, 1 lion, 3 Munch-	2 *exteriors* 3 *interiors* Munchkin farm Forest	Cyclone effect before I. Fantastic country and characters. Kansas house realistic. Scarecrow, dog, Tin Woodman, Lion costumes.

		kins	Throne room of Emerald palace / Kitchen in castle of Witch of the West / Throne room in Glinda's palace	Dance of Munchkins. Large head on throne, then a beast, then a ball of fire. Scarecrow dances. Dorothy should fly back to Kansas at end of III.
119. *The Wonderful Tang*	Bruestle, Beaumont (CTP, 1952)	19m, 6w, 1 dragon	Bare Oriental stage	Property man smokes. Stools for thrones. Brilliant oriental costumes and make-up. Attendants blow fanfares on kazoos. Many props pantomimed only: cups of tea, palanquin. Tasseled stick for horse. Some singing. A Dragon (full-sized person). Blackout of lights.
120. *Young Hickory*	McKenna, Helen (CTP, 1940)	10m, 3w, 1 boy	2 *interiors* Crude cabin Prison	2 characters hide up inside the chimney. Late 18th-century rustic and military costumes.

ℬibliography

CHILDREN'S THEATRE as a profession is young, and much of the literature in the field is of recent origin. As the movement continues to grow and spread, writers, directors, and technicians will share their research and experiences through the publication of books and articles.

This bibliography includes sources that have either proved helpful or provoked thought and experimentation. It is by no means a complete listing but is representative of the literature presently available to the reader desiring further study or information.

Four major categories are covered: children's theatre, general theatre, technical theatre, and child development and creative dramatics. Those wishing additional sources should consult the *Theatre Arts Publications in the United States, 1948–1952,* edited by William Melnitz and published by the American Educational Theatre Association, and "Creative Dramatics and Children's Theatre: A Bibliography," compiled by George L. Lewis and published in the May, 1955, issue of the *Educational Theatre Journal.*

Of further interest are the "Children's Theatre: U.S.A." reports published annually in *Theatre Arts* and the Children's Theatre Conference convention reports printed for the earlier years in *Players Magazine* and currently in the *Educational Theatre Journal.*

CHILDREN'S THEATRE

Books

Allen, John, *Going to the Theatre,* Phoenix House, 1949.

Cherniavsky, L. N. (ed.), *The Moscow Theatre for Children,* International Publishers, *c.* 1930.

Chorpenning, Charlotte, B., *Twenty-One Years with Children's Theatre,* Children's Theatre Press, 1954.

Fisher, Caroline E., and Robertson, Hazel G., *Children and the Theatre,* Stanford University Press, rev. ed., 1950.

Heniger, Alice Minnie Hertz, *The Children's Educational Theatre,* Harper, 1911.

Horton, Louise C. (ed.), *Handbook for Children's Theatre Directors,* National Thespian Society, 1949.

Kase, C. Robert, *Children's Theatre Comes of Age,* French, 1956.

Mackay, Constance D'Arcy, *Children's Theatres and Plays,* Appleton, 1927.

Mawer, Muriel, *et al., Children's Theatre Manual,* Children's Theatre Press, 1951.

Milne, Alan A., *If I May,* Dutton, 1921.

Walker, Stuart, "Preface," *Portmanteau Plays,* Stewart & Kidd, 1919.

Walton, Cecile, *The Children's Theatre Book,* Adam and Charles Black, 1949.

Ward, Winifred, *Creative Dramatics in the Upper Grades and Junior High School,* Appleton-Century, 1930.

Ward, Winifred, *Theatre for Children,* Children's Theatre Press, 3rd rev. ed., 1958.

Articles

Ausprich, Harry, "A Community Project," *Players Magazine,* October, 1957, pp. 10-11.

Blayom, Marian, "Yakima Gets Its Start," *Players Magazine,* April, 1951, p. 156.

Chase, Mary, "Writing Plays for Children," *New York Times,* February 17, 1952.

Chorpenning, Charlotte B., "Adults in Plays for Children," *Educational Theatre Journal,* May, 1951, pp. 115-118.

Chorpenning, Charlotte B., "Theatre for Young Moderns," *Journal of the American Association of University Women,* June, 1950, pp. 210-212.

Comer, Virginia Lee, "A Children's Theatre Takes to the Road," *Recreation,* September, 1940, pp. 363 ff.

Comer, Virginia Lee, "Organization Problems in Children's Theatre," *Dramatics,* November, 1948, p. 13.

Devine, George, "Theatre for Children: Art That Is Different," *World Theatre,* 1952, pp. 9 ff.

Dutton, Margaret, "Development of Work for the Children's Theatre," *Players Magazine,* October, 1951, pp. 20-21.

Forner, Marjorie M., "Children's Theatres for Personality and Culture," *Catholic School,* January, 1949, pp. 20-21.

Golden, Joseph, "Off We Go," *Players Magazine,* May, 1956, pp. 178-179.

Hayes, R., "King-Coit Children's Theatre," *Commonweal,* May 21, 1954, p. 175.

Horton, Louise C., "Children's Theatre in Your School," *American Childhood,* June, 1951, pp. 9-11.

Howard, Doris, and Johnson, E., "Trouping the Children's Theatre," *Players Magazine,* February, 1948, pp. 114-115.

Kozelka, Edwin Paul, "Children and the Theatre," *Teachers College Record,* November, 1949, pp. 106-109.

Lewis, George L., "Values From C.T. Work for High School Students," *Players Magazine,* April, 1957, pp. 159-160.

Major, Clare Tree, "Child's Play," *Theatre Arts,* October, 1952, p. 32.

Maxwell, James A., "Children Scare Me!" *The Saturday Evening Post,* March 8, 1958, pp. 24 ff.

Newmeyer, Sara, "For Children It Is Not Make-Believe," *New York Times Magazine,* December 5, 1948, pp. 24-26.

Oberreich, Bob, "Unique Children's Theatre," *Recreation,* November, 1951, p. 319.

Owen, Hal, "Writing Plays for Children," *California Journal of Elementary Education,* February, 1957, pp. 246-251.

Reed, Frieda E., "Children's Theatre as a Community Service," *Dramatics,* May, 1956, pp. 20-21.

Reed, Frieda E., "Dance-Pantomime," *Dramatics,* January, 1956, pp. 14-15.

Reed, Frieda E., "Director with Imagination, Training, and Devotion Develops Unique Project," *Dramatics,* November, 1956, pp. 12-13.

Reed, Frieda E., "The Original Script for Children's Theatre," *Dramatics,* March, 1956, pp. 18-19.

Soule, Martha, "Children's Trailer Theatre, Portland, Maine," *Recreation,* April, 1949, pp. 24-27.

Spencer, Sara, "Children's Theatre, Past and Present," *Educational Theatre Journal,* March, 1956, pp. 44 ff.

Strawbridge, Edwin, "Do Your Play For, Not To, the Children," *Recreation,* October 6, 1954, pp. 484-486.

Viola, Ann, "Drama With and For Children: An Interpretation of Terms," *Educational Theatre Journal,* May, 1956, pp. 139 ff.

Wilson, Margery, "Children's Theatre in the Round," *Educational Theatre Journal,* May, 1950, pp. 104-107.

GENERAL THEATRE

BOOKS

Albright, H. D., *Working Up a Part,* Houghton Mifflin, rev. ed., 1959.

Albright, H. D., Halstead, William, and Mitchell, Lee, *Principles of Theatre Art,* Houghton Mifflin, 1955.

Busfield, Roger M., Jr., *The Playwright's Art,* Harper, 1958.

Dean, Alexander, *Fundamentals of Play Directing,* Farrar & Rinehart, 1945.

Dietrich, John E., *Play Direction,* Prentice-Hall, 1953.
Dolman, John, *The Art of Play Production,* Harper, rev. ed., 1946.
Gallaway, Marian, *Constructing a Play,* Prentice-Hall, 1950.
Gassner, John (ed.), *Producing the Play: With the New Scene Technician's Handbook, by Philip Barber,* Dryden Press, rev. ed., 1953.
Jones, Robert Edmond, *The Dramatic Imagination,* Duell, Sloan, & Pearce, 1941.
McGaw, Charles J., *Acting Is Believing,* Rinehart, 1955.
Ommanney, Katherine, and Ommanney, Pierce C., *The Stage and the School,* Harper, 2nd rev. ed., 1950.
Oxenford, Lyn, *Playing Period Plays,* 3 vols. Coach House Press, 1957.
Whiting, Frank M, *An Introduction to the Theatre,* Harper, 1954.
Wright, Edward A., *A Primer for Playgoers,* Prentice-Hall, 1958.

ARTICLES

Boyle, Walden, "On the Nature of Artistic Representation in the Theatre," *Quarterly Journal of Speech,* October, 1944, pp. 316-320.
McGaw, John C., "Against the Illusionistic Approach to Directing," *Educational Theatre Journal,* March, 1950, pp. 66-71.

TECHNICAL THEATRE

BOOKS

Adix, Vern, *Theatre Scenecraft,* Children's Theatre Press, 1956.
Barton, Lucy, *Historic Costume for the Stage,* Walter H. Baker, 1935.
Bowman, Wayne, *Modern Theatre Lighting,* Harper, 1957.
Burris-Meyer, Harold, and Cole, Edward C., *Scenery for the Theatre,* Little, Brown, 1951.

Burris-Meyer, Harold, and Mallory, Vincent, *Sound in the Theatre,* Audio, 1959.

Cornberg, Sol, and Gebauer, Emanuel L., *A Stage Crew Handbook,* Harper, 1941.

Corson, Richard, *Stage Make-up,* Appleton-Century-Crofts, Inc., 1960.

Corson, Richard, *Styles in Scene Design,* National Thespian Society, 1948.

Dabney, Edith, and Wise, C. M., *Dramatic Costume for Children,* Educational Publishers, 1950.

Friederick, Willard J., *The Styles of Scenery Design,* National Thespian Society, 1951.

Friederick, Willard J., and Fraser, John H., *Scenery Design for the Amateur Theatre,* Macmillan, 1950.

Gillette, Arnold, *Stage Scenery: Its Construction and Rigging,* Harper, 1959.

Healy, Daty, *Dress the Show,* Row, Peterson, 1948.

McCandless, Stanley, *A Method of Lighting the Stage,* Theatre Arts, rev. ed., 1947.

Philippi, Herbert, *Stagecraft and Scene Design,* Houghton Mifflin, 1953.

Rubin, Joel E., and Watson, Leland H., *Theatrical Lighting Practice,* Theatre Arts, 1954.

Selden, Samuel, and Sellman, Hunton D., *Stage Scenery and Lighting,* Appleton-Century-Crofts, 3rd ed., 1959.

Simonson, Lee, *The Art of Scenic Design,* Harper, 1950.

Simonson, Lee, *The Stage Is Set,* Harcourt, Brace, 1932.

Walkup, Fairfax Proudfit, *Dressing the Part,* Crofts, 1938.

ARTICLES

Davis, Jed H., "The Portal: A Partial Answer," *Players Magazine,* January, 1958, pp. 79 ff.

Meikle, James, "A Dragon Mask," *Players Magazine,* May, 1956, p. 186.

Reed, Frieda E., "First-Aid for the Children's Theatre Actor (Make-up)," *Dramatics,* December, 1956, pp. 14-15.

CHILD DEVELOPMENT AND CREATIVE DRAMATICS

Books

Allstrom, E. C., *Let's Play a Story,* Friendship Press, 1957.
Andrews, Gladys, *Creative Rhythmic Movement for Children,* Prentice-Hall, 1954.
Arnheim, Rudolf, *Art and Visual Perception,* University of California Press, 1954.
Burger, Isabel B., *Creative Play Acting,* A. S. Barnes, 1950.
Cole, Natalie, *The Arts in the Classroom,* Day, 1940.
Durland, F. C., *Creative Dramatics for Children,* Antioch Press, 1952.
Fitzgerald, Burdette, *Let's Act the Story,* Fearon, 1957.
Gale, Ann VanNice, *Children's Preferences for Colors, Color Combinations, and Color Arrangements,* University of Chicago Press, 1933.
Garry, Ralph (project director), *Television for Children,* Foundation for Character Education, n. d.
Haaga, Agnes, and Randles, Patricia A., *Supplementary Materials for Use in Creative Dramatics with Younger Children,* University of Washington Press, 1952.
Hartley, R. E., and Goldenson, Robert M., *The Complete Book of Children's Play,* Crowell, 1957.
Lease, Ruth Gonser, and Siks, Geraldine Brain, *Creative Dramatics in Home, School, and Community,* Harper, 1952.
Lowenfeld, Viktor, *Creative and Mental Growth,* Macmillan, rev. ed., 1952.
Mearns, Hughes, *Creative Power,* Dover, 2d rev. ed., 1959.
Mellinger, Bonnie E., *Children's Interests in Pictures,* Contributions to Education No. 516, Bureau of Publications, Teachers College, Columbia University, 1932.
Siks, Geraldine Brain, *Creative Dramatics: An Art for Children,* Harper, 1958.
Slade, Peter, *Introduction to Child Drama,* University of London Press, 1958.

Walker, Pamela, *Seven Steps to Creative Children's Dramatics,* Hill and Wang, 1957.

Ward, Winifred, *Creative Dramatics in the Upper Grades and Junior High School,* Appleton-Century, 1930.

Ward, Winifred, *Playmaking with Children,* Appleton-Century-Crofts, 2nd ed., 1957.

Ward, Winifred, *Stories to Dramatize,* Children's Theatre Press, 1952.

ARTICLES

Anderson, John E., "Psychological Aspects of the Child Audience," *Educational Theatre Journal,* December, 1950, pp. 285-291.

Bowen, Frances C., "The Place of Creative Dramatics," *Players Magazine,* January, 1951, pp. 86-87.

Brown, Ida Stewart, "How We Act in Groups," *Childhood Education,* October, 1950, pp. 150-160.

Fleigler, Louis A., "Play Acting with the Mentally Retarded Children," *Exceptional Children,* November, 1952, pp. 56-60.

Haaga, Agnes, "Creative Dramatics in the Recreation Program," *Recreation,* May, 1951, p. 2.

Kupper, Herbert, "Fantasy and the Theatre Arts," *Educational Theatre Journal,* March, 1952, pp. 33-38.

McSwain, E. T., "The Art Experience in the Development of the Child's Personality," *Educational Theatre Journal,* May, 1953, pp. 125 ff.

Meier, Norman Charles, "Studies in the Psychology of Art," *Psychological Monographs,* 1933, entire issue.

Index

Accounting, 273-274
Acting, 110-142
  comment in, 137-138
  sincerity, 86, 127-128, 135, 141
  style, 133-142
  technique, 135-142
  vitality, 86-87, 127-128, 141
Acting areas, 102
  blocking, 104-107
  lighting, 231
Adams, Maude, 186
Adaptation, defined, 61
Admissions, 269-270
Adult actors, attitudes, 126-128
  casting, 85-90
  rehearsal schedule, 111-112
Aesthetic distance, 135
Alice in Wonderland, 4, 6, 174
American Educational Theatre Association, 13
Animal characters, 132
  costuming, 219-220
  make-up, 220
Assistant director, 115, 203-205
Attention span, 25, 75, 104, 158
Aucassin and Nicolette, 9
Audience, 22-50
  and acting style, 134-135
  attitude toward, 126-128
  contacts with, 147, 254-255
  controlling response, 138-146
  management, 142-146, 274-278
  training, 143-146
  transportation, 272-273
Audience reactions, 23-24, 26-50, 138-142
  boredom, 27, 45-47, 140-141

Audience reactions *(Continued)*
  control, 138-142
  embarrassment, 47-48
  excitement, 42-43, 139-140
  fear, 43-45, 68-69, 140
  humor, 41-42, 139
  loss of attention, 46-47, 140-142
  suspense, 41-42, 139-140
  tension release, 45-47, 140-142
  value of study, 49-50
  variations in, 48, 139
Autograph parties, 147

Backdrop, 179-180
Backstage management, 123, 203-210
Balance, 109, 129
Barrie, James M., 127
"Based upon," defined, 61
Beauty and the Beast, 86, 108
Birthday of the Infanta, The, 238
Black light, 233
Blocking, 99-100
  crowd scenes, 107
  entrances, 106
  notation, 101-103, 115
  preblocking, 100-103
  principles, 103-109, 117-118, 141
  rehearsals, 114-115
Blue Bird, The, 4, 44, 161
Bookings, 268-269
Bookkeeping, 273-274
Box office, 271-272
Briggs Management, 14
Budget, 264-270
  producing organizations, 265-268
  sponsoring organizations, 264-265

Burnett, Francis Hodgson, 170
Business management, 257-274

Cain Park Theatre, 12, 13
Casting, 81-96
  adults, 85-90
  children, 90-96
  criteria, 85-96
  mixed cast, 96, 112, 113, 148
Casting committee, 84
Ceiling, 177
Celastic, 219
Characterization, bases, 128-129, 131-133
  consistency, 140
  period plays, 120-121
  rehearsals, 115, 118-121
  role of costume, 186
  selectivity, 134
  stereotypes, 128
Characters, antagonistic, 38, 39, 45, 68-70, 86, 140
  major, 64-66, 105, 187
  minor, 70-71, 107-108, 187
  playwriting, 64-72
Chase sequences, 108
Child actors, acting style, 121, 133
  age, 90-91
  concentration, 131
  discipline, 123
  obligations to, 125-126
  rehearsal schedule, 111-112
  relation to audience, 146, 148
  relation to visual elements, 159
  securing, 254
  selection, 90-96
  supervision, 148-149
  value to, 19-20, 248
Children's Educational Theatre, 5-6
Children's Playhouse, 4
Children's theatre board, 252-253
Children's theatre committee, 250-252
Children's Theatre Conference, 13, 14, 90
Children's theatre history, 1-14
Children's theatre organizations, 3-14, 247-256
Children's theatre standards, 21, 159, 290

Children's World Theatre, 13
Chorpenning, Charlotte B., 8, 11, 68, 69, 74, 108, 159, 223
Christmas Nightingale, The, 238
Cinderella, 52, 69, 108, 223
Cleveland Playhouse, 11
Climax, 54-55, 57, 74
Coit, Dorothy, 9
Color, 175, 187, 188, 189-193
Color plates, 195
Comic characters, 41, 68-69
Comment, acting, 137-138
  costumes, 185
  design, 172, 175
Composition, blocking, 103-104
  color, 189-193
  costume design, 195
  scene design, 172
Concentration, 122, 130-131
Condescension, 42, 85, 86, 126, 137, 172
Conflict, 52, 54, 57
Costumer, 205-206
Costumes, 154-158, 159, 184-189
  animal, 219-220
  rehearsals, 120, 123
  relation to scenery, 172
  special demands, 222
  transformations, 221
Cover scenes, 75-76, 144-146
Creative dramatics, 18-19, 90-91
Crews, 91, 162, 205-211, 222-230, 239-241
Crisis, 54-55, 74
Cue sheets, lights, 316-319
  sound, 241
Curtain call, 55, 146-147
Curtain speeches, 142-143

Dance, 26, 71-72, 199
Designer, 153-198, 205, 223
Deus ex machina, 53-54
Developmental group interests, 10, 25-35, 40-41, 55
Dialogue, 58, 72-73, 118-119
Dimmers, 236
Director, 78-109, 110-152, 203
  on tour, 280-282
  professional obligations, 294-295

Discipline, performance, 148-149, 151-152
  rehearsals, 112, 123, 124-128
  touring, 280-282
Disney, Walt, 68, 160, 186
Double casting, 94-95
Dramatization, defined, 61
Duels, 108
Dunham, Dick, 13

Edwin Strawbridge Lyric Theatre, 11
Elevator stage, 178
Elves and the Shoemaker, The, 74
Emerson College, 6
Empathy, 15-18, 35-37, 38-40, 42-43, 86, 135
Emperor's New Clothes, The, 11, 68
Ensemble, 87-88, 89, 122, 129-130
Entrances, 99, 106
Equity Library Children's Theatre, 14
Evaluation, 150, 278
Evans, Dina Rees, 12, 13
Evanston Children's Theatre, 8
Evernden, Marjorie, 158, 238
Exits, 106
Exposition, 60, 154-158, 184
Expressionism, 173-174, 182
Extended run, 150-152

Facilities, 200-203
Fairy tale plays, 27-28, 54, 87, 132, 134
False proscenium (portal), 232, 285
Federal Theatre, 11
Financial report, 273-274
Financing, 248-249, 264-270
Five Little Peppers, The, 68
"Flash pots," 234
Floor plans, 96-100, 154, 193-195, 230
Fly loft, 180, 244
Flying, 226, 242-244
Focus, acting, 129-130
  blocking, 106
  child actors, 159
  color, 189
  costumes, 188

Focus *(Continued)*
  lighting, 183
  stage levels, 156
Form, costumes, 188
  scene design, 172, 173, 175, 176-182
Formalism, 165, 175-176, 178
Frank, Yasha, 11
Fry, Emma S., 5

Gerstenberg, Alice, 6
Goodman Theatre, 8, 9
Grace Price Productions, 12
Greensleeves' Magic, 238
Groff, Phyllis N., 238

Heckscher Foundation Children's Theatre, 7
Helga and the White Peacock, 161
Heniger, Alice Minnie Herts, 5-6
Historical plays, *see* Period plays
Hogel, Imogene, 6
House lights, 142-143, 145
House management, 271, 274-278
Huckleberry Finn, 74, 76, 157

Identification, 38-40, 147
  See also Empathy
Illustrations, 164, 172, 174
Image of Artemes, The, 9
Impressionism, 169, 182
Improvisation, 87-88, 129
Intermissions, 144-146, 162-163, 238

Jefferson, Joseph, 4
Junior Programs, Inc., 10, 11

Kai Khosru, 9
King, Edith, 9
King-Coit Theatre, 9
King of the Golden River, The, 158

Lantz, Walter, 68
Levels (platforms), 156, 159, 176, 177, 178, 283-285
Levels of meaning, 32, 156-158
Light plot, 197-198, 308-319

Lighting, 230-237
  color, 190-191
  contributions, 154-158
  effects, 217
  mood, 159
  scene shifts, 162
  scenic forms, 179-182
  scenic styles, 164-176
  scrims, 216-217
  simplification, 183
Lighting designer, 205-206
Line, costumes, 185, 186, 187, 188
  scenery, 173, 177
Lines, *see* Dialogue
Liquid latex, 220
Little Black Sambo, 11
Little Lame Prince, The, 228
Little Lord Fauntleroy, 4
Little Princess, The, 170
Little Women, 4

MacAlvay, Nora T., 74, 108
McCaslin, Nellie, 14
McFadden, Dorothy L., 10
Mackay, Constance D'Arcy, 6
Maeterlinck, Maurice, 161
Magic effects, 153, 162, 181
  appearances and disappearances,
    244
  flying, 226, 242-244
  shrinking and growing, 245
  spinning wheel, 224-225
  transformations, 221
  transparencies, 216-218
Major, Clare Tree, 7, 8, 14
Make-up, 154-158, 206, 220, 221
Mascots, 143-144
Meacham, Monte, 13, 14
Meigs, Cornelia, 161
Merry Wanderers, 13
Minnesota, University of, 13
Mitchell, Albert, 57, 76
Moralizing, 53, 63-64
Moscow Art Theatre, 44
Motivation, 71-72, 104, 107, 115, 128-
    130, 132
Music, 26, 71-72, 119, 141, 142, 143,
    145, 153, 162, 237-241

Musil, Rosemary, 76, 108

Nala and Damayanti, 9
National Youth Theatre, 13
Naturalism, 165, 166, 179

Ohio Wesleyan Players, 13
Omaha Community Theatre, 11
Overstimulation, 43

Pace, Gian, 13
Pageantry, 108-109, 156
Papier maché, 219, 225
Period plays, 28-30, 120-121, 132,
    137, 163, 185-186
Peter Pan, 4, 243
Peter, Peter, Pumpkin Eater, 74
Pinocchio, 11
Plastic stage, 175
Play construction, 51-64
Play titles, 76-77
Playscript, 51-77
  acting style, 133-134
  characterization, 128-129, 131-133,
    136-137
  selection, 78-80, 189, 258-259
Playwriting, 51-77
Plot, 29-30, 52-63, 74
"Plugs," 178-179
Portmanteau Theatre, 4-5
Preblocking, 100-103
Preperformance entertainment, 143-
    144
Presentation curtain, 162
Presentational acting, 133-142
Presentational design, 165, 171-176
Prince and the Knight, The, 57
Prince and the Pauper, The, 41, 57, 69
Producing organizations, 247-248,
    253-257, 265-268
Production concept, 80, 164, 176, 186
Production organization, 203-210
Production schedule, 210-213
Programs, 277-278
Projection, acting, 81, 140
Projections, lighting, 235-236
Promotion, 257-264

Prompt book, 103, 118, 300-307
Properties, 95, 99, 119, 153, 154-158, 159, 189, 195, 222-230
Proportion, 160, 161, 245
Protagonist, 39-40, 54, 58, 66-68, 86
"Psychological crowd," 33-34
Psychological needs, 35-40
Publicity, 260-263
Pyrotechnics, 233-235

Racketty Packetty House, 4
Radio Rescue, 159
Realism, 25-26, 28-30, 132, 167, 177, 178, 179, 180, 182
    simplified, 168
Rehearsals, 110-128
    blocking, 114-115
    characterization and line, 115, 118-121
    child casts, 115, 118-121
    dress, 123-124, 205
    polishing, 121-122
    reading, 113-114
    scheduling, 111-113, 116-117
    space, 110-111
    technical, 122-123, 162, 205
Representational acting, 134-135
Representational design, 165-171
Revolving stage, 178, 215
Rhythm, 34, 74-75, 122, 193
Rickert, Corinne, 74, 76, 157
Rip Van Winkle, 4
Robertson, Hazel G., 12, 13
Robin Hood, 76, 108
Romanticism, 27, 30, 154, 160, 187
Running time, 75, 145, 158

Scenery, 153-184
    forms, 176-182
    styles, 164-176
    touring, 282, 285
Scrim, 216-218
Seating, 274-275
Selectivity, acting, 136-138
    design, 171-176
    playwriting, 64-66
Sergel, Kristin, 220
Set properties, *see* Properties

Settings, 98, 153-184
    book, 181
    box, 177, 178
    drop-wing-border, 174
    fragmentary, 182
    minimum, 182
    outline, 181
    painted scrims, 217
    screen, 180
    simplification, 183-184
    simultaneous, 179
    stock, 160, 161
    transformations, 221-222
    unit, 178
Shifting, 123, 145, 161, 162, 177-182, 214-218, 230, 283
Simplification, 183-184
Sketches, 114, 196
Sleeping Beauty, The, 68
Sliding panels, 218, 244
Snow White and the Seven Dwarfs, 4, 69, 108, 160
Sound, 119, 237-241
Spinning wheel, 224, 225
Sponsorship, 224-225
    bookings, 268-269
    budget, 264-265
Stage conventions, 172, 180, 183
Stage management, 123, 206-208
Stage movement, 86-87, 135-136, 159
Stage picture, 103-104, 156, 158, 188
Staging, 153, 176
Standards, 21, 290
Story in children's plays, 52-63
Story, Josephine L., 9
Style, acting, 133-138
    design, 164-176
Stylization, acting, 132
    costumes, 185-186
    design, 171-172, 177-179, 182
"Suggested by," defined, 62
Symbolism, 157
    abstract, 170
    color, 187
    costumes, 185
    literal, 171

Technical director, 205-206, 208

Tempo, 122, 140, 141
Tenniel, John, 174
Theatricalism, 174-175, 177-182
Theme, 57, 62-64, 157
Ticket sales, 270-273
Tom Sawyer, 4
Touring, 279-288
  bookings, 268-269
Town Theatre, 12
Transformations, 221-222
Treasure Island, 4
Tryouts, 81-96
  cards, 82-83, 92, 93
    See also Casting
Tully, Nora, 74, 108

Tulsa, University of, 9

Ushers, 275-276
Utah Trail, The, 68

Voice, 81, 88, 89-90

Wagons, 178, 214-215, 283, 285
Walker, Stuart, 4-5, 238
Ward, Winifred, 8, 13
Washburn, Annette, 6
Whiting, Frank M, 74, 76, 157
Winnie-the-Pooh, 220
Working drawings, 196-197